# Sources for
# Western Society

**Volume 1: From Antiquity to the Enlightenment**

# Sources for
# Western Society

**Volume 1: From Antiquity
to the Enlightenment**

Thirteenth Edition

THE COMPANION READER FOR
*A HISTORY OF WESTERN SOCIETY*

THIRTEENTH EDITION

Merry E. Wiesner-Hanks
Clare Haru Crowston
Joe Perry
John P. McKay

bedford/st.martin's
Macmillan Learning
Boston | New York

For Bedford/St. Martin's

Vice President, Editorial, Macmillan Learning Humanities: Edwin Hill
Senior Program Director for History: Michael Rosenberg
Senior Executive Program Manager for History: William J. Lombardo
History Marketing Manager: Melissa Rodriguez
Director of Content Development, Humanities: Jane Knetzger
Associate Development Editor: Stephanie Sosa
Senior Content Project Manager: Christina M. Horn
Assistant Content Project Manager: Natalie Jones
Senior Workflow Project Manager: Jennifer Wetzel
Production Coordinator: Brianna Lester
Advanced Media Project Manager: Sarah O'Connor Kepes
Media Editor: Mary P. Starowicz
Editorial Services: Lumina Datamatics, Inc.
Composition: Lumina Datamatics, Inc.
Text Permissions Manager: Kalina Ingham
Text Permissions Editor: Michael McCarty
Executive Permissions Editor: Robin Fadool
Director of Design, Content Management: Diana Blume
Text Design: Lumina Datamatics, Inc.
Cover Design: William Boardman
Cover Image: Metropolitan Museum of Art, New York, USA/Bridgeman Images
Printing and Binding: LSC Communications

Manufactured in the United States of America.

1  2  3  4  5  6      24  23  22  21  20  19

For information, write: Bedford/St. Martin's, 75 Arlington Street, Boston, MA 02116

ISBN 978-1-319-22976-4

**Acknowledgments**
Text acknowledgments and copyrights appear at the back of the book on pages 263–265, which constitute an extension of the copyright page. Art acknowledgments and copyrights appear on the same page as the art selections they cover.

# PREFACE

This updated edition of *Sources for Western Society* gathers a diverse array of primary sources from Western history that brings the past to life for students. Recognizing that history is shaped by the many as much as it is shaped by the few, *Sources for Western Society* includes the voices of men and women from across the social spectrum offering their own unique perspective on the events and developments of their times. Designed specifically to be used with all versions of *A History of Western Society*, Thirteenth Edition, the collection mirrors and complements each chapter of the parent textbooks, encouraging students to place the viewpoints of individual authors and artists in the context of the changing world in which they lived.

With input from current instructors of the Western civilization survey course, these documents have been compiled with one goal in mind: to make history's most compelling voices accessible to students, from the most well-known thinkers of their times to the most put-upon commoner. This emphasis on accessibility is crucial, since the reader is designed to challenge students to put aside their own preconceptions and to see history from the point of view of the people of the past. In Chapter 15, for example, students have the opportunity to read Jean Domat's 1689 argument supporting absolute monarchy in France and compare it to the English Bill of Rights from the same year, which limited the king's power. Written from different perspectives, these documents help students to develop a nuanced, multisided picture of this seminal development in Western history.

To allow instructors flexibility in assigning individual sources while providing opportunities for students to focus on a document-based issue through analysis of multiple sources, each chapter provides a selection of individual documents that illuminate the variety of major developments and themes from the textbook, as well as a "Sources in Conversation" feature that allows students to examine an issue from multiple perspectives. Selections range widely in length to allow for a range of class assignments.

This companion reader steps back from drawing conclusions and instead provides just enough background to facilitate students' own analyses of the sources at hand. Chapter introductions set the context of the documents that follow within the framework of the corresponding textbook chapter. A concise headnote for each document provides key information about the author and the circumstances surrounding the document's creation, while helpful gloss notes aid comprehension of unfamiliar terms and references. Each document is followed by Reading Questions that promote understanding and critical analysis of the material. In addition, new Read and Compare questions in the "Sources in Conversation" feature guide students in their comparison of the sources provided. Finally, chapter-concluding Comparative and Discussion Questions encourage students to contemplate the harmony and discord among the sources within and across the chapters.

## New to This Edition

More than thirty new documents—including several compelling images—have been added to the Thirteenth Edition of *Sources*, offering increased representation of women and minority, particularly Muslim, perspectives. For example, Chapter 4 includes a new source describing the Jewish response to being ruled by the Greeks during the Hellenistic era; Chapter 9 now includes a Muslim account comparing two sieges of Jerusalem during the Crusades, one by the Catholics in 1099 and the other by the Muslims in 1187; Chapter 22 features an excerpt from Emmeline Pankhurst's speech made when she was sentenced to prison for having fought for voting rights for women; and Chapter 30 provides an excerpt of writings from Abdolkarim Soroush, an Iranian Muslim reformist scholar, who addresses militant secularism and the role it plays in contemporary society.

One of the most significant changes in the new edition is the addition of Read and Compare questions to the "Sources in Conversation" feature. Placed before the collected sources, these questions help students read the sources with purpose and consider their similarities and differences. For example, "Assyrian, Persian, and Hebrew Perceptions of Monarchy" in Chapter 2 asks students to think about the different expectations of kingship in three different societies, as well as the tone of the documents themselves; and "Debating the 'Iron Curtain'" in Chapter 28 invites students to compare Winston Churchill's and Joseph Stalin's speeches discussing the division of eastern and western Europe, specifically asking about their methods of addressing the audience and the ways in which their speeches reflect their positions of power.

## Affordability Option

*Sources for Western Society,* Thirteenth Edition, is now offered in two low-cost e-books, and also as part of our Bedford Select for History affordability program, alongside the Value edition of *A History of Western Society,* Thirteenth Edition. Bedford Select lets you put together the ideal set of print materials for your course by allowing you to choose the chapters, readings, skills-based tutorials, and document projects you want—and even add your own resources as well. Instructors with enrollments as low as twenty-five students can take advantage of the options within Bedford Select to save students money. Visit macmillanlearning.com/bedfordselect to learn more.

## Acknowledgments

Thanks to the instructors whose insightful comments and thoughtful suggestions helped shape the Thirteenth Edition: William Wantland, Mount Vernon Nazarene University; Ginette Aley, Kansas State University; Jennifer Foray, Purdue University; Kelley Obernuefemann, Lewis and Clark Community College; James Kabala, Community College of Rhode Island; Gesche Peters, Dawson College; Jeffrey Michael Long, Front Range Community College; Robert Janda, Cameron University; Jonathan Hall, Union County College; Laura Wertheimer, Cleveland State University; and George Gerdow, Northeastern Illinois University.

Special thanks go to Jeffrey Michael Long from Front Range Community College for his excellent and substantive contributions to this reader. Many thanks also to development editor Stephanie Sosa, William Lombardo, Heidi Hood, and Natalie Jones.

# CONTENTS

# Origins

## to 1200 B.C.E.

By 3000 B.C.E., two contrasting agricultural societies had developed in Mesopotamia and Egypt. Mesopotamia was located between the Tigris and Euphrates Rivers, which were a challenge to navigate and needed to be channeled into complicated irrigation systems. The area possessed few natural defenses against invasion, and its various city-states warred against one another for domination. Egypt, in contrast, was largely protected by desert, and the flooding of the Nile was fairly regular and could be managed with relative ease. The pharaohs were able to create a unified kingdom at an early point in Egypt's history, in part because the current of the Nile made travel up and down the river feasible.

The writings these cultures left are among the earliest records of Western society. The following documents are, for the most part, concerned with two basic questions: how did the gods create and govern the world, and what sort of life should mortals lead to fulfill their duties to the gods and one another? As you read the documents, compare the answers Egyptians and Mesopotamians gave to these questions. What might explain the similarities and differences you note?

### 1-1 | A Mesopotamian Creation Myth

### *The Battle Between Marduk and Tiamat*
### (ca. 2000–1000 B.C.E.)

Creation myths offer supernatural explanations for the origins of the earth, heavens, and life in the natural world. This Mesopotamian creation myth, known as the *Enuma Elish*, portrays the struggle of the sun-god Marduk, the patron god of Babylon, with Tiamat the sea-goddess,

---

Republished by permission of Princeton University Press from James B. Pritchard, ed., *Ancient Near Eastern Texts Relating to the Old Testament*, 3rd ed. (Princeton, N.J.: Princeton University Press, 1955); permission conveyed through Copyright Clearance Center, Inc.

mother of all gods. As Babylon came to dominate the other cities of the Euphrates Valley, Marduk defeated Tiamat to become the chief of all the gods.

Naught but primordial Apsu, their begetter,
[And] Mummu-Tiamat, she who bore them all,
Their waters commingling as a single body;
No reed hut had been matted, no marsh land had appeared,
When no gods whatever had been brought into being,
Uncalled by name, their destinies undetermined —
Then it was that the gods were formed within them. . . .

[Several generations of gods are descendants of Tiamat and Apsu, some of whom, particularly the gods Anu and Nudimmud, surpass the other gods in strength.]

The divine brothers [Anu and Nudimmud] banded together.
They disturbed Tiamat as they surged back and forth,
Yea, they troubled the mood of Tiamat
By their hilarity in the Abode of Heaven.
Apsu could not lessen their clamor
And Tiamat was speechless at their [ways].
Their doings were loathsome. . . .
Unsavory were their ways; they were overbearing.

[And so begins a war among the gods. Apsu is killed during the war, so Tiamat creates monsters to help her destroy her rivals. Ea, a leading god among Tiamat's opponents, asks his son Marduk to join the war.]

"My son, thou who knowest all wisdom,
Calm [Tiamat] with thy holy spell. . . ."
The lord [rejoiced] at the word of his father.
His heart exulting, he said to his father:
"Creator of the gods, destiny of the great gods,
If I indeed, as your avenger,
Am to vanquish Tiamat and save your lives,
Set up the Assembly [of gods], proclaim supreme my destiny!
When jointly in Ubshukinna[1] you have sat down rejoicing,
Let my word, instead of you, determine the fates.
Unalterable shall be what I may bring into being;
Neither recalled nor changed shall be the command of my lips!" . . .

[Marduk defeats Tiamat's army and then finally battles the goddess herself.]

---

[1]**Ubshukinna**: The meeting hall of the gods.

They strove in single combat, locked in battle. . . .
He released the arrow, it tore her belly,
It cut through her insides, splitting the heart.
Having thus subdued her, he extinguished her life.
He cast down her carcass to stand upon it. . . .
He split her like a shellfish into two parts:
Half of her he set up and ceiled it as sky,
Pulled down the bar and posted guards.
He bade them to allow not her waters to escape.
He crossed the heavens and surveyed the regions. . . .
Opening his mouth, he addresses Ea
To impart the plan he had conceived in his heart:
"Blood I will mass and cause bones to be.
I will establish a savage, man shall be his name.
Truly, savage-man I will create.
He shall be charged with the service of the gods
That they might be at ease!"

## READING QUESTIONS

1. According to this account, how is the world created?

2. Central to this creation story is a struggle to the death between two gods. What might the focus on battle reveal about Mesopotamian beliefs?

3. How and why are human beings created? What does this story reveal about how Mesopotamians understood the relationship between humans and the gods?

## 1-2 | The Quest for Eternal Life
### *The Epic of Gilgamesh* (ca. 2750 B.C.E.)

*The Epic of Gilgamesh is one of the oldest surviving stories in world history. Fragments of the story can be found on tablets throughout the Mesopotamian region, but the most complete version of the text comes from twelve tablets written in the Akkadian language and dating to 1300 B.C.E. The epic tells the tale of Gilgamesh, the part-human, part-divine king of Uruk. In these excerpts, Gilgamesh meets his friend Enkidu. Together, they confront Ishtar, the goddess of war and fertility. After Enkidu dies, Gilgamesh sets out to find the secret of immortality. On his journey, he encounters Siduri, the tavern-keeper, who challenges him to reconsider why he wants eternal life.*

[This is the story of]
how Gilgamesh went through every hardship.

Supreme over other kings, lordly in appearance,
he is the hero. . . .
He walks out in front, the leader,
and walks at the rear, trusted by his companions.
Mighty net, protector of his people,
raging flood-wave who destroys even walls of stone! . . .
It was he who crossed the ocean, the vast seas, to the rising sun,
who explored the world regions, seeking life. . . .
Who can say like Gilgamesh: "I am King!"?

[The legend of Gilgamesh's adventures begins with the people of his kingdom complaining about their king. They accuse him of taking away their sons, possibly as conscripts for his army, and of sexually exploiting young women. The people ask the gods to intervene with Gilgamesh. The goddess Aruru creates Enkidu to distract the king.]

In the wilderness (?) she created valiant Enkidu,
born of Silence, endowed with strength. . . .
His whole body was shaggy with hair,
he had a full head of hair like a woman,
his locks billowed in profusion. . . .
He knew neither people nor settled living. . . .
He ate grasses with the gazelles,
and jostled at the watering hole with the animals. . . .

[The local populace is afraid of Enkidu, and eventually Gilgamesh is called upon to defend them from the wild man. After a brief struggle, Gilgamesh defeats Enkidu in a fight, and the two become best friends. They fight monsters and have many adventures together, including the following encounter with the goddess Ishtar.]

When Gilgamesh placed his crown on his head,
Princess Ishtar raised her eyes to the beauty of Gilgamesh.
    "Come along, Gilgamesh, be you my husband,
    to me grant your lusciousness.
    Be you my husband, and I will be your wife. . . .
    Bowed down beneath you will be kings, lords, and princes.
    The Lullubu people[1] will bring you the produce of the mountains and
        countryside as tribute." . . .
Gilgamesh addressed Princess Ishtar saying:
    "What would I have to give you if I married you?
    Do you need oil or garments for your body?
    Do you lack anything for food or drink?
    I would gladly feed you food fit for a god,
    I would gladly give you wine fit for a king. . . .

---

[1]**Lullubu people**: The Lullubi were a wild, nomadic people of the mountains.

See here now, I will recite the list of your lovers . . .
Tammuz, the lover of your earliest youth,
for him you have ordained lamentations year upon year! . . .
You loved the stallion, famed in battle,
yet you ordained for him the whip, the goad, and the lash. . . ."
When Ishtar heard this,
in a fury she went up to the heavens,
going to Anu, her father, and crying,
going to Anrum, her mother, and weeping:
"Father, Gilgamesh has insulted me over and over,
Gilgamesh has recounted despicable deeds about me,
despicable deeds and curses!"
Anu addressed Princess Ishtar, saying:
"What is the matter? Was it not you who provoked King Gilgamesh?
So Gilgamesh recounted despicable deeds about you,
despicable deeds and curses!"
Ishtar spoke to her father, Anu, saying:
"Father, give me the Bull of Heaven,
so he can kill Gilgamesh in his dwelling.
If you do not give me the Bull of Heaven
I will knock down the Gates of the Netherworld,
I will smash the door posts, and leave the doors flat down,
and will let the dead go up to eat the living!
And the dead will outnumber the living!"
Anu addressed Princess Ishtar, saying:
"If you demand the Bull of Heaven from me,
there will be seven years of empty husks for the land of Uruk.
Have you collected grain for the people?
Have you made grasses grow for the animals?"
Ishtar addressed Anu, her father, saying:
"I have heaped grain in the granaries for the people,
I made grasses grow for the animals,
in order that they might eat in the seven years of empty husks.
I have collected grain for the people,
I have made grasses grow for the animals." . . .

[About six lines are missing here.]

When Anu heard her words,
he placed the nose rope of the Bull of Heaven in her hand.
Ishtar led the Bull of Heaven down to the earth.
When it reached Uruk it climbed down to the Euphrates. . . .
At the snort of the Bull of Heaven a huge pit opened up,
and 100 young men of Uruk fell in.
At his second snort a huge pit opened up,

and 200 young men of Uruk fell in.
At his third snort a huge pit opened up,
and Enkidu fell in up to his waist.
Then Enkidu jumped out and seized the Bull of Heaven by its horns. . . .
Enkidu stalked and *hunted down* the Bull of Heaven.
He grasped it by the thick of its tail
*and held onto it with both his hands* (?),
while Gilgamesh, like *an expert butcher,*
boldly and *surely approached the Bull of Heaven.* . . .
He thrust his sword.
After they had killed the Bull of Heaven, . . .
Then the brothers sat down together.
Ishtar went up onto the top of the Wall of Uruk-Haven,
cast herself into the pose of mourning, and hurled her woeful curse:
    "Woe unto Gilgamesh who slandered me and killed the Bull of Heaven!"
When Enkidu heard this pronouncement of Ishtar,
    he wrenched off the Bull's hindquarter and flung it in her face:
    "If I could only get at you I would do the same to you!
    I would drape his innards over your arms!"
The men of Uruk gathered together, staring at them.
Gilgamesh said to the palace retainers:
    "Who is the bravest of the men?
    Who is the boldest of the males?"

[Enkidu reveals that he is dying, and that the afterlife will be a place of sorrow. After Enkidu dies, Gilgamesh goes on a journey to find the secret of eternal life. He travels for some time and encounters Siduri, who owns a tavern.]

Gilgamesh said to the tavern-keeper:
    "I am Gilgamesh . . .
    I grappled with the Bull that came down from heaven, and killed him."
The tavern-keeper spoke to Gilgamesh, saying:
    "If you are Gilgamesh, . . . why are your cheeks emaciated, your expression
        desolate?
    Why is your heart so wretched, your features so haggard?
    Why is there such sadness deep within you?
    Why do you look like one who has been traveling a long distance
        so that ice and heat have seared your face?" . . .
Gilgamesh spoke to her, to the tavern-keeper he said:
    "Tavern-keeper, should not my cheeks be emaciated?
    Should my heart not be wretched, my features not haggard?
    Should there not be sadness deep within me?
    Should I not look like one who has been traveling a long distance,
    and should ice and heat not have seared my face?
    My friend, . . . Enkidu, the wild ass who chased the wild donkey,
    panther of the wilderness,

we joined together, and went up into the mountain.
We grappled with and killed the Bull of Heaven. . . .
Enkidu, whom I love deeply, who went through every hardship with me,
the fate of mankind has overtaken him.
Six days and seven nights I mourned over him
and would not allow him to be buried
until a maggot fell out of his nose.
I was terrified by his *appearance* (?),
I began to fear death, and so roam the wilderness.
How can I stay silent, how can I be still?
My friend whom I love has turned to clay.
Am I not like him? Will I lie down, never to get up again?"

[The tavern-keeper sends Gilgamesh to find the one man, Utnapishtim (oot-nuh-PISH-tim), who has been granted immortality by the gods. She warns him, however, about what he will find on the journey.]

The tavern-keeper spoke to Gilgamesh, saying: . . .
  "The crossing is difficult, its ways are treacherous —
  and in between are the Waters of Death that bar its approaches!
  And even if, Gilgamesh, you should cross the sea,
  when you reach the Waters of Death what would you do?"

[After his long, arduous journey Gilgamesh finally finds Utnapishtim, who tells him that no human can be immortal. He does, however, tell Gilgamesh of a plant that will restore his youth. Utnapishtim instructs a ferryman, Urshanabi, to take Gilgamesh back to Uruk after Gilgamesh finds the plant.]

[Gilgamesh says,] "[T]his plant is a plant against decay
by which a man can attain his survival.
I will bring it to Uruk and have an old man eat the plant to test it.
The plant's name is 'The Old Man Becomes a Young Man.'
Then I will eat it and return to the condition of my youth." . . .
Seeing a spring and how cool its waters were,
Gilgamesh went down and was bathing in the water.
A snake smelled the fragrance of the plant,
silently came up and carried off the plant. . . .
At that point Gilgamesh sat down, weeping,
his tears streaming over the side of his nose.
"Counsel me, O ferryman Urshanabi!
For whom have my arms labored, Urshanabi!
For whom has my heart's blood roiled!
I have not secured any good deed for myself. . . ."
They arrived in Uruk. Gilgamesh said to Urshanabi, the ferryman:
"Go up, Urshanabi, onto the wall of Uruk and walk around.
Examine its foundation, inspect its brickwork thoroughly. . . ."

## READING QUESTIONS

1. At the beginning of the epic, what kind of king is Gilgamesh? Does he stay the same in the story, or does he change?

2. What happens when Gilgamesh rejects Ishtar? Who suffers because of her anger?

3. What kind of advice does Gilgamesh get from the tavern-keeper? What lesson is she trying to teach him?

4. What does this story tell us about the Mesopotamians' perceptions of their gods and the concept of the afterlife? What does it tell us about their perception of kingship?

# 1-3 | Society and Law in Ancient Babylonia
## *The Code of Hammurabi* (ca. 1780 B.C.E.)

As king of Babylon, one of the first great cities in the world, Hammurabi (hahm-moo-RAH-bee) (r. ca. 1792–1750 B.C.E.) created an empire that extended throughout Mesopotamia. During his reign, Hammurabi compiled a well-known law code and ordered it to be carved on stone tablets and set up in a public space. The inscriptions were in Akkadian, the daily language of the people. Although it is not known how many Babylonians were literate at this time, ordinary people might have had a general sense of what was written there.

3. If any one bring an accusation of any crime before the elders, and does not prove what he has charged, he shall, if it be a capital offense charged, be put to death. . . .

5. If a judge try a case, reach a decision, and present his judgment in writing; if later error shall appear in his decision, and it be through his own fault, then he shall pay twelve times the fine set by him in the case, and he shall be publicly removed from the judge's bench, and never again shall he sit there to render judgment. . . .

15. If anyone take a male or female slave of the court, or a male or female slave of a freed man, outside the city gates, he shall be put to death.

16. If anyone receive into his house a runaway male or female slave of the court, or of a freed man, and does not bring it out at the public proclamation of the major domus,[1] the master of the house shall be put to death.

17. If anyone find runaway male or female slaves in the open country and bring them to their masters, the master of the slaves shall pay him two shekels of silver. . . .

---

From James B. Pritchard, ed., *Ancient Near Eastern Texts Relating to the Old Testament*, 3d ed. (Princeton, N.J.: Princeton University Press, 1969), pp. 166–175. Permission conveyed through Copyright Clearance Center, Inc.

[1]**major domus**: In this context, an official in charge of overseeing slaves.

25. If fire break out in a house, and some one who comes to put it out cast his eye upon the property of the owner of the house, and take the property of the master of the house, he shall be thrown into that self-same fire. . . .

30. If a chieftain or a man leave his house, garden, and field and hires it out, and some one else takes possession of his house, garden, and field and uses it for three years: if the first owner return and claims his house, garden, and field, it shall not be given to him, but he who has taken possession of it and used it shall continue to use it. . . .

108. If a tavern-keeper (feminine) does not accept corn according to gross weight in payment of drink, but takes money, and the price of the drink is less than that of the corn, she shall be convicted and thrown into the water.

109. If conspirators meet in the house of a tavern-keeper, and these conspirators are not captured and delivered to the court, the tavern-keeper shall be put to death.

110. If a sister of a god[2] open a tavern, or enter a tavern to drink, then shall this woman be burned to death. . . .

128. If a man take a woman to wife, but have no intercourse with her, this woman is no wife to him.

129. If a man's wife be surprised with another man, both shall be tied and thrown into the water, but the husband may pardon his wife and the king his slaves.

130. If a man violate the wife (betrothed or child-wife) of another man, who has never known a man, and still lives in her father's house, and sleep with her and be surprised, this man shall be put to death, but the wife is blameless.

131. If a man bring a charge against one's wife, but she is not surprised with another man, she must take an oath and then may return to her house.

132. If the "finger is pointed" at a man's wife about another man, but she is not caught sleeping with the other man, she shall jump into the river for her husband. . . .

137. If a man wish to separate from a woman who has borne him children, or from his wife who has borne him children: then he shall give that wife her dowry, and a part of the usufruct of field, garden, and property, so that she can rear her children. When she has brought up her children, a portion of all that is given to the children, equal as that of one son, shall be given to her. She may then marry the man of her heart.

138. If a man wishes to separate from his wife who has borne him no children, he shall give her the amount of her purchase money and the dowry which she brought from her father's house, and let her go.

139. If there was no purchase price he shall give her one mina of gold as a gift of release. . . .

141. If a man's wife, who lives in his house, wishes to leave it, plunges into debt, tries to ruin her house, neglects her husband, and is judicially convicted: if

---

[2]**sister of a god**: A woman dedicated to the service of a god or goddess.

her husband offer her release, she may go on her way, and he gives her nothing as a gift of release. If her husband does not wish to release her, and if he take another wife, she shall remain as servant in her husband's house. . . .

144. If a man take a wife and this woman give her husband a maid-servant, and she bear him children, but this man wishes to take another wife, this shall not be permitted to him; he shall not take a second wife.

145. If a man take a wife, and she bear him no children, and he intend to take another wife: if he take this second wife, and bring her into the house, this second wife shall not be allowed equality with his wife. . . .

195. If a son strike his father, his hands shall be hewn off.

196. If a man put out the eye of another man, his eye shall be put out.

197. If he break another man's bone, his bone shall be broken.

198. If he put out the eye of a freed man, or break the bone of a freed man, he shall pay one gold mina.

199. If he put out the eye of a man's slave, or break the bone of a man's slave, he shall pay one-half of its value.

200. If a man knock out the teeth of his equal, his teeth shall be knocked out.

201. If he knock out the teeth of a freed man, he shall pay one-third of a gold mina.

202. If anyone strike the body of a man higher in rank than he, he shall receive sixty blows with an ox-whip in public.

203. If a free-born man strike the body of another free-born man of equal rank, he shall pay one gold mina.

204. If a freed man strike the body of another freed man, he shall pay ten shekels in money.

205. If the slave of a freed man strike the body of a freed man, his ear shall be cut off. . . .

209. If a man strike a free-born woman so that she lose her unborn child, he shall pay ten shekels for her loss.

210. If the woman die, his daughter shall be put to death.

211. If a woman of the free class lose her child by a blow, he shall pay five shekels in money.

212. If this woman die, he shall pay half a mina.

213. If he strike the maid-servant of a man, and she lose her child, he shall pay two shekels in money.

214. If this maid-servant die, he shall pay one-third of a mina. . . .

### READING QUESTIONS

1. What do these laws reveal about the social structure of Babylon? How is the role of social rank in Babylonian society reflected in these laws?

2. What do these laws reveal about contemporary family life? What do they reveal about the status of women and children?

3. From these laws, what can we surmise about a person's responsibilities to the community as a whole?

# 1-4 | A Declaration of Innocence
## *The Egyptian Book of the Dead* (ca. 2100–1800 B.C.E.)

The Egyptian *Book of the Dead* comprises texts that were placed in tombs and describes how a dead person should overcome various obstacles in the afterlife. Although there was no standard *Book of the Dead* (this was not a name used by the Egyptians), many of the same texts appear in tombs dating from shortly after 2000 B.C.E. until the adoption of Christianity. One such text, the "Declaration of Innocence," is remarkable for the detail with which it describes the possible sins of the deceased Egyptian. Its list of undesirable acts creates an outline of what Egyptians considered acceptable social behavior. As you read, consider what it tells you about what the Egyptians believed the gods expected from them.

To be said on reaching the Hall of the Two Truths[1] so as to purge [name] of any
    sins committed and to see the face of every god:
Hail to you, great God, Lord of the Two Truths!
I have come to you, my Lord,
I was brought to see your beauty.
I know you, I know the names of the forty-two gods
Who are with you in the Hall of the Two Truths,
Who live by warding off evildoers,
Who drink of their blood,
On that day of judging characters before Wennofer [Osiris]. Lo, your name is
    "He-of-Two-Daughters,"
[And] "He-of-Maat's[2]-Two-Eyes."
Lo, I come before you,
Bringing Maat to you,
Having repelled evil for you.
I have not done crimes against people,
I have not mistreated cattle,
I have not sinned in the Place of Truth,
I have not known what should not be known,
I have not done any harm.
I did not begin a day by exacting more than my due,
My name did not reach the bark of the mighty ruler.

---

The Egyptian Book of the Dead. Republished with permission of University of California Press from *Ancient Egyptian Literature: A Book of Readings, Volume 2*, edited by Miriam Lichtheim, copyright © 1973 by the Regents of the University of California; permission conveyed through Copyright Clearance Center, Inc.

[1]**Hall of the Two Truths**: A place of judgment after death. Upon reaching the Hall of the Two Truths, ancient Egyptians would stand before a jury of gods, hear a recounting of their life's deeds, and have their hearts literally weighed by the god Osiris on the scales of justice. A heart heavy with guilt meant the owner would be devoured by the demon Ammit.

[2]**Maat** (muh-AHT): Egyptian goddess who personified truth, cosmic order, and justice. Her followers were considered upholders of the universal order.

I have not blasphemed a god,
I have not robbed the poor.
I have not done what the god abhors,
I have not maligned a servant to his master.
I have not caused pain,
I have not caused tears.
I have not killed,
I have not ordered to kill,
I have not made anyone suffer.
I have not damaged the offerings in the temples,
I have not depleted the loaves of the gods,
I have not stolen the cakes of the dead.
I have not copulated nor defiled myself.
I have not increased nor reduced the measure,
I have not diminished the arura [land].
I have not cheated in the fields.
I have not added to the weight of the balance,
I have not falsified the plummet of the scales.
I have not taken milk from the mouths of children,
I have not deprived cattle of their pasture.
I have not snared birds in the reeds of the gods,
I have not caught fish in their ponds.
I have not held back water in its season,
I have not dammed a flowing stream,
I have not quenched a needed fire.
I have not neglected the days of meat offerings,
I have not detained cattle belonging to the god,
I have not stopped a god in his procession.
I am pure, I am pure, I am pure, I am pure!

## READING QUESTIONS

1. What kinds of offenses are included in the list? What might explain the fact that so many have to do with economic fairness?

2. Based on this document, how would you describe the "perfect" Egyptian? What does the document tell you about the qualities and characteristics the Egyptians valued most?

3. What does the list tell you about the place of ethics in Egyptian religion? From the Egyptian perspective, was it possible to respect the gods without respecting one's fellow human beings?

## 1-5 | Life Lessons from an Ancient Egyptian
### *The Precepts of Ptahotep* (ca. 2650 B.C.E.)

Ancient Egyptian society was organized into a rigid class hierarchy with the semidivine pharaoh at the apex of the social pyramid. There were very clear directions about the responsibilities of people to the gods and to the pharaoh. Lofty ethical standards also guided the daily lives and social interactions of Egyptians. The following list of principles is attributed to a man who lived during the fifth dynasty. As you read, note how his advice addresses social hierarchy and family relationships.

If you find a wise man, a leader whose understanding is greater than yours, bend your arms and bow your back [to support him].

If you find a wise man who is your equal, speak out when he speaks evil. Those who hear you will approve, and the princes will hear of your good deeds.

If you find a wise man who is poor, do not be overbearing when he falls on hard times.

If you sit at the feet of a man who is greater than you, take what he gives, look at what you have in front of you, and don't stare at him, and don't speak until he asks you to. You do not know what is displeasing to his heart. Speak when he greets you, and then he will enjoy what you say.

If you are a messenger sent by a prince to another prince, repeat his words exactly, and don't alter a word of it.

If you are insignificant, follow an able man and everything you do will be good before the god.

If you are an able man, pay attention to what your son does.

If you are a leader, listen carefully and kindly to the speech of the petitioner.

If you want to establish friendship in a house, whether you are a lord, a brother, or a friend, beware of approaching the women. A thousand men are undone to enjoy a brief moment like a dream. Men gain only death for knowing them.

If you want your procedure to be good, avoid evil and greed. It corrupts fathers, mothers, and mother's brothers. It divides wife and man.

Do not be greedy in dividing, do not be greedy towards your kin. The gentle are more famous than the harsh.

If you are successful, establish your house. Love your wife in a husbandly embrace, fill her body, clothe her back. Provide ointment for her limbs. Gladden her heart as long as you live. She is a profitable field for her lord.

Satisfy those that come to your office with what you have.

Do not repeat a word of hearsay.

From George A. Barton, *Archaeology and the Bible* (Philadelphia: American Sunday-School Union, 1917), pp. 409–411. Language modernized by J. Michael Long.

If you are an able man who sits in the council of his lord, be silent and judicious.

If you are a strong man, earn respect by showing wisdom and quiet speech.

If you become great after you were little, and wealthy when you were once poor, do not be proud about your wealth. It has only come to you as a gift from the god.

Bend your back to your superior, the overseer of the king's house, and your house will endure because of his possessions. It is evil to show disobedience to a superior.

Do not corrupt children.

If you search the character of a friend, speak of it with him when he is alone.

Know your merchants when your fortunes are evil.

Let your face be bright your whole lifetime. That which goes out of the storehouse doesn't go back in, and he that is concerned with loaves already distributed still has an empty stomach.

How good it is when a son listens to what his father says! He will live long as a result. The god hates one who does not listen.

If a son listens to what his father says, none of his plans will fail. Instruct men who listen to you as if they were your son, whom the princes will judge successful. How many misfortunes happen to men who do not listen!

The fool who does not listen accomplishes nothing. He sees wisdom as ignorance, and good fortune as bad. His life is death. Men avoid him, because of the multiple evils he carries every day.

A son who listens is a follower of Horus. He prospers after he listens, lives a long life, and is revered. He teaches his children the same. Attain character . . . make righteousness to flourish and your children shall live.

Live your life so your lord will say to you, "How well his father taught him!" According to what I have attained, you will live as long as I have lived. I have lived one hundred ten years, and the king praised me above the ancestors in the vizier's[1] office because I served him righteously to his grave.

## READING QUESTIONS

1. According to the reading, what qualities are most essential for a man to have?

2. What seem to be the levels of hierarchy that are being described, and how should people of lower and higher rank treat each other? What rewards are promised to a man who follows this advice?

3. What does the reading reflect about family relationships? What members of the family seem to be most important, and why do you think that is?

---

[1]**vizier:** The highest-ranking official that served the Egyptian pharaoh.

# The Great and Terrible Power of the Gods

Both the Egyptians and the Mesopotamians believed that their prosperity and well-being depended on the gods. The gods had created the universe, and all the forces of nature and the cosmos were theirs to command. Thus, it was only through their benevolence that crops grew, disease was kept at bay, and enemies were defeated. If the gods, for whatever reason, chose to withdraw their favor, catastrophe was sure to follow. The following two documents illustrate Egyptian and Mesopotamian beliefs about the power of the gods. As you read them, ask yourself what light they shed on Egyptian and Mesopotamian religion. What similarities do you note? What differences in Mesopotamian and Egyptian outlooks do they suggest?

### READ AND COMPARE

1. What does the monotheistic message of Akhenaton suggest about Egyptian society and politics at that time, as opposed to the polytheistic message from Mesopotamia?

2. What is different in the tone of the two documents, and what does this suggest about the differences between Egyptian and Mesopotamian society?

## 1-6 | AKHENATON, *The Hymn to Aton* (ca. 1350 B.C.E.)

This hymn is attributed to the pharaoh Akhenaton (ah-keh-NAH-tuhn) (r. ca. 1367–1350 B.C.E.). When he became pharaoh, Akhenaton abandoned the traditional Egyptian gods and replaced them with the worship of Aton, a single, universal god. The change, although deeply unpopular and rejected after Akhenaton's death, was not as dramatic as it first appears. Akhenaton's Aton performed by himself all the tasks that a host of gods had performed in the past. Thus, traditional Egyptian beliefs about the relationship between humans, nature, and the divine remained largely intact. The hymn offers praise to Aton for bringing order, balance, and abundance to the world. As you read it, consider what it tells us about the way that Egyptians saw their society and their land.

Your rising is beautiful in the horizon of heaven, O Aton, ordainer of life.
You rise in the eastern horizon, filling every land with your radiance.
You are beautiful, great, splendid, and raised up above every land.

---

From Sir Ernest Alfred Wallis Budge, *The Gods of the Egyptians, or Studies in Egyptian Mythology*, vol. 1 (London: Methuen and Co., 1904), pp. 75–78. Text modernized by Amy R. Caldwell.

Your rays, like those of Ra,[1] deck every land you have made,

You have taken [the lands], and have made them subject to your son [i.e., Akhenaton].

You are far away, but your beams are on the earth;

You are on [people's] faces, they [admire] your goings.

When you set in the west, the earth is dark as with death.

Men lie down in their cabins shrouded in wrappings;

One cannot see his companion, and if all the goods that are under their heads are carried off, they cannot see [the thief]. . . .

You rise up in the horizon at dawn

You shine in the disk in the day

You scatter the darkness

You send out your rays, the Two Lands[2] rejoice,

Men wake up and stand on their feet,

For you raise them.

All beasts and cattle turn into their pastures,

The grass and herbs flourish,

The waterfowl fly over their marshes, their feathers praising your Ka.[3] . . .

How many are the things which you have made! . . .

O God, one who has no counterpart!

You, existing alone, did by your heart create the earth and everything that is thereon.

Men, cattle, beasts, and creatures of all kinds that move on feet,

All the creatures of the sky that fly with wings,

The deserts of Syria and Kush, and the land of Egypt

You have assigned to everyone his place,

Providing the daily food, each receiving his destined share;

You decree his span of life.

The speech and characteristics of men vary, as do their skins,

The dwellers in foreign lands having their distinguishing marks. . . .

O Lord of every land, you shine upon them,

O Aton of the day, you mighty one of majesty.

You create the life.

Of the foreign desert, and of all deserts, O Lord of the way

You create their life.

You have set a Nile in heaven, it descends upon them.

It makes on the mountains a flood like the great, green sea,

It waters the fields around their villages.

How perfect, wholly perfect, are your plans, O lord of eternity!

You are a Nile in the sky for all those who dwell in the deserts of foreign lands.

---

[1]**Ra**: Traditional Egyptian god of the sun.

[2]**Two Lands**: Upper and Lower Egypt, which formed one united kingdom at this time.

[3]**Ka**: The soul or spirit.

## READING QUESTIONS

1. What benefits does Aton bring? What might Aton expect humans to do to remain in his favor?

2. What does the hymn tell us about the Egyptian view of society? What are the implications of the claim that Aton has "assigned to everyone his place," providing everyone with "his destined share"?

3. What image does the hymn create of the Egyptian natural environment? What might explain the benevolent picture of nature painted by the hymn?


# 1-7    | *Lamentation over the Destruction of Sumer and Ur* (ca. 2000–1700 B.C.E.)

The "Lamentation over the Destruction of Sumer and Ur," created during the early second millennium B.C.E., was part of the long-standing Mesopotamian literary tradition of the "city lament," epic poems that linked a city's misfortune to the displeasure of the gods. Following the pattern typical of such works, it told how the gods An and Enlil decreed that the various gods of Sumer must abandon their cities, related the consequences of that decree for the city of Ur, and concluded with the intervention by the god Nanna on his city's behalf. The passages from the "Lamentation" included here describe Ur's devastation by Enlil, Enlil's rejection of Nanna's initial plea to spare his city, and Enlil's change of heart in response to Nanna's second appeal. As you read the passages, consider what they tell us about the relationship of the Mesopotamian gods to each other, to their cities, and to the people who worshipped them.


[The devastation of Ur.]


After Ur has stood [as] a great ox (noble on its own) —
the seedling city of lordship and kingship built on virgin soil —
to quickly subdue it [with] a rope like an ox, to bring its neck to the ground:
An, Enlil, Enki, and Ninmah determined its fate.
Who [can] overturn its fate, something that cannot be altered?
Who [can] oppose the pronouncement of An and Enlil?
An terrified Sumer in its dwelling place; the people were afraid.
Enlil brought a bitter storm; silence was established in the city.
Nintu blocked off the womb of the land.
Enki stopped up the water in the Tigris and Euphrates.
Utu removed the pronouncements of righteousness and just rulings.
Inanna granted battle and strife to a rebellious land.
Ningirsu poured Sumer to the dogs like milk.
Rebellion fell upon the land, something which no one [had] known.
It was something which had not been seen, something unspeakable, something
     that could not be grasped.

---

From Mark W. Chavalas, ed., *Historical Sources in Translation: The Ancient Near East* (Malden, Mass.: Blackwell Publishing, 2006), pp. 69–71. Permission conveyed through Copyright Clearance Center, Inc.

All the lands were confounded in their fear.
The gods of the city turned away; the shepherd fell away.
The population breathed in fear.
The storm immobilized them; daylight would not return for them.
With no daylight returning from them to their dwelling,
this is what Enlil, the shepherd of the black-headed ones,[1] did:

[The devastation of Ur continued.]


In Ur no one went for food, no one went for water.
Its people wandered[?] like water poured into a well.
Having no strength, they do not [even] travel.
Enlil installed a pestilent famine in the city.
He installed a city destroyer and a temple destroyer in the city.
He installed something no weapon could withstand in the city.
He installed impropriety and shiftiness in the city.
In Ur, like a single planted reed, he was establishing fear.
Its people, like fish seized with the hand, gasped for breath.
[People] small and great were spread about; no one [could] rise.
At the "royal station,"[2] which was atop the portico, there was no food.
The king, who [usually] ate fine food, [could] take only a morsel.
As the day grew dark . . . they knew hunger.
There was no beer in the brewery, there was no malt.
There was no food for him in his palace; it was unsuitable.
No grain filled his magnificent storehouse; he [could] not bear his life.
From the large granary to the small granary of Nanna there was no grain. . . .
The boat of the first fruits did not bring first fruits to the father who begat him
       [Nanna].
Its food offerings could not enter for Enlil [in] Nippur.

[Enlil rejects Nanna's appeal.]


"There is mourning in the midst of the haunted city. Reeds of tears are growing
       there. . . .
In its midst [the people] pass the day in lament.
O my son, noble one. . . . Why are you in tears?
O Nanna, noble one. . . . Why are you in tears?
There is no revoking the verdict, the command of the assembly.
The pronouncement of An and Enlil knows no overturning.

---

[1]**the black-headed ones**: The Sumerians.
[2]**"royal station"**: A place of offering on top of the central ziggurat, or temple, of Ur.

Ur was indeed given kingship, but it was not given an everlasting reign.

From [the time] the land was established ages ago until the people were multiplied,

who has seen a reign of kingship that has emerged for preeminence?

Its kingship, its reign, was long [but] grew tired.

My Nanna, do not grow tired [yourself], [but] leave your city!"

[Enlil relents and Ur is restored.]

"My son, the city that was [indeed] built for you in prosperity and joy is your reign.

The destroyed city, the great wall, the walls with leveled ramparts . . . all these were aside from the reign.

That which was arranged for you there, a reign of dark days . . . was created[?] for you.

Take a seat in your Etemennigur,[3] righteously built!

Let Ur be [re]built in joy; let the people lie down before you!

Let it have substance in its foundation! Let Ashnan dwell there with it!

Let there be joy in its branches! Let Utu rejoice there!

Let an abundance of grain overflow its table!

Let Ur, the city [for which] An decreed fate, be restored for you!"

Enlil, proclaiming his blessing, stretched his neck to the heavens:

Let the land be organized [from] south [to] north for Nanna!

For Suen, let the road of the land be set in order!

Like a cloud, like one hugging the earth, they will lay hands on him!

By the order of An and Enlil, let them set a righteous hand on him."

### READING QUESTIONS

1. What happens to Ur when the gods leave the city? What are the consequences of this catastrophe for the city's inhabitants?

2. What do Nanna's efforts to intervene on Ur's behalf tell you about the relationships between the gods? Between a god and his or her favored city?

3. What lessons might a Mesopotamian audience have taken from this lamentation?

---

[3]**Etemennigur:** The ziggurat of Ur.

## ▪ COMPARATIVE AND DISCUSSION QUESTIONS ▪

1. In what ways is the relationship between gods and humans in the Mesopotamian sources different from the relationship in the Egyptian documents? What role might geography and climate play in explaining the differences you note?

2. What role do goddesses play in the "Mesopotamian Creation Myth" and *The Epic of Gilgamesh*? What connections can you make between the depiction of goddesses in these documents and the Mesopotamian attitudes toward women revealed in Hammurabi's code?

3. Based on the documents, what would you list as the top priorities of a model Egyptian or Mesopotamian citizen? List at least three priorities each for Egyptians and Mesopotamians.

4. Compare and contrast the view of nature presented in Akhenaton's "Hymn to Aton" and the "Lamentation over the Destruction of Sumer and Ur." How would you explain the differences you note?

# 2

# Small Kingdoms and Mighty Empires in the Near East

## 1200–510 B.C.E.

The following documents explore the beliefs of the Hebrew people and help connect their story to the political consolidation and military conflict that shaped the development of the Near East. Unified by their distinctive faith, the Hebrews defeated a number of enemies to build a "small kingdom" in Palestine. The kingdom of Israel flourished under Kings David and Solomon, whose heirs split the kingdom into two states — Israel and Judah — around 925 B.C.E. These smaller states proved tempting targets for the region's powerful empires, and both eventually lost their independence. The northern kingdom, Israel, fell to the Assyrians, while around 587 B.C.E. the remnants of the southern kingdom were defeated by the Babylonian king Nebuchadnezzar (ne-buh-kuhd-NEH-zuhr) and exiled to his capital. The Hebrews were forced to reside in Babylon until its capture by the new Persian ruler, Cyrus the Great. Although Cyrus practiced the dualistic religion known as Zoroastrianism, he let the people he conquered maintain their religious traditions and allowed the Hebrews to return to Jerusalem, their homeland. His was a very different kind of empire than that of the Assyrians, and the emergence of the Persian Empire marked the beginning of a new chapter in the history of the region.

## 2-1   |   The Hebrews Explain Creation
### *Book of Genesis* (ca. 950–450 B.C.E.)

The following passage is the beginning of Genesis, the first book of the Hebrew Bible, or Torah. The range of dates given for this selection reveals something about the hotly debated issue of how the Hebrew Bible was created. Modern historians believe that by about 450 B.C.E. the book of Genesis existed in something close to the form we now possess. At the same time, it is known that some passages of Genesis are much older. As you read the passage, think about other Near Eastern creation stories to which you have been exposed (for example, the Mesopotamian creation myth included in Chapter 1 of this sourcebook). How is Genesis similar to those stories? What aspects of it are unique?

In the beginning God created the heavens and the earth.

Now the earth was formless and empty, darkness was over the surface of the deep, and the Spirit of God was hovering over the waters.

And God said, "Let there be light," and there was light. God saw that the light was good, and He separated the light from the darkness. God called the light "day," and the darkness he called "night." And there was evening, and there was morning—the first day.

And God said, "Let there be an expanse between the waters to separate water from water." So God made the expanse and separated the water under the expanse from the water above it. And it was so. God called the expanse "sky." And there was evening, and there was morning—the second day.

And God said, "Let the water under the sky be gathered to one place, and let dry ground appear." And it was so. God called the dry ground "land," and the gathered waters he called "seas." And God saw that it was good.

Then God said, "Let the land produce vegetation: seed-bearing plants and trees on the land that bear fruit with seed in it, according to their various kinds." And it was so. The land produced vegetation: plants bearing seed according to their kinds and trees bearing fruit with seed in it according to their kinds. And God saw that it was good. And there was evening, and there was morning—the third day.

And God said, "Let there be lights in the expanse of the sky to separate the day from the night, and let them serve as signs to mark seasons and days and years, and let them be lights in the expanse of the sky to give light on the earth." And it was so. God made two great lights—the greater light to govern the day and the lesser light to govern the night. He also made the stars. God set them in the expanse of the sky to give light on the earth, to govern the day and the night, and to separate light from darkness. And God saw that it was good. And there was evening, and there was morning—the fourth day.

And God said, "Let the water teem with living creatures, and let birds fly above the earth across the expanse of the sky." So God created the great

From Genesis 1:1–31; 2:1–7.

creatures of the sea and every living and moving thing with which the water teems, according to their kinds, and every winged bird according to its kind. And God saw that it was good. God blessed them and said, "Be fruitful and increase in number and fill the water in the seas, and let the birds increase on the earth." And there was evening, and there was morning—the fifth day.

And God said, "Let the land produce living creatures according to their kinds: livestock, creatures that move along the ground, and wild animals, each according to its kind." And it was so. God made the wild animals according to their kinds, the livestock according to their kinds, and all the creatures that move along the ground according to their kinds. And God saw that it was good.

Then God said, "Let us make man in our image, in our likeness, and let them rule over the fish of the sea and the birds of the air, over the livestock, over all the earth, and over all the creatures that move along the ground."

So God created man in his own image, in the image of God he created him; male and female he created them.

God blessed them and said to them, "Be fruitful and increase in number; fill the earth and subdue it. Rule over the fish of the sea and the birds of the air and over every living creature that moves on the ground."

Then God said, "I give you every seed-bearing plant on the face of the whole earth and every tree that has fruit with seed in it. They will be yours for food. And to all the beasts of the earth and all the birds of the air and all the creatures that move on the ground—everything that has the breath of life in it—I give every green plant for food." And it was so.

God saw all that he had made, and it was very good. And there was evening, and there was morning—the sixth day.

Thus the heavens and the earth were completed in all their vast array. By the seventh day God had finished the work he had been doing; so on the seventh day he rested from all his work. And God blessed the seventh day and made it holy, because on it he rested from all the work of creating that he had done.

This is the account of the heavens and the earth when they were created. When the Lord God made the earth and the heavens—and no shrub of the field had yet appeared on the earth and no plant of the field had yet sprung up, for the Lord God had not sent rain on the earth and there was no man to work the ground, but streams came up from the earth and watered the whole surface of the ground—the Lord God formed the man from the dust of the ground and breathed into his nostrils the breath of life, and the man became a living being.

### READING QUESTIONS

1. Consider the stages of creation. What does their order reveal about the Hebrew faith?

2. God creates man on the sixth day, but a few verses later the text states that "there was not a man to till the ground"; then streams watered the earth and

God formed man from the dust of the ground. Why does God seem to create man twice, and what could this indicate about the way the text was created?

3.  Explain the following passage: "Be fruitful and increase in number; fill the earth and subdue it." What does this indicate about how the Hebrews understood the relationship between their God and humanity?

4.  Given that all of God's creations through the sixth day are described as "good," what does that suggest about the source of evil in the world? Does evil come from nature, from God, or from human beings?

## 2-2    |    The Hebrew Law and Covenant

### *Exodus and Deuteronomy* (ca. 950–450 B.C.E.)

Moses, the greatest of the Hebrew prophets, is revered by Jews, Christians, and Muslims alike. After Moses led his people out of bondage in Egypt, the Hebrew God revealed a series of commandments to Moses on Mount Sinai. This was not the first occasion when their God handed down moral commandments to his people, but it was here that he forbade his people to worship other gods. The passage thus establishes monotheism, the worship of and belief in only one god, as the central tenet of the Hebrew religion. At the same time, it identifies the Hebrews as God's chosen people.

On the morning of the third day there was thunder and lightning, with a thick cloud over the mountain, and a very loud trumpet blast. Everyone in the camp trembled. Then Moses led the people out of the camp to meet with God, and they stood at the foot of the mountain. Mount Sinai was covered with smoke, because the Lord descended on it in fire. The smoke billowed up from it like smoke from a furnace, the whole mountain trembled violently, and the sound of the trumpet grew louder and louder. Then Moses spoke and the voice of God answered him.

The Lord descended to the top of Mount Sinai and called Moses to the top of the mountain. So Moses went up and the Lord said to him, "Go down and warn the people so they do not force their way through to see the Lord and many of them perish. Even the priests, who approach the Lord, must consecrate themselves, or the Lord will break out against them."

Moses said to the Lord, "The people cannot come up Mount Sinai, because you yourself warned us, 'Put limits around the mountain and set it apart as holy.'"

The Lord replied, "Go down and bring Aaron[1] up with you. But the priests and the people must not force their way through to come up to the Lord, or he will break out against them."

---

From Exodus 19:16–25; 20:1–21; Deuteronomy 28:1–9, 15–26.

[1]**Aaron**: Moses's brother and high priest of the Hebrews.

So Moses went down to the people and told them.

And God spoke all these words:

"I am the Lord your God, who brought you out of Egypt, out of the land of slavery.

"You shall have no other gods before me.

"You shall not make for yourself an idol in the form of anything in heaven above or on the earth beneath or in the waters below. You shall not bow down to them or worship them; for I, the Lord your God, am a jealous God, punishing the children for the sin of the fathers to the third and fourth generation of those who hate me, but showing love to a thousand [generations] of those who love me and keep my commandments.

"You shall not misuse the name of the Lord your God, for the Lord will not hold anyone guiltless who misuses his name.

"Remember the Sabbath day by keeping it holy. Six days you shall labor and do all your work, but the seventh day is a Sabbath to the Lord your God. On it you shall not do any work, neither you, nor your son or daughter, nor your man-servant or maidservant, nor your animals, nor the alien within your gates. For in six days the Lord made the heavens and the earth, the sea, and all that is in them, but he rested on the seventh day. Therefore the Lord blessed the Sabbath day and made it holy.

"Honor your father and your mother, so that you may live long in the land the Lord your God is giving you.

"You shall not murder.

"You shall not commit adultery.

"You shall not give false testimony against your neighbor.

"You shall not covet your neighbor's house. You shall not covet your neighbor's wife, or his manservant or maidservant, his ox or donkey, or anything that belongs to your neighbor."

When the people saw the thunder and lightning and heard the trumpet and saw the mountain in smoke, they trembled with fear. They stayed at a distance and said to Moses, "Speak to us yourself and we will listen. But do not have God speak to us or we will die."

Moses said to the people, "Do not be afraid. God has come to test you, so that the fear of God will be with you to keep you from sinning."

The people remained at a distance, while Moses approached the thick darkness where God was.

[After giving the Hebrews the law, Moses also tells the Hebrews what will happen if they obey or disobey their God.]

If you fully obey the Lord your God and carefully follow all his commands I give you today, the Lord your God will set you high above all the nations on earth. All these blessings will come upon you and accompany you if you obey the Lord your God:

You will be blessed in the city and blessed in the country.

The fruit of your womb will be blessed, and the crops of your land and the young of your livestock — the calves of your herds and the lambs of your flocks.

Your basket and your kneading trough will be blessed.

You will be blessed when you come in and blessed when you go out.

The Lord will grant that the enemies who rise up against you will be defeated before you. They will come at you from one direction but flee from you in seven.

The Lord will send a blessing on your barns and on everything you put your hand to. The Lord your God will bless you in the land he is giving you.

The Lord will establish you as his holy people, as he promised you on oath, if you keep the commands of the Lord your God and walk in his ways. . . .

However, if you do not obey the Lord your God and do not carefully follow all his commands and decrees I am giving you today, all these curses will come upon you and overtake you:

You will be cursed in the city and cursed in the country.

Your basket and your kneading trough will be cursed.

The fruit of your womb will be cursed, and the crops of your land, and the calves of your herds and the lambs of your flocks.

You will be cursed when you come in and cursed when you go out.

The Lord will send on you curses, confusion and rebuke in everything you put your hand to, until you are destroyed and come to sudden ruin because of the evil you have done in forsaking him. The Lord will plague you with diseases until he has destroyed you from the land you are entering to possess. The Lord will strike you with wasting disease, with fever and inflammation, with scorching heat and drought, with blight and mildew, which will plague you until you perish. The sky over your head will be bronze, the ground beneath you iron. The Lord will turn the rain of your country into dust and powder; it will come down from the skies until you are destroyed.

The Lord will cause you to be defeated before your enemies. You will come at them from one direction but flee from them in seven, and you will become a thing of horror to all the kingdoms on earth. Your carcasses will be food for all the birds of the air and the beasts of the earth, and there will be no one to frighten them away.

## READING QUESTIONS

1. Consider the description of God's descent upon Mount Sinai and the following passage: "And the Lord said to [Moses], 'Go down and warn the people so they do not force their way through to see the Lord and many of them perish.'" What does this passage reveal about the Hebrews' conception of their God's power?

2. Why does God forbid the creation and worship of idols?

3. What incentives are there for the Hebrews to obey their God's commands?

SOURCES IN CONVERSATION

# Assyrian, Persian, and Hebrew Perceptions of Monarchy

In the eyes of their countrymen, the high kings of Assyria and Cyrus the Great (r. 559–530 B.C.E.), the founder of the Persian Empire, earned their titles on the battlefield. However, as important as Cyrus's military victories were, his accomplishments as a ruler were perhaps even more impressive. Through his policies, he laid the foundation of a lasting state, binding together far-flung and diverse peoples and harnessing their energies and resources to the royal will. Assyrian kings relied much more upon brute force, though they also used some innovative and relatively progressive tactics to maintain their empire. In contrast, the first king of the Hebrews came to power reluctantly, as the Hebrews believed that their god Yahweh was omnipotent and their worship of him should not be diluted by revering a human king. The united kingdom of Israel was short-lived in comparison to the Assyrian and Persian Empires, though the cultural legacy the Hebrews left to the world far surpassed the legacy of Persia or Assyria.

## READ AND COMPARE

1. What do these three documents reveal about the different expectations of kingship for Assyrians, Persians, and Hebrews?

2. How does the tone of the three documents vary, and what does that variance in tone tell you about the experiences of the various societies?

## 2-3 | *Assyrian Kings Proclaim Their Greatness*
### (ca. 1220–1070 B.C.E.)

From the point of view of the Hebrews, Assyrian expansion was an unqualified evil. Some claimed that conquest by the Assyrians was a punishment inflicted on the Hebrews for allowing moral and spiritual decay to infect their society, but that did not make the Assyrians themselves any less wicked. Needless to say, the Assyrians saw things differently. The two documents included are Assyrian royal inscriptions, written accounts of the accomplishments of the rulers who ordered their creation. In the first, Tukulti-Ninurta I (r. 1243–1207 B.C.E.) describes his construction of a new capital, Kar-Tukulti-Ninurta. In the second, Tiglath-pilesar I (r. 1115–1077 B.C.E.) gives an account of his conquests. As you read these documents, note the similarities. What qualities did both kings claim for themselves? What do the documents tell you about what, from the Assyrian perspective, made a king "great"?

From Mark W. Chavalas, ed., *The Ancient Near East: Historical Sources in Translation* (Malden, Mass.: Blackwell Publishing, 2006), pp. 155–158. Permission conveyed through Copyright Clearance Center, Inc.

## [Tukulti-Ninurta Builds a Capital]

Then the god Ashur[1] my lord requested of me a cult center across [the river] from my city, which was chosen by the gods, and he commanded me to build his temple. At the command of the god Ashur, the god who loves me, on the other side [of the river] from Assur, my city, I indeed built a city for the god Ashur on the opposite bank of the Tigris, in the barren steppes and meadows where no house or dwelling had previously existed. No ruin mound or debris was piled up there, no bricks were laid. I named it Kar-Tukulti-Ninurta. I sliced straight through the hills, I hewed out high mountain passes with chisels. I channeled a stream that brings abundance, making secure the life of the land. I transformed the environs of my city into irrigated land. From the abundant yield of the waters of that canal I prepared perpetual offerings for the god Ashur and the great gods, my lords.

Then I built in my city — Kar-Tukulti-Ninurta, the cult center that I constructed — a pure temple, an awe-inspiring sanctuary for the dwelling of the god Ashur, my lord. I named it Ekurmesharra. Within it I completed a great ziggurat[2] as the cult platform for the god Ashur, my lord, and I deposited my inscriptions.

May a later ruler restore this ziggurat and temple of the god Ashur, my lord, when they become dilapidated. May he anoint my inscriptions with oil, may he offer sacrifices, and may he return [them] to their proper places. The gods Ashur, Enlil, and Shamash will listen to his prayers.

He who does not restore the ziggurat and the temple of Ashur my lord; who removes my inscriptions and inscribed name; who destroys it by inattention, neglect, or disrepair; who plans any evil matter or makes trouble for this ziggurat and for this temple of the god Ashur my lord; may the gods Ashur, Enlil, and Shamash — the gods who are my help — lead him into distress and sorrow. Wherever battle and conflict are found, may they break his weapons. May they bring about the defeat of his army. May they hand him over to a king who is his adversary and make him live in bondage in the land of his enemies. May they overthrow his reign, and may they destroy his name and his progeny from the land.

## [Tiglath-pilesar Conquers His Enemies]

At that time, by the exalted might of Ashur, my lord, with the authoritative consent of Shamash, the warrior, with the support of the great gods by which I have just authority in the four quarters and have neither competitor in battle nor rival in combat, Ashur, my lord, commissioned me to march to the Nairi lands, whose distant kings on the Upper Sea coast in the west, have not known submission. I passed through treacherous roads and narrow passes — whose interior no king had previously known — blocked roads and closed remote mountain regions: the mountains of Elama, Amadanu, Elhish, Sherabeli, Tarhuna, Terkahuli, Kisra, Tarhanabe, Elula, Hashtarae, Shahishara, Ubera, Miadruni, Shulianzi, Nubanashe, and Sheshe.

---

[1]**Ashur**: The chief god of the Assyrian pantheon.
[2]**ziggurat**: A pyramid-shaped temple, often located in the center of a city.

Sixteen rugged mountains became smooth terrain in my chariot because I hacked that difficult terrain with bronze mattocks. I felled the Urumu trees of the mountains. I constructed bridges for the passage of my chariots and troops.

I crossed the Euphrates. The king of Tummu, the king of Tunubu, the king of Tualu, the king of Dardaru, the king of Uzula, the king of Unzamunu, the king of Andiabu, the king of Piladarnu, the king of Adurginu, the king of Kulibarzinu, the king of Shinibirnu, the king of Himua, the king of Paiteru, the king of Uiram, the king of Shururia, the king of Abaenu, the king of Adaenu, the king of Kirinu, the king of Albaya, the king of Ugina, the king of Nazabia, the king of Abarsiunu, the king of Dayenu—a total of 23 kings of the Nairi lands—mustered their chariotry and their troops within their lands. They advanced in order to wage warfare, battle, and combat.

I attacked them with the fury of my fierce weaponry. I brought about the slaughter of their vast armies like a deluge of Adad.[3] I laid out like sheaves the corpses of their warriors in the plains, on the heights of the mountains, and in the vicinity of their cities. I seized 120 of their wooden chariots in the midst of battle. I pursued the 60 kings of the Nairi lands, including those who had come to their aid, at the tip of my arrow as far as the Upper Sea.

I conquered their great towns. I removed their booty, their property, and their possessions. Their cities I burned with fire, leveled, and demolished. I turned them into a mound and ruin heap. I brought back multitudinous herds of horses, mules, and donkeys and innumerable livestock from their pastures.

I personally captured alive all of the kings of the Nairi lands. I showed mercy on those kings and spared their lives. I released them from their captivity and bondage in the presence of Shamash, my lord. I made them swear by my great gods an oath of permanent vassalage. I seized their royal male progeny as hostages. I imposed upon them a tribute of 1,200 horses and 2,000 cattle. I released them to their lands.

Sheni, the king of Dayenu, had not been submissive to Ashur, my lord, so I brought him into captivity and bondage to my city. I showed him mercy and released him alive from my city, Ashur, in order to proclaim the glory of the great gods. I ruled the vast Nairi lands in their entirety and subjugated all their kings at my two feet.

## READING QUESTIONS

1. How would you describe the language used to discuss each king's accomplishments? What does this tell you about Assyrian ideas of kingship?

2. What role did Assyrian technology play in each accomplishment? What light do the inscriptions shed on the importance of such technology to the Assyrians' success?

3. What role did religion play in each accomplishment? In this context, what goals were served by both the construction of a capital and a successful military campaign?

---

[3]**Adad**: The Assyrian storm-god.

**30** Chapter 2 Small Kingdoms and Mighty Empires, 1200–510 B.C.E.

**SOURCES IN CONVERSATION**

## 2-4 | CYRUS OF PERSIA, *Ruling an Empire* (ca. 550 B.C.E.)

An important part of Cyrus's imperial strategy, and one that would be continued by his successors, was to present Persian kings as righteous rulers. Thus, Cyrus's generous treatment of the Jews of Babylonia was more than an act of kindness. By returning the Jews to their homeland and helping them rebuild their temple, Cyrus presented himself as a champion of right order. As you read the royal inscription included below, compare it to those of the Assyrian kings above and the passage from the book of Samuel from the Hebrew Bible below. How do they differ? What do the differences tell you about the governing strategies of the two empires?

I am Cyrus, king of the world, great king, legitimate king, king of Babylon, king of Sumer and Akkad, king of the four rims [of the earth], son of Cambyses, great king, king of Anshan, grandson of Cyrus, great king, king of Anshan, descendant of Teispes, great king, king of Anshan, of a family [which] always [exercised] kingship; whose rule Bel and Nabu[1] love, whom they want as king to please their hearts.

When I entered Babylon as a friend and [when] I established the seat of government in the palace of the ruler under jubilation and rejoicing, Marduk,[2] the great lord (induced) the magnanimous inhabitants of Babylon (to love me), and I was daily endeavoring to worship him. My numerous troops walked around in Babylon in peace, I did not allow anybody to terrorize [any place] of the [country of Sumer] and Akkad. I strove for peace in Babylon, [I abolished] the [labor tribute] which was against their [social] standing. I brought relief to their dilapidated housings, putting an end to their complaints. Marduk, the great Lord, was well pleased with my deeds and sent friendly blessings to myself, Cyrus, the king who worships him, to Cambyses, my son, the offspring of my loins, as well as to all my troops, and we all [praised] his great [godhead] joyously, standing before him in peace.

All the kings of the entire world from the Upper to the Lower Sea, those who are seated in throne rooms, [those who] live in other [types of buildings as well as] all the kings of the West land living in tents, brought their heavy tributes and kissed my feet in Babylon. [As to the region] from . . . as far as Ashur and Susa, Agade, Eshnuna, the towns of Zamban, Me-Turnu, Der, as well as the region of the Gutium, I returned to [these] sacred cities on the other sides of the Tigris, the sanctuaries of which have been ruins for a long time, the images which [used] to live therein and established for them permanent sanctuaries. I [also] gathered all their [former] inhabitants and returned [to them] their habitations. Furthermore, I resettled upon the command of Marduk, the great lord, all the gods of Sumer and Akkad who Nabonidus[3] has brought into Babylon to

From James B. Pritchard, ed., *Ancient Near Eastern Texts Relating to the Old Testament*, 3d ed. (Princeton, N.J.: Princeton University Press, 1969), pp. 315–316. Permission conveyed through Copyright Clearance Center, Inc.

[1]**Bel and Nabu**: Babylonian gods.
[2]**Marduk**: The Mesopotamian god who created humans. See Document 1-1.
[3]**Nabonidus**: The last king of the Neo-Babylonian empire, whom Cyrus overthrew.

the anger of the lord of the gods, unharmed, in the [former] chapels, the places which make them happy.

May all the gods whom I have resettled in their sacred cities ask daily Bel and Nabu for a long life for me and may they recommend me [to him]; to Marduk, my lord, they may say this: "Cyrus, the king who worships you, and Cambyses, his son, . . . all of them I settled in a peaceful place . . . ducks and doves . . . I endeavored to repair their dwelling places. . . ."

### READING QUESTIONS

1. Why does Cyrus claim that he entered Babylon as a friend, and what orders did he give his troops about how to treat the Babylonians?

2. What reforms and improvements did Cyrus bring to Babylon? Why would Cyrus solve problems that he had not created in the first place?

3. How did Cyrus treat people who had been displaced from their homes? How did he treat the gods of the people he conquered?

## 2-5 | *Book of Samuel 8:1–10:27* (ca. 630–540 B.C.E.)

According to the book of Samuel in the Hebrew Bible, Saul, the first king of Israel, was chosen by a judge named Samuel, but the Hebrews were hesitant to follow a mortal king and Saul did not initially consider himself worthy of the honor either. After a string of military victories, he lost the support of Yahweh and ultimately killed himself during a battle to avoid becoming a prisoner to the Philistines. He was eventually succeeded by his son-in-law David. As you read the following passage, pay attention to the changing perceptions of the Hebrews, Samuel, and Saul about the prospect of kingship.

And it came to pass, when Samuel was old, that he made his sons judges over Israel. Now the name of his first-born was Joel; and the name of his second, Abijah: they were judges in Beer-sheba. And his sons walked not in his ways, but turned aside after lucre,[1] and took bribes, and perverted justice.

Then all the elders of Israel gathered themselves together, and came to Samuel unto Ramah; and they said unto him, Behold, thou art old, and thy sons walk not in thy ways: now make us a king to judge us like all the nations. But the thing displeased Samuel, when they said, Give us a king to judge us. And Samuel prayed unto Jehovah. And Jehovah said unto Samuel, Hearken unto the voice of the people in all that they say unto thee; for they have not rejected thee, but they have rejected me, that I should not be king over them. According to all the works which they have done since the day that I brought them up out of Egypt even unto this day, in that they have forsaken me, and served other gods, so do they also unto thee. Now therefore hearken unto their voice: howbeit thou

---

From 1 Samuel 8:1–10:27. American Standard Version.

[1]**lucre**: Money gained in an immoral way.

**32** Chapter 2 Small Kingdoms and Mighty Empires, 1200–510 B.C.E.

**SOURCES IN CONVERSATION**

shalt protest solemnly unto them, and shalt show them the manner of the king that shall reign over them.

And Samuel told all the words of Jehovah unto the people that asked of him a king. And he said, This will be the manner of the king that shall reign over you: he will take your sons, and appoint them unto him, for his chariots, and to be his horsemen; and they shall run before his chariots; and he will appoint them unto him for captains of thousands, and captains of fifties; and he will set some to plow his ground, and to reap his harvest, and to make his instruments of war, and the instruments of his chariots. And he will take your daughters to be perfumers, and to be cooks, and to be bakers. And he will take your fields, and your vineyards, and your oliveyards, even the best of them, and give them to his servants. And he will take the tenth of your seed, and of your vineyards, and give to his officers, and to his servants. And he will take your men-servants, and your maid-servants, and your goodliest young men, and your asses, and put them to his work. He will take the tenth of your flocks: and ye shall be his servants. And ye shall cry out in that day because of your king whom ye shall have chosen you; and Jehovah will not answer you in that day.

But the people refused to hearken unto the voice of Samuel; and they said, Nay: but we will have a king over us, that we also may be like all the nations, and that our king may judge us, and go out before us, and fight our battles. And Samuel heard all the words of the people, and he rehearsed them in the ears of Jehovah. And Jehovah said to Samuel, Hearken unto their voice, and make them a king.

Now there was a man of Benjamin, whose name was Kish . . . and he had a son, whose name was Saul, a young man and . . . goodly . . . from his shoulders and upward he was higher than any of the people. And the asses of Kish, Saul's father, were lost. And Kish said to Saul his son, Take now one of the servants with thee, and arise, go seek the asses. And he passed through the hill-country of Ephraim, and passed through the land of Shalishah, but they found them not: then they passed through the land of Shaalim, and there they were not: and he passed through the land of the Benjamites, but they found them not.

When they were come to the land of Zuph, Saul said to his servant that was with him, Come, and let us return, lest my father leave off caring for the asses, and be anxious for us. And he said unto him, Behold now, there is in this city a man of God, and he is a man that is held in honor; all that he saith cometh surely to pass: now let us go thither; peradventure he can tell us concerning our journey whereon we go.

. . .

And they went up to the city; and as they came within the city, behold, Samuel came out toward them, to go up to the high place.

Now Jehovah had revealed unto Samuel a day before Saul came, saying, To-morrow about this time I will send thee a man out of the land of Benjamin, and thou shalt anoint him to be prince over my people Israel; and he shall save my people out of the hand of the Philistines: for I have looked upon my people, because their cry is come unto me. And when Samuel saw Saul, Jehovah said unto him, Behold, the man of whom I spake to thee! this same shall have authority over my people. Then Saul drew near to Samuel in the gate, and said, Tell me, I pray thee, where the seer's house is. And Samuel answered Saul, and said, I am the seer; go up before me unto the high place, for ye shall eat with me to-day: and in the morning I will let thee go, and will tell thee all that is in thy heart. And as for thine asses that were lost three days ago, set not thy mind on them; for they are found. And for whom is all that is desirable in Israel? Is it not for thee, and for all thy father's house? And Saul answered and said, Am not I a Benjamite, of the smallest of the tribes of Israel? and my family the least of all the families of the tribe of Benjamin? wherefore then speakest thou to me after this manner?

. . .

As they were going down at the end of the city, Samuel said to Saul, Bid the servant pass on before us (and he passed on), but stand thou still first, that I may cause thee to hear the word of God.

. . .

Then Samuel took the vial of oil, and poured it upon his head, and kissed him, and said, Is it not that Jehovah hath anointed thee to be prince over his inheritance? When thou art departed from me to-day, then thou shalt find two men by Rachel's sepulchre, in the border of Benjamin at Zelzah; and they will say unto thee, The asses which thou wentest to seek are found; and, lo, thy father hath left off caring for the asses, and is anxious for you, saying, What shall I do for my son? Then shalt thou go on forward from thence, and thou shalt come to the oak of Tabor; and there shall meet thee there three men going up to God to Beth-el, one carrying three kids, and another carrying three loaves of bread, and another carrying a bottle of wine: and they will salute thee, and give thee two loaves of bread, which thou shalt receive of their hand. After that thou shalt come to the hill of God, where is the garrison of the Philistines: and it shall come to pass, when thou art come thither to the city, that thou shalt meet a band of prophets coming down from the high place with a psaltery, and a timbrel, and a pipe, and a harp, before them; and they will be prophesying: and the Spirit of Jehovah will come mightily upon thee, and thou shalt prophesy with them, and shalt be turned into another man. And let it be, when these signs are come unto thee, that thou do as occasion shall serve thee; for God is with thee.

And it was so, that, when he had turned his back to go from Samuel, God gave him another heart: and all those signs came to pass that day. And when they came thither to the hill, behold, a band of prophets met him; and the Spirit of God came mightily upon him, and he prophesied among them. And it came to pass, when all that knew him beforetime saw that, behold, he prophesied with the prophets, then the people said one to another, What is this that is come unto the son of Kish? Is Saul also among the prophets?

. . .

And Samuel called the people together unto Jehovah to Mizpah; and he said unto the children of Israel, Thus saith Jehovah, the God of Israel, I brought up

Israel out of Egypt, and I delivered you out of the hand of the Egyptians, and out of the hand of all the kingdoms that oppressed you: but ye have this day rejected your God, who himself saveth you out of all your calamities and your distresses; and ye have said unto him, Nay, but set a king over us. Now therefore present yourselves before Jehovah by your tribes, and by your thousands. So Samuel brought all the tribes of Israel near, and the tribe of Benjamin was taken. And he brought the tribe of Benjamin near by their families; and the family of the Matrites was taken; and Saul the son of Kish was taken: but when they sought him, he could not be found. Therefore they asked of Jehovah further, Is there yet a man to come hither? And Jehovah answered, Behold, he hath hid himself among the baggage. And they ran and fetched him thence; and when he stood among the people, he was higher than any of the people from his shoulders and upward. And Samuel said to all the people, See ye him whom Jehovah hath chosen, that there is none like him among all the people? And all the people shouted, and said, Long live the king.

### READING QUESTIONS

1. Why were the Hebrews hesitant to embrace a human king, and what changed their minds about it?

2. What aspects of the Hebrew perception of kingship were similar to Persian ideas about it, and how was their perception different?

3. Why do you suppose the Hebrew perception of kingship was different than Persian or Assyrian perceptions of monarchy?

## 2-6 | A Choice Between Good and Evil

### ZOROASTER, *Gatha 30: Good Thoughts, Good Words, Good Deeds* (ca. 600 B.C.E.)

The Persian priest Zoroaster (zo-ro-ASS-tuhr), also known as Zarathustra (zar-uh-THUH-struh), reformed the religion of his people, separating the traditional deities into two groups. One group, led by Ahuramazda (ah-HOOR-uh-MAZ-duh), promoted goodness and ethical behavior; the other, led by Ahriman (AH-ree-mahn), was the force behind all evil. The names of the other gods were often personifications of an inner quality, such as Good Thought and Piety. Embraced by King Darius (dah-REE-uhs) (r. 521–486 B.C.E.), Zoroastrianism (zo-ro-ASS-tree-uh-nihz-uhm) remained a dominant belief in Persia for centuries. The following passage is Gatha 30, one of seventeen poems believed to be written by Zoroaster himself. The Gathas are part of a larger text known as the Yasna, which contains liturgical services, prayers, and hymns to the good gods.

From Charles F. Horne, ed., *The Sacred Books and Early Literature of the East* (New York: Park, Austin, and Lipscombe, 1917), pp. 23–25.

Now will I proclaim to those who will hear the things that the understanding man should remember, for hymns unto Ahura and prayers to Good Thought; also the joy that is with the heavenly lights, which through Right shall be beheld by him who wisely thinks.

Hear with your ears the best things; look upon them with clear-seeing thought, for decision between the two Beliefs, each man for himself before the Great Consummation,[1] bethinking you that it be accomplished to our pleasure.

Now the two primal Spirits, who revealed themselves in vision as Twins, are the Better and the Bad in thought and word and action. And between these two the wise once chose aright, the foolish not so.

And when these twin Spirits came together in the beginning, they established Life and Not-Life, and that at the last the Worst Existence shall be to the followers of the Lie, but the Best Thought to him that follows Right.

Of these twin Spirits he that followed the Lie chose doing the worst things; the holiest Spirit chose Right, he that clothes himself with the heavens as a garment. So likewise they that are eager to please Ahura Mazda [choose] dutiful actions.

Between these two the demons also chose not aright, for infatuation came upon them as they took counsel together, so that they chose the Worst Thought. Then they rushed together to Violence, that they might enfeeble the world of man.

And to them [humans] came Dominion, Good Thought, and Right; and Piety gave continued life of their bodies and indestructibility. . . .

So when there comes the punishment of these evil ones, then, O Mazda, at thy command shall Good Thought establish the Dominion. . . .

So may we be those that make this world advance! O Mazda, and you other Ahuras,[2] gather together the Assembly, . . . that thoughts may meet where Wisdom is at home.

Then truly on the Lie shall come destruction [but those who choose good] shall be partakers in the promised reward in the fair abode of Good Thought, of Mazda, and of Right.

If, O mortals, you follow those commandments that Mazda hath ordained — of happiness and pain, the long punishment for the liars, and blessings for the righteous — then hereafter shall ye have bliss.

## READING QUESTIONS

1. How does Zoroaster explain the creation of all things that exist? What role do humans play in creation?

2. What are the attributes of the good gods and the evil gods?

3. How does a person become a follower of either the good gods or the bad gods? What happens to the good people and the evil people at the end of the world?

---

[1]**Great Consummation:** The end of the world.
[2]**Ahuras:** The good gods.

## ▪ COMPARATIVE AND DISCUSSION QUESTIONS ▪

1. What are some differences or similarities between the Mesopotamian (Document 1-1), Hebrew, and Zoroastrian explanations for creation? How do the tones of each document compare?

2. What, if any, differences can you find between man as created by God in Genesis and man as commanded by God in Exodus and Deuteronomy? What kind of god is the God in each document?

3. How do the "Hymn to Aton" (Document 1-6) and the "Hebrew Law and Covenant" (Document 2-2) compare in their attitudes toward foreign peoples?

4. How could the "Hebrew Law and Covenant" be used to explain the Hebrews' deliverance from the Assyrians? How could it explain Cyrus's restoration of Jerusalem to the Hebrews?

# 3

# The Development of Greek Society and Culture

## ca. 3000–338 B.C.E.

The earliest literature of the Greek civilization reflects the Greeks' intense interest in examining the world as a way to understand themselves, their gods, and their surroundings. Through their epic poems, written around 800 B.C.E., Homer and Hesiod provided explanations for how the gods worked in the world and how humans should behave. Around this time the Greeks developed the polis system, in which independent communities defined their own political systems and societies. The poleis differed widely in their ideas of what made for an effective government, however, and their independent spirit made alliances with other communities difficult to maintain. Conflict between the two greatest poleis, Athens and Sparta, eventually led to the destruction of much of Greece's progress. However, the warfare also marked a time of intellectual and cultural flourishing, as philosophers sought rational explanations for human nature and the world around them, lyric poets explored human thoughts and emotions in verse, and historians recorded the triumphs and failures of their civilization. The documents in this chapter address the Greek interest in individuals and communities and the proper relationship between the two. In a related theme, they also discuss the definition of justice in a civilized world.

## 3-1 | A Long Journey Home

### HOMER, *The Odyssey: Odysseus and the Sirens* (ca. 800 B.C.E.)

Homer's *Odyssey*, a masterwork of Western literature and an important cultural, religious, and social record of Greek civilization, is one of the few historical documents that survive from the early period of Greek history. Composed in dactylic hexameter, a form of verse that is usually sung, the *Odyssey* was probably passed down orally. It tells the story of hero Odysseus's ten-year journey home to Ithaca after his victory in the Trojan War (possibly 1200 or 1100 B.C.E.). The *Odyssey* begins in the middle of this journey, and Homer uses flashback to supply background information as his protagonist's struggles unfold. In the following passage, Odysseus tells his men how the goddess Circe (SIR-see) warned him about the dangers they will encounter on their journey.

At last, and sore at heart, I told my shipmates,
"Friends . . . it's wrong for only one or two
to know the revelations that lovely Circe
made to me alone. I'll tell you all,
so we can die with our eyes wide open now
or escape our fate and certain death together.
First, she warns, we must steer clear of the Sirens,
their enchanting song, their meadow starred with flowers.
I alone was to hear their voices, so she said,
but you must bind me with tight chafing ropes
so I cannot move a muscle, bound to the spot,
erect at the mast-block, lashed by ropes to the mast.
And if I plead, commanding you to set me free,
then lash me faster, rope pressing on rope."
So I informed my shipmates point by point,
all the while our trim ship was speeding toward
the Sirens' island, driven by the brisk wind.
But then—the wind fell in an instant,
all glazed to a dead calm . . .
a mysterious power hushed the heaving swells.
The oarsmen leapt to their feet, struck the sail,
stowed it deep in the hold and sat to the oarlock,
thrashing with polished oars, frothing the water white.
Now with a sharp sword I sliced an ample wheel of beeswax
down into pieces, kneaded them in my two strong hands
and the wax grew soft, worked by my strength
and Helios'[1] burning rays, the sun at high noon,

---

From Homer, *The Odyssey*, trans. Robert Fagles (London: Penguin Books, 1996), pp. 276–279.

[1]**Helios**: Greek sun-god.

and I stopped the ears of my comrades one by one.
They bound me hand and foot in the tight ship—
erect at the mast-block, lashed by ropes to the mast—
and rowed and churned the whitecaps stroke on stroke.
We were just offshore as far as a man's shout can carry,
scudding close, when the Sirens sensed at once a ship
was racing past and burst in their high, thrilling song:
"Come closer, famous Odysseus—Achaea's[2] pride and glory—
moor your ship on our coast so you can hear our song!
Never has any sailor passed our shores in his black craft
until he has heard the honeyed voices pouring from our lips,
and once he hears to his heart's content sails on, a wiser man.
We know all the pains that the Greeks and Trojans once endured
on the spreading plain of Troy when the gods willed it so—
all that comes to pass on the fertile earth, we know it all!"
So they sent their ravishing voices out across the air
and the heart inside me throbbed to listen longer.
I signaled the crew with frowns to set me free—
they flung themselves at the oars and rowed on harder,
Perimedes and Eurylochus springing up at once
to bind me faster with rope chafing on rope.
But once we'd left the Sirens fading in our wake,
once we could hear their song no more, their urgent call—
my steadfast crew was quick to remove the wax I'd used
to seal their ears and loosed the bonds that lashed me.

[Now Odysseus must decide how to navigate his ship past two monsters, Scylla, who is close to the rocks, and Charybdis, who creates a whirlpool. Circe warned him that if he avoids one, he will come too close to the other. She suggested sailing past Scylla as quickly as possible, instructing Odysseus not to waste time putting on armor.]

We'd scarcely put that island astern when suddenly
I saw smoke and heavy breakers, heard their booming thunder.
The men were terrified—oarblades flew from their grip,
clattering down to splash in the vessel's wash.
She lay there, dead in the water . . .
no hands to tug the blades that drove her on.
But I strode down the decks to rouse my crewmen,
halting beside each one with a bracing, winning word:
"Friends, we're hardly strangers at meeting danger—
and this is no worse than what we faced

---

[2]**Achaea:** Greece.

when Cyclops penned us up in his vaulted cave
with crushing force! But even from there my courage,
my presence of mind and tactics saved us all,
and we will live to remember this someday,
I have no doubt. Up now, follow my orders,
all of us work as one! . . .
You, helmsman, here's your order—burn it in your mind,
the steering-oar of our rolling ship is in your hands.
Keep her clear of that smoke and surging breakers,
head for those crags or she'll catch you off guard,
she'll yaw over there—you'll plunge us all in ruin!"
So I shouted. They snapped to each command.
No mention of Scylla—how to fight that nightmare?—
for fear the men would panic, desert their oars
and huddle down and stow themselves away.
But now I cleared my mind of Circe's orders—
cramping my style, urging me not to arm at all.
I donned my heroic armor, seized long spears
in both my hands and marched out on the half-deck,
forward, hoping from there to catch the first glimpse
of Scylla, ghoul of the cliffs, swooping to kill my men.
But nowhere could I make her out—and my eyes ached
scanning that mist-bound rock face top to bottom.
Now wailing in fear, we rowed on up those straits,
Scylla to starboard, dreaded Charybdis off to port,
her horrible whirlpool gulping the sea-surge down, down
but when she spewed it up—like a cauldron over a raging fire,
all her churning depths would seethe and heave—exploding spray
showering down to splatter the peaks of both crags at once!
But when she swallowed the sea-surge down her gaping maw
the whole abyss lay bare and the rocks around her roared,
terrible, deafening—

    bedrock showed down deep, boiling
black with sand—

    and ashen terror gripped the men.
But now, fearing death, all eyes fixed on Charybdis—
now Scylla snatched six men from our hollow ship,
the toughest, strongest hands I had, and glancing
backward over the decks, searching for my crew
I could see their hands and feet already hoisted,
flailing, high, higher, over my head, look—
wailing down at me, comrades riven in agony,
shrieking out my name for one last time! . . . so now they writhed,
gasping as Scylla swung them up her cliff and there
at her cavern's mouth she bolted them down raw—

screaming out, flinging their arms toward me,
lost in that mortal struggle. . . .
Of all the pitiful things I've had to witness,
suffering, searching out the pathways of the sea,
this wrenched my heart the most.

### READING QUESTIONS

1. What kind of a leader is Odysseus? How do his decisions affect his men? How does he balance their needs with his own plans?

2. Why does Odysseus ignore Circe's advice about Scylla and Charybdis, even though her plan for escaping the Sirens worked?

3. Of all the Greek heroes, Odysseus is described as the most resourceful. In what ways does this passage support that assessment?

4. Why might Homer have composed this story? Is it meant to be a history lesson, or is it for instruction, entertainment, or some other purpose?

## 3-2 | Moral Instruction and Good Advice
### HESIOD, *Works and Days* (ca. 800 B.C.E.)

Hesiod, along with Homer, is one of the earliest known sources for Greek civilization. His *Theogony* covers the history of the gods, while his *Works and Days* addresses how humans should act. Along with moral instructions, Hesiod also provides recommendations on how to manage farms and households. The text is addressed to his younger brother, Perses, who cheated Hesiod out of his inheritance. When Hesiod took the matter to the judges, Perses bribed them to decide in his favor.

But you, Perses, listen to right and do not foster violence; for violence is bad for a poor man. Even the prosperous cannot easily bear its burden, but is weighed down under it when he has fallen into delusion. The better path is to go by on the other side towards justice. . . .

But they who give straight judgments to strangers and to the men of the land, and go not aside from what is just, their city flourishes, and the people prosper in it: Peace, the nurse of children, is abroad in their land, and all-seeing Zeus[1] never decrees cruel war against them. Neither famine nor disaster ever haunt men who do true justice; but lightheartedly they tend the fields which are all their care. The earth bears them victual in plenty, and on the mountains the oak bears acorns upon the top and bees in the midst. Their woolly sheep are

---

From *Hesiod, the Homeric Hymns, and Homerica*, trans. Hugh Gerald Evelyn-White (New York: G. P. Putnam's Sons, 1920), pp. 19–33.

[1]**Zeus**: Leading god in the Greek pantheon.

laden with fleeces; their women bear children like their parents. They flourish continually with good things, and do not travel on ships, for the grain-giving earth bears them fruit. . . .

And there is virgin Justice, the daughter of Zeus, who is honored and reverenced among the gods who dwell on Olympus, and whenever anyone hurts her with lying slander, she sits beside her father, Zeus the son of Cronos, and tells him of men's wicked heart, until the people pay for the mad folly of their princes who, evilly minded, pervert judgment and give sentence crookedly. Keep watch against this, you princes, and make straight your judgments, you who devour bribes; put crooked judgments altogether from your thoughts. . . .

To you, foolish Perses, I will speak good sense. Badness can be got easily . . . : the road to her is smooth, and she lives very near us. But between us and Goodness the gods have placed the sweat of our brows: long and steep is the path that leads to her, and it is rough at the first; but when a man has reached the top, then is she easy to reach, though before that she was hard.

That man is altogether best who considers all things himself and marks what will be better afterwards and at the end; and he, again, is good who listens to a good adviser; but whoever neither thinks for himself nor keeps in mind what another tells him, he is an unprofitable man. But do you at any rate, always remembering my charge, work, high-born Perses, that Hunger may hate you, and venerable Demeter[2] richly crowned may love you and fill your barn with food; for Hunger is altogether a good comrade for the sluggard. Both gods and men are angry with a man who lives idle, for in nature he is like the stingless drones who waste the labor of the bees, eating without working; but let it be your care to order your work properly, that in the right season your barns may be full of victual. Through work men grow rich in flocks and substance, and working they are much better loved by the immortals. Work is no disgrace: it is idleness which is a disgrace. . . .

Let the wage promised to a friend be fixed; . . . and get a witness; for trust and mistrust, alike ruin men. . . .

First of all, get a house, and a woman and an ox for the plough—a slave woman and not a wife, to follow the oxen as well—and make everything ready at home, so that you may not have to ask of another, and he refuse you, and so, because you are in lack, the season pass by and your work come to nothing. Do not put your work off till tomorrow and the day after; for a sluggish worker does not fill his barn, nor one who puts off his work: industry makes work go well, but a man who puts off work is always at hand-grips with ruin.

## READING QUESTIONS

1. According to this document, what kind of society do the Greeks have? What ranks does Greek society include?

2. According to Hesiod, what sort of behavior do the gods expect of humanity?

---

[2]**Demeter**: Goddess of agriculture and fertility.

3. What qualities does Hesiod value in a person?

4. How does Hesiod define justice?


## 3-3 | A Clash of Loyalties

### SOPHOCLES, *Antigone* (441 B.C.E.)

Sophocles's *Antigone* is an exploration of the tensions between one's duty to the gods, to the law, to the community, and to one's self. At its heart is a conflict between Antigone and Creon, the king of Thebes, who has ordered that the body of Polyneices, Antigone's brother, be left unburied and dishonored. Antigone defies Creon, buries Polyneices, and carries out the proper funeral rituals, knowing full well that in so doing she has signed her death warrant. Two passages from the play are included here. In the first, from the opening scene of the play, Antigone's sister Ismene makes a fruitless effort to convince Antigone to give up her plan to bury Polyneices. In the second, Antigone justifies her actions to Creon, who offers his response in an aside to the audience. As you read the passages, consider how these characters see their obligations to themselves, to the community, and to the gods. Pay particular attention to the way ideas about proper gender roles shape each character's perspective.


[Ismene pleads with Antigone.]


ISMENE: Alas. Remember, sister, how our father[1]
   perished abhorred, ill-famed.
   Himself with his own hand, through his own curse
   destroyed both eyes.
   Remember next his mother and his wife
   finishing life in the shame of the twisted strings,
   And third two brothers on a single day,
   Poor creatures, murdering, a common doom
   each with his arm accomplished on the other.
   And now look at the two of us alone.
   We'll perish terribly if we force law
   and try to cross the royal vote and power.
   We must remember that we two are women
   so not to fight with men.
   And that since we are subject to strong power
   we must hear these orders, or any that may be worse.


---

From Peter J. Steinberger, ed., *Readings in Classical Political Thought* (Indianapolis, Ind.: Hackett Publishing Company, 2000), pp. 118, 123–124.

   [1]**our father**: Antigone and Ismene's father is Oedipus, a mythical king of Thebes. *Antigone* is the third play in a trilogy by Sophocles that includes *Oedipus the King* and *Oedipus at Colonus.*

So I shall ask of them beneath the earth
forgiveness, for in these things I am forced,
and shall obey the men in power. I know
that wild and futile action makes no sense.

ANTIGONE: I wouldn't urge it. And if now you wished
to act, you wouldn't please me as a partner.
Be what you want to; but that man shall I
bury. For me, the doer, death is best.
Friend shall I lie with him, yes friend with friend,
when I have dared the crime of piety.
Longer the time in which to please the dead
than that for those up here.
There shall I lie forever. You may see fit
to keep from honor what the gods have honored.

ISMENE: I shall do no dishonor. But to act
against the citizens. I cannot.

ANTIGONE: That's your protection. Now I go, to pile
the burial-mound for him, my dearest brother.

[Creon confronts Antigone.]

CREON (*to Antigone*): You—tell me not at length but in a word.
You knew the order not to do this thing?

ANTIGONE: I knew, of course I knew. The word was plain.

CREON: And still you dared to overstep these laws?

ANTIGONE: For me it was not Zeus who made that order.
Nor did that Justice who lives with the gods below
mark out such laws to hold among mankind.
Nor did I think your orders were so strong
that you, a mortal man, could over-run
the gods' unwritten and unfailing laws.
Not now, nor yesterday's, they always live,
and no one knows their origin in time.
So not through fear of any man's proud spirit
would I be likely to neglect these laws,
draw on myself the gods' sure punishment.
I knew that I must die; how could I not?
even without your warning. If I die
before my time, I say it is a gain.
Who lives in sorrows many as are mine
how shall he not be glad to gain his death?
And so, for me to meet this fate, no grief.
But if I left that corpse, my mother's son,
dead and unburied I'd have cause to grieve
as now I grieve not.

And if you think my acts are foolishness
    the foolishness may be in a fool's eye.
CHORUS: The girl is bitter. She's her father's child.
    She cannot yield to trouble; nor could he.
CREON: These rigid spirits are the first to fall.
    The strongest iron, hardened in the fire,
    most often ends in scraps and shatterings.
    Small curbs bring raging horses back to terms.
    Slave to his neighbor, who can think of pride?
    This girl was expert in her insolence
    when she broke bounds beyond established law.
    Once she had done it, insolence the second,
    to boast her doing, and to laugh in it.
    I am no man and she the man instead
    if she can have this conquest without pain.
    She is my sister's child, but were she child
    of closer kin than any at my hearth,
    she and her sister should not so escape
    their death and doom. I charge Ismene too.
    She shared the planning of this burial.
    Call her outside. I saw her in the house,
    maddened, no longer mistress of herself.
    The sly intent betrays itself sometimes
    before the secret plotters work their wrong.
    I hate it too when someone caught in crime
    then wants to make it seem a lovely thing.
ANTIGONE: Do you want more than my arrest and death?
CREON: No more than that. For that is all I need.
ANTIGONE: Why are you waiting? Nothing that you say
    fits with my thought. I pray it never will.
    Nor will you ever like to hear my words.
    And yet what greater glory could I find
    than giving my own brother funeral?
    All these would say that they approved my act
    did fear not mute them.
    (A king is fortunate in many ways,
    and most, that he can act and speak at will.)
CREON: None of these others see the case this way.
ANTIGONE: They see, and do not say. You have them cowed.
CREON: And you are not ashamed to think alone?
ANTIGONE: No, I am not ashamed. When was it shame
    to serve the children of my mother's womb?

## READING QUESTIONS

1. What arguments does Ismene use in her effort to convince Antigone to change her mind?

2. On what basis does Antigone justify her violation of Creon's decree?

3. How do ideas about proper roles for men and women shape both Creon's and Ismene's reactions to Antigone's decision?

4. What does Creon's mistaken assumption that Ismene shared in Antigone's crime tell us about his character?

5. What lessons might an Athenian audience have drawn from this play? What parallels might they have seen between their own history and the events portrayed in the play?

## SOURCES IN CONVERSATION

# Political Philosophy

The same probing, rational spirit that led Greek thinkers and philosophers to delve into nature's laws, to seek the fundamental substances and patterns that shaped the cosmos, led them to examine their own governments — to ask what forms states took, what ties bound the inhabitants of a state together, and why one state was better than another. The exploration and articulation of political philosophy took many forms, and its practitioners reached a variety of conclusions. Such efforts were, however, bound together by a shared interest in discovering the relationship between the organization of the state on the one hand, and the level of prosperity, achievement, and social harmony achieved by the state on the other.

## READ AND COMPARE

1. What is similar about the analyses of Pericles and Plato concerning Greek rationality, and where do they differ?

2. Does it seem that Plato and Pericles had similar ideas about how to achieve social harmony? If not, how are they different?

## 3-4 | THUCYDIDES, *The History of the Peloponnesian War: Pericles's Funeral Oration* (ca. 400 B.C.E.)

Thucydides (thoo-SIH-dih-deez) was an Athenian general who lost a battle in the early years of the Peloponnesian War (431–404 B.C.E.). Exiled from Athens, he spent the remainder of the war tracking the progress of the conflict and ultimately wrote its history. The selection

From Thucydides, *The History of the Peloponnesian War*, 2d ed., trans. Benjamin Jowett (London: Henry Frowde, 1900), pp. 126–132.

that follows is from the first years of the war, when Pericles (PEHR-uh-kleez), the leading Athenian statesman, gave this eulogy in memory of those who died in the war. In it, Pericles makes a direct connection between Athenian government and Athenian success.

But before I praise the dead, I should like to point out by what principles of action we rose to power, and under what institutions and through what manner of life our empire became great. . . .

Our form of government does not enter into rivalry with the institutions of others. Our government does not copy our neighbors, but is an example to them. It is true that we are called a democracy, for the administration is in the hands of the many and not of the few. But while the law secures equal justice to all alike in their private disputes, the claim of excellence is also recognized; and when a citizen is in any way distinguished, he is preferred to the public service, not as a matter of privilege, but as the reward of merit. Neither is poverty a bar, but a man may benefit his country whatever the obscurity of his condition. There is no exclusiveness in our public life, and in our private intercourse we are not suspicious of one another, nor angry with our neighbor if he does what he likes; we do not put on sour looks at him which, though harmless, are not pleasant. While we are thus unconstrained in our private intercourse, a spirit of reverence pervades our public acts; we are prevented from doing wrong by respect for the authorities and for the laws, having an especial regard to those which are ordained for the protection of the injured as well as those unwritten laws which bring upon the transgressor of them the reprobation of the general sentiment.

And we have not forgotten to provide for our weary spirits many relaxations from toil; we have regular games and sacrifices throughout the year; our homes are beautiful and elegant; and the delight which we daily feel in all these things helps to banish melancholy. Because of the greatness of our city the fruits of the whole earth flow in upon us; so that we enjoy the goods of other countries as freely as our own.

Then, again, our military training is in many respects superior to that of our adversaries. Our city is thrown open to the world, and we never expel a foreigner and prevent him from seeing or learning anything of which the secret if revealed to an enemy might profit him. We rely not upon management or trickery, but upon our own hearts and hands. And in the matter of education, whereas they from early youth are always undergoing laborious exercises which are to make them brave, we live at ease, and yet are equally ready to face the perils which they face. And here is the proof: The Lacedaemonians[1] come into Attica not by themselves, but with their whole confederacy following; we go alone into a neighbor's country; and although our opponents are fighting for their homes and we on a foreign soil, we have seldom any difficulty in overcoming them. Our enemies have never yet felt our united strength, the care of a navy divides our attention, and on land we are obliged to send our own citizens everywhere. But they, if they meet and defeat a part of our army, are as proud as if they had routed us all, and when defeated they pretend to have been vanquished by us all.

---

[1]**Lacedaemonians**: Spartans.

If then we prefer to meet danger with a light heart but without laborious training, and with a courage which is gained by habit and not enforced by law, are we not greatly the gainers? Since we do not anticipate the pain, although, when the hour comes, we can be as brave as those who never allow themselves to rest; thus too our city is equally admirable in peace and in war. For we are lovers of the beautiful, yet simple in our tastes, and we cultivate the mind without loss of manliness. Wealth we employ, not for talk and ostentation, but when there is a real use for it. To avow poverty with us is no disgrace; the true disgrace is in doing nothing to avoid it. An Athenian citizen does not neglect the state because he takes care of his own household; and even those of us who are engaged in business have a very fair idea of politics. We alone regard a man who takes no interest in public affairs, not as a harmless, but as a useless character; and if few of us are originators, we are all sound judges of a policy. The great impediment to action is, in our opinion, not discussion, but the want of that knowledge which is gained by discussion preparatory to action. For we have a peculiar power of thinking before we act, and of acting, too, whereas other men are courageous from ignorance but hesitate upon reflection. And they are surely to be esteemed the bravest spirits who, having the clearest sense both of the pains and pleasures of life, do not on that account shrink from danger. In doing good, again, we are unlike others; we make our friends by conferring, not by receiving favors. . . .

To sum up: I say that Athens is the school of Hellas,[2] and that the individual Athenian in his own person seems to have the power of adapting himself to the most varied forms of action with the utmost versatility and grace. This is no passing and idle word, but truth and fact; and the assertion is verified by the position to which these qualities have raised the state. For in the hour of trial Athens alone among her contemporaries is superior to the report of her. . . .

I have dwelt upon the greatness of Athens because I want to show you that we are contending for a higher prize than those who enjoy none of these privileges, and to establish by manifest proof the merit of these men whom I am now commemorating. Their loftiest praise has been already spoken. For in magnifying the city I have magnified them, and men like them whose virtues made her glorious.

### READING QUESTIONS

1. According to Pericles, what makes Athens so great? What does democracy mean to him?

2. How is Athens different from other Greek cities? What do Athenians care about that other Greeks don't?

3. What is the relationship between the individual and the community in Athens? Which is more important to Pericles?

---

[2]**Hellas:** Greece.

# 3-5 | PLATO, *The Republic: The Allegory of the Cave* (ca. 360 B.C.E.)

The Peloponnesian War ended badly for the Athenians: they lost to the Spartans, the Athenian democracy fell, and the city came under the rule of tyrants. The Athenian democracy was eventually restored, but it was unstable. During that time, the philosopher Socrates (SOK-ruh-teez) (ca. 470–399 B.C.E.) gathered a following of young Athenians as he pointed out the shortcomings of the wealthy, powerful, and wise. Socrates was put on trial and executed for impiety and corrupting the youth. After his death, his student Plato (PLAY-toh) (427–347 B.C.E.) wrote *The Republic*, which is perhaps the best-known example of Greek political philosophy. In it, Plato emphasizes not so much what kind of state is best, but what kind of people make the best leaders. The section included below is a discussion between Socrates and Plato's older brother, Glaucon. Much of the dialogue is taken up with an extended allegory about the difficulties humans face as they struggle to see things as they really are. As the allegory comes to a conclusion, its political implications become clear. In Plato's view, very few people succeed in the quest for truth, and the best states are those that ensure that these few, most enlightened citizens take up the mantle of leadership.

SOCRATES: And now, let me show in a figure how far our nature is enlightened or unenlightened:—Behold! human beings living in an underground den, which has a mouth open towards the light and reaching all along the den; here they have been from their childhood, and have their legs and necks chained so that they cannot move, and can only see before them, being prevented by the chains from turning round their heads. Above and behind them a fire is blazing at a distance, and between the fire and the prisoners there is a raised way; and you will see, if you look, a low wall built along the way, like the screen which marionette players have in front of them, over which they show the puppets.

GLAUCON: I see.

SOCRATES: And do you see men passing along the wall carrying all sorts of vessels, and statues and figures of animals made of wood and stone and various materials, which appear over the wall? Some of them are talking, others silent.

GLAUCON: You have shown me a strange image, and they are strange prisoners.

SOCRATES: Like ourselves, and they see only their own shadows, or the shadows of one another, which the fire throws on the opposite wall of the cave?

GLAUCON: True; how could they see anything but the shadows if they were never allowed to move their heads?

SOCRATES: And of the objects which are being carried in like manner they would only see the shadows?

GLAUCON: Yes.

SOCRATES: And if they were able to converse with one another, would they not suppose that they were naming what was actually before them?

---

From Plato, *The Dialogues of Plato*, vol. 2, trans. Benjamin Jowett (New York: Charles Scribner's Sons, 1914), pp. 265–274.

GLAUCON: Very true.

SOCRATES: And suppose further that the prison had an echo which came from the other side, would they not be sure to fancy when one of the passers-by spoke that the voice which they heard came from the passing shadow?

GLAUCON: No question.

SOCRATES: To them . . . the truth would be literally nothing but the shadows of the images.

GLAUCON: That is certain.

SOCRATES: And now look again, and see what will naturally follow if the prisoners are released and disabused of their error. At first, when any of them is liberated and compelled suddenly to stand up and turn his neck round and walk and look towards the light, he will suffer sharp pains; the glare will distress him, and he will be unable to see the realities of which in his former state he had seen the shadows; and then conceive some one saying to him, that what he saw before was an illusion, but that now, when he is approaching nearer to being and his eye is turned towards more real existence, he has a clearer vision,—what will be his reply? And you may further imagine that his instructor is pointing to the objects as they pass and requiring him to name them,—will he not be perplexed? Will he not fancy that the shadows which he formerly saw are truer than the objects which are now shown to him?

GLAUCON: Far truer.

SOCRATES: And if he is compelled to look straight at the light, will he not have a pain in his eyes which will make him turn away to take refuge in the objects of vision which he can see, and which he will conceive to be in reality clearer than the things which are now being shown to him?

GLAUCON: True.

SOCRATES: And suppose once more, that he is reluctantly dragged up a steep and rugged ascent, and held fast until he's forced into the presence of the sun himself, is he not likely to be pained and irritated? When he approaches the light his eyes will be dazzled, and he will not be able to see anything at all of what are now called realities.

GLAUCON: Not all in a moment.

SOCRATES: He will require to grow accustomed to the sight of the upper world. And first he will see the shadows best, next the reflections of men and other objects in the water, and then the objects themselves; then he will gaze upon the light of the moon and the stars and the spangled heaven; and he will see the sky and the stars by night better than the sun or the light of the sun by day?

GLAUCON: Certainly.

SOCRATES: Last of all he will be able to see the sun, and not mere reflections of him in the water, but he will see him in his own proper place, and not in another; and he will contemplate him as he is.

GLAUCON: Certainly.

SOCRATES: He will then proceed to argue that this is he who gives the season and the years, and is the guardian of all that is in the visible world, and in a certain way the cause of all things which he and his fellows have been accustomed to behold?

GLAUCON: Clearly . . . he would first see the sun and then reason about it.

SOCRATES: And when he remembered his old habitation, and the wisdom of the den and his fellow-prisoners, do you not suppose that he would felicitate himself on the change, and pity them?

GLAUCON: Certainly, he would.

SOCRATES: And if they were in the habit of conferring honors among themselves on those who were quickest to observe the passing shadows and to remark which of them went before, and which followed after, and which were together; and who were therefore best able to draw conclusions as to the future, do you think that he would care for such honors and glories, or envy the possessors of them? . . .

GLAUCON: . . . . I think that he would rather suffer anything than entertain these false notions and live in this miserable manner.

SOCRATES: Imagine once more . . . such a one coming suddenly out of the sun to be replaced in his old situation; would he not be certain to have his eyes full of darkness?

GLAUCON: To be sure.

SOCRATES: And if there were a contest, and he had to compete in measuring the shadows with the prisoners who had never moved out of the den, while his sight was still weak, and before his eyes had become steady . . . would he not be ridiculous? Men would say of him that up he went and down he came without his eyes; and that it was better not even to think of ascending; and if any one tried to loose another and lead him up to the light, let them only catch the offender, and they would put him to death.

GLAUCON: No question.

SOCRATES: The prison-house is the world of sight, the light of the fire is the sun, and you will not misapprehend me if you interpret the journey upwards to be the ascent of the soul into the intellectual world according to my poor belief, which, at your desire, I have expressed whether rightly or wrongly God knows. But, whether true or false, my opinion is that in the world of knowledge the idea of good appears last of all, and is seen only with an effort; and, when seen, is also inferred to be the universal author of all things beautiful and right, parent of light and of the lord of light in this visible world, and the immediate source of reason and truth in the intellectual; and that this is the power upon which he who would act rationally, either in public or private life, must have his eye fixed.

GLAUCON: I agree as far as I am able to understand you.

SOCRATES: Moreover . . . you must not wonder that those who attain to this beatific vision are unwilling to descend to human affairs; for their souls are ever hastening into the upper world where they desire to dwell; which desire of theirs is very natural, if our allegory may be trusted.

GLAUCON: Yes, very natural.

SOCRATES: And is there anything surprising in one who passes from divine contemplations to the evil state of man, behaving himself in a ridiculous manner; if, while his eyes are blinking and before he has become accustomed to the surrounding darkness, he is compelled to fight in courts of law, or in other places, about the images or the shadows of images of justice, and is endeavoring to meet the conceptions of those who have never yet seen absolute justice?

GLAUCON: Anything but surprising. . . .

SOCRATES: Whereas, our argument shows that the power and capacity of learning exists in the soul already; and that just as the eye was unable to turn from darkness to light without the whole body, so too the instrument of knowledge can only by the movement of the whole soul be turned from the world of becoming into that of being, and learn by degrees to endure the sight of being, and of the brightest and best of being, or in other words, of the good.

And there is another thing which is likely or rather a necessary inference from what has preceded, that neither the uneducated and uninformed of the truth, nor yet those who never [finish] their education, will be able ministers of State. . . .

GLAUCON: Very true.

SOCRATES: Then . . . the business of us who are the founders of the State will be to compel the best minds to attain that knowledge which we have already shown to be the greatest of all—they must continue to ascend until they arrive at the good; but when they have ascended and seen enough we must not allow them to do as they do now.

GLAUCON: What do you mean?

SOCRATES: I mean that they remain in the upper world: but this must not be allowed; they must be made to descend again among the prisoners in the den, and partake of their labors and honors, whether they are worth having or not.

GLAUCON: But is not this unjust; ought we to give them a worse life, when they might have a better?

SOCRATES: You have again forgotten, my friend . . . the intention of the legislator, who did not aim at making any one class in the State happy above the rest; the happiness was to be in the whole State, and he held the citizens together by persuasion and necessity, making them benefactors of the State, and therefore benefactors of one another; to this end he created them, not to please themselves, but to be his instruments in binding up the State. . . .

And will our pupils, when they hear this, refuse to take their turn at the toils of State, when they are allowed to spend the greater part of their time with one another in the heavenly light?

GLAUCON: Impossible, for they are just men, and the commands which we impose upon them are just; there can be no doubt that every one of them will take office as a stern necessity, and not after the fashion of our present rulers of State.

SOCRATES: Yes, my friend . . . ; and there lies the point. You must contrive for your future rulers another and a better life than that of a ruler, and then you may have a well-ordered State; for only in the State which offers this, will they rule who are truly rich, not in silver and gold, but in virtue and wisdom, which are the true blessings of life. Whereas if they go to the administration of public affairs, poor and hungering after their own private advantage, thinking that hence they are to snatch the chief good, order there can never be; for they will be fighting about office, and the civil and domestic broils which thus arise will be the ruin of the rulers themselves and of the whole State.

GLAUCON: Most true.

### READING QUESTIONS

1. What is the condition of the people in the cave? How does their condition affect the way they understand the world?

2. How does the one who leaves the cave react to the things he encounters? Why does he go back into the cave?

3. How do the people in the cave treat the one who left? Why?

4. What is Plato saying about the balance between the needs of an individual and the needs of the state? How does he think justice can be found for both individuals and states?

## 3-6 | Choosing the Best State

### ARISTOTLE, *Politics: Democracy* (ca. 340 B.C.E.)

Aristotle (EH-ruh-STAH-tuhl) (384–322 B.C.E.), a student of Plato, is one of the most important philosophers in Western civilization — in the Middle Ages he was known simply as "The Philosopher." His extensive body of work attempts to classify and study all things known to exist, but he was particularly well known for his ideas about science, ethics, and politics. *Politics* explains the types of state that exist as well as their merits and shortfalls. In the passage that follows, he considers which kind of state is best.

We have now to inquire what is the best constitution for most states, and the best life for most men, neither assuming a standard of virtue which is above ordinary persons, nor an education which is exceptionally favored by nature

From *The Politics of Aristotle*, trans. Benjamin Jowett (Oxford: Clarendon Press, 1885), pp. 126–129.

and circumstances, nor yet an ideal state which is an aspiration only, but having regard to the life in which the majority are able to share, and to the form of government which states in general can attain. . . .

Now in all states there are three elements: one class is very rich, another very poor, and a third in a mean.[1] It is admitted that moderation and the mean are best, and therefore it will clearly be best to possess the gifts of fortune in moderation; for in that condition of life men are most ready to follow rational principle. But he who greatly excels in beauty, strength, birth, or wealth, or on the other hand who is very poor, or very weak, or very much disgraced, finds it difficult to follow rational principle. Of these two the one sort grow into violent and great criminals, the others into rogues and petty rascals. And two sorts of offenses correspond to them, the one committed from violence, the other from roguery. Again, the middle class is least likely to shrink from rule, or to be over-ambitious for it; both of which are injuries to the state. Again, those who have too much of the goods of fortune, strength, wealth, friends, and the like, are neither willing nor able to submit to authority. The evil begins at home; for when they are boys, by reason of the luxury in which they are brought up, they never learn, even at school, the habit of obedience. On the other hand, the very poor, who are in the opposite extreme, are too degraded. So that the one class cannot obey, and can only rule despotically; the other knows not how to command and must be ruled like slaves. Thus arises a city, not of freemen, but of masters and slaves, the one despising, the other envying; and nothing can be more fatal to friendship and good fellowship in states than this: for good fellowship springs from friendship; when men are at enmity with one another, they would rather not even share the same path. But a city ought to be composed, as far as possible, of equals and similars; and these are generally the middle classes. . . .

Thus it is manifest that the best political community is formed by citizens of the middle class, and that those states are likely to be well-administered in which the middle class is large, and stronger if possible than both the other classes, or at any rate than either singly; for the addition of the middle class turns the scale, and prevents either of the extremes from being dominant. Great then is the good fortune of a state in which the citizens have a moderate and sufficient property; for where some possess much, and the others nothing, there may arise an extreme democracy, or a pure oligarchy; or a tyranny may grow out of either extreme—either out of the most rampant democracy, or out of an oligarchy; but it is not so likely to arise out of the middle constitutions and those akin to them. . . .

These considerations will help us to understand why most governments are either democratical or oligarchical. The reason is that the middle class is seldom numerous in them, and whichever party, whether the rich or the common people, transgresses the mean and predominates, draws the constitution its own way, and thus arises either oligarchy or democracy. There is another reason—the poor

---

[1]**in a mean**: Average; neither rich nor poor.

and the rich quarrel with one another, and whichever side gets the better, instead of establishing a just or popular government, regards political supremacy as the prize of victory, and the one party sets up a democracy and the other an oligarchy. Further, both the parties which had the supremacy in Hellas looked only to the interest of their own form of government, and established in states, the one, democracies, and the other, oligarchies; they thought of their own advantage, of the public not at all. . . . But it has now become a habit among the citizens of states, not even to care about equality; all men are seeking for dominion, or, if conquered, are willing to submit.

What then is the best form of government, and what makes it the best, is evident; and of other constitutions, since we say that there are many kinds of democracy and many of oligarchy, it is not difficult to see which has the first and which the second or any other place in the order of excellence, now that we have determined which is the best. For that which is nearest to the best must of necessity be better, and that which is furthest from it worse, if we are judging absolutely and not relatively to given conditions: I say "relatively to given conditions," since a particular government may be preferable, but another form may be better for some people.

### READING QUESTIONS

1. What happens to a state dominated by the rich?

2. What happens to a state dominated by the poor?

3. According to Aristotle, which kind of state is best? What makes it the best?

4. How do Aristotle's ideas reflect what he knew about the history of Athens? Since he tutored Alexander the Great, what would he have to say about the Hellenistic kingdoms that resulted from Alexander's conquests?

## ■ COMPARATIVE AND DISCUSSION QUESTIONS ■

1. Compare and contrast the characteristics of a Greek hero, as seen in Homer, with the characteristics of a good person as seen in Hesiod. How do Greek heroes compare with Mesopotamian heroes (Document 1-1)?

2. What do these documents reveal about the Greeks' ideas about the relationship between the individual and the community?

3. How does the excerpt from *Antigone* complicate the picture of a Greek community painted by Pericles? What kinds of tensions and conflicts within Greek city-states threatened the unanimity and consensus Pericles celebrated?

4. Compare and contrast Pericles, Plato, and Aristotle. How would each one define good government? Is Plato's notion of ideal justice compatible with the beliefs of Pericles or Aristotle? Do Pericles and Aristotle have the same definition of democracy?

# 4

# Life in the Hellenistic World

## 338–30 B.C.E.

In 338 B.C.E., Philip II, king of Macedonia, defeated the armies of Athens and Thebes at the battle of Chaeronea (kehr-uh-NEE-uh) and established a Common Peace, a new political system that maintained each Greek city-state's right to its own laws and customs. Following Philip II's assassination in 336 B.C.E., his young son Alexander set about to finish his father's plans and conquer Persia. By the time of his premature death in 323 B.C.E., Alexander had conquered the entire Persian Empire and taken his army through Afghanistan into what is now northwestern India. The newly connected reaches of the expanded Greek Empire became a melting pot of culture in what is commonly referred to as the Hellenistic period (336–30 B.C.E.). Although Alexander's empire quickly broke up into smaller states, Greek rulers dominated most of the eastern Mediterranean and spread Greek culture, or Hellenism, far into the East. New schools of philosophy took root and gained followers, and educated people throughout the Mediterranean world adopted the Greek language. Yet the divided empire never regained the strength and stability it had possessed under Alexander, and the Hellenistic period was characterized by constant warfare.

## 4-1 | Remembering a Legend

### EPHIPPUS OF OLYNTHUS, *On the Burial of Alexander and Hephaestion: Ephippus of Olynthus Remembers Alexander the Great* (ca. 323 B.C.E.)

Even before his death in 323 B.C.E., Alexander the Great had become a legend, the hero for whom the defeat of the mighty Persian Empire was only the first step toward the conquest of the known world. Alexander, who thought of himself as the son of Zeus, encouraged this belief in his superhuman abilities, emphasizing in his manner and dress the connection between himself and the gods. The following excerpt from a treatise by Ephippus of Olynthus captures Alexander's style. As you read it, ask yourself why Alexander behaved as he did. What political advantages might he have gained by his overt claims to semidivine status?

Concerning the luxury of Alexander the Great, Ephippus of Olynthus, in his treatise *On the Burial of Alexander and Hephaestion*, relates that he had in his park a golden throne and couches with silver feet, on which he used to sit while transacting business with his companions. Nicobule[1] says, moreover, that while he was at supper all the dancers and athletes sought to amuse the king. At his very last banquet, Alexander, remembering an episode in the *Andromeda*[2] of Euripides, recited it in a declamatory manner, and then drank a cup of unmixed wine with great zest, and compelled all the rest to do the same. Ephippus tells us, too, that Alexander used to wear at his entertainments even the sacred vestments. Sometimes he would put on the purple robe, cloven sandals, and horns of Ammon,[3] as if he had been the god. Sometimes he would imitate Artemis,[4] whose dress he often wore while driving in his chariot; at the same time he had on a Persian robe, which displayed above his shoulders the bow and javelin of the goddess. At times also he would appear in the guise of Hermes;[5] at other times, and in fact nearly every day, he would wear a purple cloak, a chiton shot with white, and a cap with a royal diadem attached. When too he was in private with his friends he wore the sandals of Hermes, with the petasus[6] on his head and the caduceus[7] in hand. Often however he wore a lion's skin and carried a club like Heracles.[8] . . .

From G. W. Botsford and E. G. Sihler, eds., *Hellenic Civilization* (New York: Columbia University Press, 1915), pp. 682–683.

[1]**Nicobule**: Greek female historian to whom a biography of Alexander is ascribed.

[2]*Andromeda*: Euripides's play of approximately 412 B.C.E., in which the hero Perseus saves Andromeda from being sacrificed to a sea monster.

[3]**horns of Ammon**: Symbolized the Greco-Egyptian "composite god" Zeus-Ammon, a king of all other gods.

[4]**Artemis**: Daughter of Zeus and goddess of fertility and the hunt.

[5]**Hermes**: Messenger of the gods.

[6]**petasus**: Flat hat, typically worn by the god Hermes.

[7]**caduceus**: Wand of the god Hermes, a staff with two serpents wrapping around it.

[8]**Heracles**: A half-god and the son of Zeus, Heracles was worshipped for his incomparable strength, courage, and cleverness.

Alexander used also to have the floor sprinkled with exquisite perfumes and with fragrant wine; and myrrh and other kinds of incense were burned before him, while all the bystanders kept silence or spoke words only of good omen because of fear. For he was an extremely violent man with no regard for human life, and gave the impression of a man of choleric temperament.

### READING QUESTIONS

1. According to this source, in what ways did Alexander seek to glorify himself? What do Alexander's choices reveal about Greek attitudes toward the gods?

2. How would you explain Alexander's choice to associate himself with the gods? How was his style of rule different from that of earlier Greek and Macedonian leaders?

3. How would you describe the author's (or authors') view of Alexander? Point to specific passages to support your argument.

## 4-2   |   A Jewish Response to Hellenistic Rule

### *First and Second Books of the Maccabees*
### (ca. 124–100 B.C.E.)

The Levant, or the area that eventually became the Roman province of Judaea, was ruled by outside powers for many centuries, and the Jewish people did not have their own state until the creation of Israel in 1948 C.E. During the Hellenistic era, Jews in the Levant were able to worship relatively freely until the Seleucid king Antiochus IV began to feel pressured by the growing power of the Roman Empire and thus started to restrict the religious freedom of Jews in the area. The following apocryphal document, which serves as official scripture for Jews and Catholics, recounts the attempts of Antiochus IV to impose Hellenistic religion upon the Jews, along with a description of the Maccabee revolt against his actions.

And he called his servants, nobles who were raised with him from his youth. And he divided his kingdom to them, while he was still alive.

And Alexander reigned twelve years, and then he died.

And his servants obtained his kingdom, each one in his place.

And there went forth from among them a sinful root, Antiochus the illustrious, the son of king Antiochus, who had been a hostage at Rome. And he reigned in the one hundred and thirty-seventh year of the kingdom of the Greeks.

In those days, there went forth from Israel sons of iniquity, and they persuaded many, saying: "Let us go and negotiate a covenant with the Gentiles that are all around us. For since we have withdrawn from them, many evils have found us."

And the word seemed good in their eyes.

And some of the people determined to do this, and they went to the king. And he gave them the power to act according to the justice of the Gentiles.

From 1 Maccabees 1:7–16; 2 Maccabees 4:10–17, 6:1–6, 10:1–8. Sacred Bible: Catholic Public Domain.

And they built a sports arena in Jerusalem, according to the laws of the Nations.

And they made themselves uncircumcised, and they withdrew from the holy covenant, and they were joined to the nations, and they were sold into evil-doing.

When the king had assented, and he had obtained the leadership, he immediately began to transfer his subjects to the rituals of the heathens.

. . .

And taking away those things that had been established by the kings, by reason of the humanitarianism of the Jews, through John, the father of Eupolemus, who formed a friendship and alliance with the Romans, he discharged the legitimate legislations, voiding the oaths of the citizens, and he sanctioned depraved customs.

For he even had the audacity to set up, below the very stronghold, a sports arena, and to place all of the best adolescent boys in brothels.

Now this was not the beginning, but a certain increase and progression of heathenism and foreign practices, due to the nefarious and unheard of wickedness of the impious non-priest Jason, so much so that now the priests were not devoted to the concerns of services at the altar, but, despising the temple and neglecting the sacrifices, they hurried to become participants of the wrestling school, and of its prohibited injustices, and of the training of the discus.

And, even holding the honors of their fathers to be nothing, they esteemed the glories of the Greeks as best.

For the sake of these, they held a dangerous competition, and were imitators of their practices, and so, in all things, they desired to be similar to those who had been their enemies and destroyers.

But acting impiously against the divine laws does not go unpunished, as these subsequent events will reveal.

. . .

But not much time later, the king sent a certain elder of Antioch, who compelled the Jews to transfer themselves from the laws of God and of their fathers. . . and also to contaminate the temple that was in Jerusalem, and to name it "Jupiter of Olympus," and in Garizim, "Jupiter of Hospitality," exactly like those who inhabited the place.

Yet the worst and most grievous thing of all was the onrush of evils.

For the temple was full of the luxuries and carousings of the Gentiles, and of consorting with promiscuous women. And the women hurried themselves unreservedly into the sacred buildings, bringing in things that were not lawful.

And even the altar was filled with illicit things, which were prohibited by the laws.

And also the Sabbaths were not kept, and the solemn days of the fathers were not observed, neither did anyone simply confess himself to be a Jew.

. . .

But Maccabeus and those who were with him, the Lord protecting them, even recovered the temple and the city.

Then he demolished the altars, which the foreigners had constructed in the streets, and likewise the shrines.

**60** Chapter 4 Life in the Hellenistic World, 338–30 B.C.E.

SOURCES IN
CONVERSATION

And, having purged the temple, they made another altar. And, taking glowing stones from the fire, they began to offer sacrifices again after two years, and they set out incense, and lamps, and the bread of the Presence.

Having done these things, they petitioned the Lord, lying prostrate on the ground, lest they should fall once more into such evils, but also, if they should at any time sin, that they might be chastised by him more mildly, and not be delivered over to barbarians and blasphemous men.

Then, on the day that the temple had been polluted by the foreigners, it happened on the same day that the purification was accomplished, on the twenty-fifth day of the month, which was Kislev.

And they celebrated for eight days with joy, in the manner of the Feast of Tabernacles, remembering that, a little time before, they had celebrated the solemn days of the Feast of Tabernacles in mountains and caves, in the manner of wild beasts.

Because of this, they now preferred to carry boughs and green branches and palms, for him who had prospered the cleansing of his place.

And they decreed a common precept and decree, that all the people of the Jews should keep those days every year.

### READING QUESTIONS

1. What sorts of actions by the Hellenistic regime are cited as offensive, problematic, or blasphemous? Why are they seen as such in the Jewish tradition?

2. From the story being told here, what is probably most concerning to the Jews about the incursion of Hellenistic culture in their ancestral homeland?

3. In the Jewish tradition, what is dangerous about the influence of outside cultures? According to that tradition, what were some consequences that occurred to the Hebrew people when they wavered in their faith?

### SOURCES IN CONVERSATION

# Living the Good Life

Philosophical inquiry, long a hallmark of Greek culture, took on new importance in the Hellenistic period. Unsettled by the changes that followed Alexander's conquests and no longer confident in the ability of traditional religion to provide certainty and stability, an increasing number of Greeks turned to philosophy for consolation and guidance. The following documents provide insight into three of the most important Hellenistic philosophies: Cynicism, Epicureanism, and Stoicism. Although different in many ways, all three focused on a single question: in a world of constant change, where all the old certainties seem to be disintegrating, how should one live? As you read the documents, ask yourself how each philosophy answered this question.

What advice did each offer to Hellenistic Greeks in search of happiness, contentment, and peace?

**READ AND COMPARE**

1. How did each of these philosophies attempt to attain personal happiness, contentment, and peace?

2. Which of these philosophies would have been more easily accepted by Hellenistic society, and why do you think so?

## 4-3 | DIOGENES LAERTIUS, *The Lives and Opinions of Eminent Philosophers: Diogenes of Sinope, the Cynic* (ca. 300–200 B.C.E.)

The Cynics believed that happiness could be found in the rejection of human conventions and the embrace of a life lived in accord with nature. In their view, the desire for material goods, public acclaim, and personal power was unnatural, a byproduct of social and cultural conventions that placed a false value on these things. The struggle to obtain and hold on to such things was the principal source of human unhappiness. Only when convention and custom were swept aside could one see, and obtain, that which was truly valuable. In the passage below, Diogenes Laertius, a third-century biographer of Greek philosophers, describes one of the best-known Cynics, Diogenes of Sinope. As you read it, ask yourself how Diogenes of Sinope's behavior reflected his philosophical commitments.

And when he saw a mouse running about and not seeking for a bed, nor taking care to keep in the dark, nor looking for any of those things which appear enjoyable to such an animal, he found a remedy for his own poverty. He was, according to the account of some people, the first person who doubled up his cloak out of necessity, and who slept in it; and who carried a wallet, in which he kept his food; and who used whatever place was near for all sorts of purposes, eating, and sleeping, and conversing in it. . . . He took a cask . . . for his house,[1] as he himself tells us in his letters. And during the summer he used to roll himself in the warm sand, but in winter he would embrace statues all covered with snow, practicing himself, on every occasion, to endure anything. . . .

He often condemned those who praise the just for being superior to money, but who at the same time are eager themselves for great riches. He was also very indignant at seeing men sacrifice to the Gods to procure good health, and yet at the sacrifice eating in a manner injurious to health. He often expressed his surprise at slaves, who, seeing their masters eating in a gluttonous manner, still do not themselves lay hands on any of the eatables. . . .

---

From Diogenes Laertius, *The Lives and Opinions of Eminent Philosophers*, trans. C. D. Yonge (London: George Bell and Sons, 1901), pp. 224–248.

[1]**took a cask . . . for his house**: He lived in a large barrel.

**62** Chapter 4 Life in the Hellenistic World, 338–30 B.C.E.

**SOURCES IN CONVERSATION**

Once, while he was sitting in the sun, . . . Alexander was standing by, and said to him, "Ask any favor you choose of me." And he replied, "Cease to shade me from the sun." . . .

Plato defined man thus: "Man is a two-footed, featherless animal," and was much praised for the definition; so Diogenes plucked a cock and brought it into his school, and said, "This is Plato's man." On which account this addition was made to the definition, "With broad flat nails." . . . When people were speaking of the happiness of Callisthenes,[2] and saying what splendid treatment he received from Alexander, he replied, "The man is wretched, for he is forced to breakfast and dine whenever Alexander chooses."

### READING QUESTIONS

1. How does Diogenes live his life? Why does he choose to live this way?

2. What is Diogenes's attitude toward the famous and powerful? Why does he treat them as he does?

3. Does Diogenes exhibit any of the qualities that were valued by the classical Greeks? Explain your response.

## 4-4 | EPICURUS, *The Principal Doctrines of Epicureanism* (ca. 306 B.C.E.)

Epicurus (eh-pih-KYOUR-uhs), founder of the Epicurean school of philosophy, lived from 340 to 270 B.C.E., primarily in Athens. The central principle of his teachings was to live a life that was free of pain and fear (the bad) and filled with pleasure and friendship (the good). He presented arguments that helped establish numerous principles of scientific and religious study, including the idea that one should believe only that which can be observed. His sometimes unpopular theories challenged Greek notions of the gods' power in their lives. Few of his works survive; the quotes that follow were recorded by Diogenes Laertius.

1. The blessed and immortal nature knows no trouble itself nor causes trouble to any other, so that it is never constrained by anger or favor. For all such things exist only in the weak.

2. Death is nothing to us: for that which is dissolved is without sensation; and that which lacks sensation is nothing to us. . . .

4. Pain does not last continuously in the flesh, but the acutest pain is there for a very short time, and even that which just exceeds the pleasure in the flesh does not continue for many days at once. But chronic illnesses permit a predominance of pleasure over pain in the flesh.

5. It is not possible to live pleasantly without living prudently and honorably and justly, nor again to live a life of prudence, honor, and justice without

From Whitney H. Oates, ed., *The Stoic and Epicurean Philosophers* (New York: Modern Library, 1940), pp. 35–39.

[2]**Callisthenes**: Greek historian and adviser to Alexander.

living pleasantly. And the man who does not possess the pleasant life, is not living prudently and honorably and justly, and the man who does not possess the virtuous life, cannot possibly live pleasantly. . . .

7. Some men wished to become famous and conspicuous, thinking that they would thus win for themselves safety from other men. Wherefore if the life of such men is safe, they have obtained the good which nature craves; but if it is not safe, they do not possess that for which they strove at first by the instinct of nature.

8. No pleasure is a bad thing in itself: but the means which produce some pleasures bring with them disturbances many times greater than the pleasures. . . .

10. If the things that produce the pleasures of profligates[1] could dispel the fears of the mind about the phenomena of the sky and death and its pains, and also teach the limits of desires and of pains, we should never have cause to blame them: for they would be filling themselves full with pleasures from every source and never have pain of body or mind, which is the evil of life. . . .

12. A man cannot dispel his fear about the most important matters if he does not know what is the nature of the universe but suspects the truth of some mythical story. So that without natural science it is not possible to attain our pleasures unalloyed.[2] . . .

15. The wealth demanded by nature is both limited and easily procured; that demanded by idle imaginings stretches on to infinity. . . .

17. The just man is most free from trouble, the unjust most full of trouble. . . .

21. He who has learned the limits of life knows that that which removes the pain due to want and makes the whole of life complete is easy to obtain; so that there is no need of actions which involve competition. . . .

27. Of all the things which wisdom acquires to produce the blessedness of the complete life, far the greatest is the possession of friendship. . . .

31. The justice which arises from nature is a pledge of mutual advantage to restrain men from harming one another and save them from being harmed. . . .

33. Justice never is anything in itself, but in the dealings of men with one another in any place whatever and at any time it is a kind of compact not to harm or be harmed.

## READING QUESTIONS

1. According to Epicurus, what is the relationship between pain and pleasure? What is true pleasure?

2. How does natural science contribute to true pleasure?

3. How does Epicurus define justice?

4. What principles should a human being follow to lead a fulfilled life? Which of Epicurus's principles might have upset his contemporaries, and why?

---

[1]**profligates**: Wasteful and extravagant people.
[2]**unalloyed**: Purely and completely.

**64**    Chapter 4  Life in the Hellenistic World, 338–30 B.C.E.

**SOURCES IN
CONVERSATION**

## 4-5  |  EPICTETUS, *Encheiridion, or The Manual* (ca. 100 C.E.)

Epictetus, a Greek slave and philosopher, wrote his manual for living as a Stoic during the height of the Roman Empire. After his owner freed him, Epictetus opened a school of Stoic philosophy in Rome. Stoics, like Epicureans and Cynics, believed that they were followers of Socrates's philosophy. Of the Hellenistic philosophies, Stoicism was the most popular. Rather than inspiring people to change political or social systems so that they conform to an ideal, it taught people that the best way to live was to accept things as they were.

**I**

Of things some are in our power, and others are not. In our power are opinion, movement towards a thing, desire, aversion; and in a word, whatever are our own acts: not in our power are the body, property, reputation, offices (magisterial power), and in a word, whatever are not our own acts. And the things in our power are by nature free, not subject to restraint nor hindrance: but the things not in our power are weak, slavish, subject to restraint, in the power of others. Remember then that if you think the things which are by nature slavish to be free, and the things which are in the power of others to be your own, you will be hindered, you will lament, you will be disturbed, you will blame both gods and men: but if you think that only which is your own to be your own, and if you think that what is another's, as it really is, belongs to another, no man will ever compel you, no man will hinder you, you will never blame any man, you will accuse no man, you will do nothing involuntarily [against your will], no man will harm you, you will have no enemy, for you will not suffer any harm.

If then you desire [aim at] such great things, remember that you must not [attempt to] lay hold of them with a small effort; but you must leave alone some things entirely, and postpone others for the present. But if you wish for these things also [such great things], and power [office] and wealth, perhaps you will not gain even these very things [power and wealth] because you aim also at those finer things [such great things]; certainly you will fail in those things through which alone happiness and freedom are secured. Straightway then practice saying to every harsh appearance, "You are an appearance, and in no manner what you appear to be." Then examine it by the rules which you possess, and by this first and chiefly, whether it relates to the things which are in our power or to things which are not in our power: and if it relates to any thing which is not in our power, be ready to say, that it does not concern you. . . .

From George Long, trans., *The Discourses of Epictetus: With the Encheiridion and Fragments* (London: George Bell and Sons, 1888), pp. 379–404.

## III

In everything which pleases the soul, or supplies a want, or is loved, remember to add this to the [description]; what is the nature of each thing, beginning from the smallest? If you love an earthen vessel, say it is an earthen vessel which you love; for when it has been broken, you will not be disturbed. If you are kissing your child or wife, say that it is a human being whom you are kissing, for when the wife or child dies, you will not be disturbed. . . .

## V

Men are disturbed not by the things which happen, but by the opinions about the things: for example, death is nothing terrible, for if it were, it would have seemed so to Socrates; for the opinion about death, that it is terrible, is the terrible thing. When then we are impeded or disturbed or grieved, let us never blame others, but ourselves, that is, our opinions. It is the act of an ill-instructed man to blame others for his own bad condition; it is the act of one who has begun to be instructed, to lay the blame on himself; and of one whose instruction is completed, neither to blame another, nor himself. . . .

## VII

As on a voyage when the vessel has reached a port, if you go out to get water, it is an amusement by the way to pick up a shell fish or some bulb, but your thoughts ought to be directed to the ship, and you ought to be constantly watching if the captain should call, and then you must throw away all those things, that you may not be bound and pitched into the ship like sheep: so in life also, if there be given to you instead of a little bulb and a shell a wife and child, there will be nothing to prevent [you from taking them]. But if the captain should call, run to the ship, and leave all those things without regard to them. But if you are old, do not even go far from the ship, lest when you are called you make default. . . .

## XI

Never say about anything, I have lost it, but say I have restored it. Is your child dead? It has been restored. Is your wife dead? She has been restored. Has your estate been taken from you? Has not then this also been restored? But he who has taken it from me is a bad man. But what is it to you, by whose hands the giver demanded it back? So long as he may allow you, take care of it as a thing which belongs to another, as travellers do with their inn.

## XII

If you intend to improve, throw away such thoughts as these: if I neglect my affairs, I shall not have the means of living: unless I chastise my slave, he will

**66** **Chapter 4** Life in the Hellenistic World, 338–30 B.C.E.

**SOURCES IN CONVERSATION**

be bad. For it is better to die of hunger and so to be released from grief and fear than to live in abundance with perturbation; and it is better for your slave to be bad than for you to be unhappy. Begin then from little things. Is the oil spilled? Is a little wine stolen? Say on the occasion, at such price is sold freedom from perturbation; at such price is sold tranquility, but nothing is got for nothing. And when you call your slave, consider that it is possible that he does not hear; and if he does hear, that he will do nothing which you wish. But matters are not so well with him, but altogether well with you, that it should be in his power for you to be not disturbed. . . .

## XX

Remember that it is not he who reviles you or strikes you, who insults you, but it is your opinion about these things as being insulting. When then a man irritates you, you must know that it is your own opinion which has irritated you. Therefore especially try not to be carried away by the appearance. For if you once gain time and delay, you will more easily master yourself. . . .

## XXII

If you desire philosophy, prepare yourself from the beginning to be ridiculed, to expect that many will sneer at you, and say, He has all at once returned to us as a philosopher; and whence does he got this supercilious look for us? Do you not show a supercilious look; but hold on to the things which seem to you best as one appointed by God to this station. And remember that if you abide in the same principles, these men who first ridiculed will afterwards admire you: but if you shall have been overpowered by them, you will bring on yourself double ridicule.

### READING QUESTIONS

1. According to Epictetus, what things can a person control? What things are out of one's control?

2. How should one respond to events, both good and bad?

3. What is the point of life according to the Stoics?

4. How would Stoicism have helped people with the social and political conditions that existed during the Hellenistic period?

## 4-6 | A Greek View of Byzantium

### POLYBIUS, *A Greek Historian Describes Byzantium's Contribution to Regional Trade* (ca. 170–118 B.C.E.)

Alexander's conquests paved the way for a dramatic expansion of trade throughout the Mediterranean. Vast amounts of new wealth flowed westward, creating increased demand for imported goods and providing funds for the construction of new roads and harbors. In the passage below, the Greek historian Polybius (200–118 B.C.E.) describes the important role the city Byzantium played in the Greek economy. Situated on a narrow peninsula from which it dominated the waters that connected the Mediterranean to the Black Sea, Byzantium, later re-founded and renamed Constantinople, served as a link between East and West. As you read the passage, consider what it tells us about the Hellenistic economy. How were the cities of the Hellenistic world dependent on one another for their prosperity?

As far as the sea is concerned, the Byzantines occupy a position that is more secure and more advantageous than that of any other city in our part of the world, but as regards the land that position is in both respects most unfavourable. Their situation by sea at the entrance to the Black Sea enables them to prevent any trader from sailing into or out of the Black Sea against their will. Since the Black Sea has an abundance of products which are of use to the rest of the world, the Byzantines have control over all of these. For those commodities which are indispensable to life, cattle and slaves, are supplied to us by the countries around the Black Sea, as is generally agreed, in greater quantity, and of better quality than by any others; and as far as luxuries are concerned, they supply us with honey, wax and salt-fish in abundance. In return they receive from our part of the world the surplus olive oil and every kind of wine. With corn there is interchange; they give us some on occasion and sometimes import it from us. Now the Greeks would have been deprived of all these resources or would have found trading in them quite unprofitable if the Byzantines had shown hostility and combined with the Celts, or still more with the Thracians, or had given up the place altogether. Because of the narrowness of the straits and the large number of barbarians living along its shores, the Black Sea would by common consent have become closed to navigation. The Byzantines probably draw themselves the greatest practical benefits from the peculiar situation of their town. Any surplus products they have are easily exported, while they can import easily and profitably anything they lack, without incurring any hardship or danger; but, as I have said, others derive many great advantages thanks to them. Hence as common benefactors of all, as it were, they deserve to gain not only gratitude but concerted support from the Greeks in the dangers they face from the barbarians.

POLYBIUS IV. 38. 1–10

## READING QUESTIONS

1. What products did the Greeks import from the peoples of the Black Sea? What products did the peoples of the Black Sea import from the Greeks?

2. Why did Polybius believe the Greeks owed the Byzantines their gratitude and support?

3. What light does this passage shed on the interdependence of Hellenistic cities?

## ▪ COMPARATIVE AND DISCUSSION QUESTIONS ▪

1. How would Alexander have reacted to the three philosophies highlighted in Documents 4-3 to 4-5? Which would he most like, and which would he most dislike, and why?

2. Consider the Greek city-states of the classical versus the Hellenistic period. What had changed? Why? What light do the documents included in this chapter shed on these questions?

3. All three Hellenistic philosophies mentioned in this chapter offer a way to live a good life. How does each philosophy define "the good life"? What advice does each offer for achieving this goal? How does each of them address the specific problems people would have experienced during that time?

# 5

# The Rise of Rome

## ca. 1000–27 B.C.E.

Founded around 750 B.C.E., Rome was first ruled by kings. In the sixth century B.C.E., an aristocratic revolt led to the overthrow of the monarchy and the establishment of the Roman Republic. Over the next two hundred years, Rome gained control of the whole Italian peninsula, partly by conquest and partly in alliance with other states. During these same centuries, Rome's legal and political institutions underwent substantial change, as the common people of Rome, the plebeians, fought for, and won, greater political and legal equality. In the course of three wars (264–146 B.C.E.) the Romans destroyed Carthage, the greatest power in the western Mediterranean, clearing the way for further Roman expansion. The wealth that came with the expanding empire allowed Roman culture to flourish and created more opportunities for leisure and the arts. Expansion was not, however, without costs. As the first millennium B.C.E. came to a close, republican institutions proved insufficient to cope with the growing social and economic problems created by expansion, and Rome descended into military rule and civil war.

### 5-1 | The Moral Roots of the Republic
### LIVY, *The Rape of Lucretia* (ca. 27–25 B.C.E.)

From a Roman perspective, the rape of Lucretia was a powerful story because it forged a link between the foundation of the republic and the triumph of core Roman values and beliefs. According to the story, excerpted here from Livy's (59 B.C.E.–17 C.E.) comprehensive history of Rome, the rape of the noble Roman lady Lucretia by the Etruscan prince Sextus Tarquinius sparked the rebellion that culminated in the overthrow of the Etruscan monarchy. Thus, from the beginning, honor, duty, and the sanctity of the Roman family were at the heart of the republic. The Roman aristocracy rose against the Etruscans not simply to seize power,

---

From Livy, *Ab Urbe Condita* (*History*), vol. 1, trans. George Baker (Philadelphia: T. Wardle, 1840), pp. 58–59.

but to protect Roman values. As you read the story, focus on the values it champions. What does the story tell you about the Romans' image of themselves?

A few days after, Sextus Tarquinius,[1] without the knowledge of Collatinus,[2] went to Collatia, with only a single attendant: he was kindly received by the family, who suspected not his design, and, after supper, conducted to the chamber where guests were lodged. Then, burning with desire, as soon as he thought that everything was safe, and the family all at rest, he came with his sword drawn to Lucretia, where she lay asleep, and, holding her down, with his left hand pressed on her breast, said, "Lucretia, be silent: I am Sextus Tarquinius; my sword is in my hand, if you utter a word, you die."

Terrified at being thus disturbed from sleep, she saw no assistance near, and immediate death threatening her. Tarquinius then acknowledged his passion, entreated, mixed threats with entreaties, and used every argument likely to have effect on a woman's mind: but finding her inflexible, and not to be moved, even by the fear of death, he added to that fear, the dread of dishonor, telling her that, after killing her he would murder a slave, and lay him naked by her side, that she might be said to have been slain in base adultery. The shocking apprehension, conveyed by this menace, overpowering her resolution in defending her chastity, his lust became victorious; and Tarquinius departed, applauding himself for this triumph over a lady's honor.

But Lucretia[,] plunged by such a disaster into the deepest distress, dispatched a messenger to Rome to her father, with orders to proceed to Ardea to her husband, and to desire them to come to her, each with one faithful friend; to tell them, that there was a necessity for their doing so, and speedily, for that a dreadful affair had happened. Spurius Lucretius came with Publius Valerius, the son of Volesus; Collatinus with Lucius Junius Brutus, in company with whom he chanced to be returning to Rome, when he was met by his wife's messenger.

They found Lucretia sitting in her chamber, melancholy and dejected: on the arrival of her friends, she burst into tears, and on her husband's asking, "Is all well?" "Far from it," said she, "for how can it be well with a woman who has lost her chastity? Collatinus, the impression of another man is in your bed; yet my person only has been violated, my mind is guiltless as my death will testify. But give me your right hands, and pledge your honor that the adulterer shall not escape unpunished. He is Sextus Tarquinius, who, under the appearance of a guest, disguising an enemy, obtained here last night, by armed violence, a triumph deadly to me, and to himself also, if ye be men."

They all pledged their honor, one after another, and endeavored to comfort her distracted mind, acquitting her of blame, as under the compulsion of force, and charging it on the violent perpetrator of the crime, told her, that "the mind alone was capable of sinning, not the body, and that where there was no such intention, there could be no guilt."

---

[1]**Sextus Tarquinius**: Prince of Rome, son of King L. Tarquinius Superbus (r. 535–510 B.C.E.).
[2]**Collatinus**: Lucretia's husband.

"[It is] your concern," said she, "to consider what is due to him; as to me, though I acquit myself of the guilt, I cannot dispense with the penalty, nor shall any woman ever plead the example of Lucretia, for surviving her chastity." Thus saying, she plunged into her heart a knife which she had concealed under her garment, and falling forward on the wound, dropped lifeless. The husband and father shrieked aloud.

But Brutus, while they were overpowered by grief, drawing the knife, from the wound of Lucretia, and holding it out, reeking with blood, before him, said, "By this blood, most chaste until injured by royal insolence, swear, and call you, O ye gods, to witness, that I will prosecute to destruction, by sword, fire, and every forcible means in my power, both Lucius Tarquinius the proud, and his impious wife, together with their entire race, and never will suffer one of them, nor any other person whatsoever, to be king in Rome." He then delivered the knife to Collatinus, afterwards to Lucretius, and Valerius, who were filled with amazement, as at a prodigy, and at a loss to account for this unusual elevation of sentiment in the mind of Brutus.

However, they took the oath as directed, and converting their grief into rage, followed Brutus, who put himself at their head, and called on them to proceed instantly to abolish kingly power.

They brought out the body of Lucretia from the house, conveyed it to the forum, and assembled the people, who came together quickly, in astonishment, as may be supposed at a deed so atrocious and unheard of. Every one exclaimed with vehemence against the villainy and violence of the prince: they were deeply affected by the grief of her father, and also by the discourse of Brutus, who rebuked their tears and ineffectual complaints, and advised them, as became men, as became Romans, to take up arms against those who had dared to treat them as enemies. The most spirited among the youth offered themselves with their arms, and the rest followed their example. On which, leaving half their number at the gates to defend Collatia, and fixing guards to prevent any intelligence of the commotion being carried to the princes, the rest, with Brutus at their head, marched to Rome.

When they arrived there, the sight of such an armed multitude spread terror and confusion wherever they came: but, in a little time, when people observed the principal men of the state marching at their head, they concluded, that whatever the matter was, there must be good reason for it. Nor did the heinousness of the affair raise less violent emotions in the minds of the people at Rome, than it had at Collatia: so that, from all parts of the city, they hurried into the forum; where, as soon as the party arrived, a crier summoned the people to attend the tribune of the celeres,[3] which office happened at that time to be held by Brutus.

He there made a speech, no way consonant to that low degree of sensibility and capacity, which until that day, he had counterfeited; recounting the violence and lust of Sextus Tarquinius, the shocking violation of Lucretia's chastity, and her lamentable death; the misfortune of Tricipitinus,[4] in being left childless, who

---

[3]**tribune of the celeres**: Commander of the king's body guard.
[4]**Tricipitinus**: Spurius Tricipitinus Lucretius; Lucretia's father.

must feel the cause of his daughter's death as a greater injury and cruelty, than her death itself: to these representations he added the pride of the king himself, the miseries and toils of the commons, buried under ground to cleanse sinks and sewers, saying, that ". . . citizens of Rome, the conquerors of all the neighboring nations, were, from warriors, reduced to laborers and stone cutters"; mentioned the barbarous murder of King Servius Tullius,[5] his abominable daughter driving in her carriage over the body of her father, and invoked the gods to avenge the cause of parents.

By descanting on these and other, I suppose, more forcible topics, which the heinousness or present injuries suggested at the time, but which it is difficult for writers to repeat, he inflamed the rage of the multitude to such a degree, that they were easily persuaded to deprive the king of his government, and to pass an order for the banishment of Lucius Tarquinius, his wife, and children. Brutus himself, having collected and armed such of the young men as voluntarily gave in their names, set out for the camp at Ardea, in order to excite the troops there to take part against the king. The command in the city he left to Lucretius, who had some time before been appointed by the king to the office of prefect of the city. During this tumult Tullia fled from her house; both men and women, wherever she passed, imprecating curses on her head, and invoking the furies, the avengers of parents.

### READING QUESTIONS

1.  How did Tarquinius frighten Lucretia into having sex with him?

2.  How did the men in Lucretia's family react to what had happened to her?

3.  What does the story tell you about Roman ideas about the family? About Roman values?

4.  How did Lucretia's relatives and friends connect her rape and suicide to the larger grievances of the Roman people? According to the story, what is the role of the common people in Roman politics?

## 5-2   |   Roman Family Values

### POLYBIUS, *The Histories* (ca. 160–140 B.C.E.)

Roman family values are also reflected in an account written by Polybius, a Greek from Arcadia who spent many years in the city of Rome. In *The Histories*, he recounts the events of the Punic Wars while analyzing and praising the Roman republican government, military

From Oliver J. Thatcher, *The Library of Original Sources*, vol. 3: *The Roman World* (Milwaukee, Wisc.: University Research Extension Co., 1915), pp. 187–189.

[5]**Servius Tullius**: King of Rome (r. 578–535 B.C.E.), who reorganized the Roman constitution to expand the political rights of the lower classes. He was killed by patrician conspirators, including his daughter Tullia.

prowess, and the moral virtues of the people, all of which he claims contributed to the defeat of the Carthaginians by the Italian state and to Rome becoming a regional Mediterranean power. This section describes how society, and especially family members, honored great men at their death and thereby inspired younger generations of Romans.

Now the people of Italy are by nature superior to the Carthaginians and the Africans, both in bodily strength and courage. Add to this, that they have among them certain institutions by which the young men are greatly animated to perform acts of bravery. It will be sufficient to mention one of these, as a proof of the attention that is shewn by the Roman government, to infuse such a spirit into the citizens as shall lead them to encounter every kind of danger for the sake of obtaining reputation in their country. When any illustrious person dies, he is carried in procession with the rest of the funeral pomp, to the rostra in the forum; sometimes placed conspicuous in an upright posture; and some-times, though less frequently, reclined. And while the people are all standing round, his son, if he has left one of sufficient age . . . or . . . some person of his kindred, ascends the rostra,[1] and extols the virtues of the deceased, and the great deeds that were performed by him in his life. By this discourse . . . before all the multitude [they] are moved to such sympathy or sorrow, that the acci-dent seems rather to be a public misfortune, than a private loss. He is then bur-ied with the usual rites; and afterwards an image, which both in features and complexion expresses an exact resemblance of his face, is set up in the most conspicuous part of the house, inclosed [*sic*] in a shrine of wood. Upon solemn festivals, these images are uncovered, and adorned with the greatest care. And when any other person of the same family dies, they are carried also in the funeral procession, with a body added to the bust, that the representation may be just, even with regard to size. They are dressed likewise in the habits that belong to the ranks which they severally filled when they were alive. If they were consuls[2] or praetors,[3] in a gown bordered with purple: if censors,[4] in a purple robe; and if they triumphed, or obtained any similar honor, in a vest embroidered in gold. And when they arrive at the forum, they are all seated upon chairs of ivory; and there exhibit the noblest objects that can be offered to youthful mind, warmed with the love of virtue and of glory. For who can behold without emotion the forms of so many illustrious men, thus living, as it were, and breathing together in his presence? Or what spectacle can be con-ceived more great and striking? . . . By this method, which renews continually the remembrance of men celebrated for their virtue, the fame of every great and noble action become immortal. And the glory of those, by whose services their country has benefited, is rendered familiar to the people, and delivered

---

[1]**rostra**: A large raised platform in the city of Rome where speakers would address crowds.
[2]**consuls**: Chief magistrates in Rome who were elected each year.
[3]**praetors**: Roman magistrates just below consuls in rank.
[4]**censors**: Roman magistrates who supervised population counts and public morals.

down to future time. But the chief advantage is, that by the hope of obtaining this honorable fame, which is reserved for virtue, the young men are animated to sustain all danger, in the cause of the common safety.

### READING QUESTIONS

1. What was the purpose of honoring important Roman men?
2. How would these rituals help Rome become a powerful regional empire?
3. What do these rituals suggest about social class and gender relationships in Rome?

## 5-3 | An Effort to Resolve Social Conflict
### *The Laws of the Twelve Tables* (449 B.C.E.)

It is not a coincidence that the same centuries that saw the Roman conquest of Italy also saw the Struggle of the Orders, the plebeians' long and hard-fought battle for greater legal and political equality. In some ways, the history of Rome is the history of Roman social and political adaptation to the pressures of expansion. The Laws of the Twelve Tables, codified and published in 449 B.C.E., was one of the first, and perhaps most important, patrician concessions to the new realities created by Roman conquest. As you read the excerpts below, pay particular attention to the abuses the laws sought to prevent. What conflicts in Roman society did the laws seek to remedy?

### TABLE I. Concerning the Summons to Court

Law I

When anyone summons another before the tribunal of a judge, the latter must, without hesitation, immediately appear.

Law II

If, after having been summoned, he does not appear, or refuses to come before the tribunal of the judge, let the party who summoned him call upon any citizens who are present to bear witness. Then let him seize his reluctant adversary; so that he may be brought into court, as a captive, by apparent force.

Law III

When anyone who has been summoned to court is guilty of evasion, or attempts to flee, let him be arrested by the plaintiff.

---

From S. P. Scott, ed., *The Civil Law*, vol. 1 (Cincinnati, Ohio: The Central Trust Company, 1932), pp. 57–58, 73–74.

## Law IV

If bodily infirmity or advanced age should prevent the party summoned to court from appearing, let him who summoned him furnish him with an animal, as a means of transport. If he is unwilling to accept it, the plaintiff cannot legally be compelled to provide the defendant with a vehicle constructed of boards, or a covered litter.

## Law V

If he who is summoned has either a sponsor or a defender, let him be dismissed, and his representative can take his place in court.

## Law VI

The defender, or the surety of a wealthy man, must himself be rich; but anyone who desires to do so can come to the assistance of a person who is poor, and occupy his place.

## Law VII

When litigants wish to settle their dispute among themselves, even while they are on their way to appear before the Prætor,[1] they shall have the right to make peace; and whatever agreement they enter into, it shall be considered just, and shall be confirmed.

## Law VIII

If the plaintiff and defendant do not settle their dispute, as above mentioned, let them state their cases either in the *Comitium*[2] or the Forum, by making a brief statement in the presence of the judge, between the rising of the sun and noon; and, both of them being present, let them speak so that each party may hear.

## Law IX

In the afternoon, let the judge grant the right to bring the action, and render his decision in the presence of the plaintiff and the defendant.

## Law X

The setting of the sun shall be the extreme limit of time within which a judge must render his decision. . . .

---

[1]**Prætor**: A magistrate, in some cases responsible for presiding over civil cases between citizens.

[2]*Comitium*: The location of the original founding of Rome, and subsequently a public gathering place and the site of many temples and shrines.

## TABLE IX. Concerning Public Law

Law I

No privileges, or statutes, shall be enacted in favor of private persons, to the injury of others contrary to the law common to all citizens, and which individuals, no matter of what rank, have a right to make use of.

Law II

The same rights shall be conferred upon, and the same laws shall be considered to have been enacted for all the people residing in and beyond Latium,[3] that have been enacted for good and steadfast Roman citizens.

Law III

When a judge, or an arbiter appointed to hear a case, accepts money, or other gifts, for the purpose of influencing his decision, he shall suffer the penalty of death.

Law IV

No decision with reference to the life or liberty of a Roman citizen shall be rendered except by the vote of the Greater *Comitia*.[4]

Law V

Public accusers in capital cases shall be appointed by the people.

Law VI

If anyone should cause nocturnal assemblies in the City, he shall be put to death.

Law VII

If anyone should stir up war against his country, or delivers a Roman citizen into the hands of the enemy, he shall be punished with death.

### READING QUESTIONS

1. Who was subject to the Laws of the Twelve Tables? Who, if anyone, was not?
2. What might explain the emphasis the laws placed on the speedy resolution of legal disputes? Who might have benefited from longer, more drawn-out proceedings?

---

[3]**Latium**: The region surrounding the city of Rome.
[4]**Greater *Comitia***: A legal assembly of the people.

3. What procedures and protections did the laws put in place to ensure the impartiality of Roman justice? What kinds of abuses might have made those procedures and protections necessary?

## 5-4 | Life in a Roman City

### SENECA, *The Sounds of a Roman Bath* (ca. 50 C.E.)

Personal cleanliness was imperative to both Greeks and Romans. The Greeks in particular frequently complained that barbarians were dirty. Public baths were central gathering places for Romans of many classes. The well-off frequently had baths in their own houses, but even so, they might visit the public baths to meet friends or partake in other activities. The public baths had a questionable reputation, in part because prostitutes often sought clients there. Seneca (ca. 4 B.C.E.–65 C.E.), a philosopher, orator, and eventually the chief adviser to the emperor, recorded this sketch of a bath's commotion.

I live over a bath. Imagine the variety of voices, enough noise to make you sick. When the stronger fellows are working out with heavy weights, when they are working hard or pretending to work hard, I hear their grunts; and whenever they exhale, I hear their hissing and panting. Or when some lazy type is getting a cheap rubdown, I hear the slap of the hand pounding his shoulders. . . . If a serious ballplayer comes along and starts keeping score out loud, that's the end for me. . . . And there's the guy who always likes to hear his own voice when washing, or those people who jump into the swimming pool with a tremendous splash. . . . The hair plucker keeps up a constant chatter to attract customers, except when he is plucking armpits and making his customer scream instead of screaming himself. It would be disgusting to list all the cries from the sausage seller, and the fellow hawking cakes, and all the food vendors yelling out what they have to sell, each with own special intonation.

#### READING QUESTIONS

1. What other activities took place at the public baths besides bathing?

2. How would you describe Roman notions of privacy and personal space?

3. What does it reveal about Roman urban life that someone like Seneca would live so close to the public baths?

# Political Unrest in Rome

Rome's wars of conquest brought the Romans land, power, and wealth. They also led to a social and political upheaval that culminated in the fall of the republic. The wars produced a flood of slave labor, concentrated wealth and land in the hands of the few, and created a growing class of landless citizens. The social and economic problems associated with these developments triggered political conflict, with advocates of reform battling the forces of the status quo. As the conflict continued, republican institutions began to break down and then collapsed completely, as rival generals vied for supreme power. The documents in this section shed light on this process.

## READ AND COMPARE

1. What is similar or different about the political tactics described in these two documents? Why do you think they resemble or differ from each other?

2. Do the authors seem to admire or criticize Tiberius Gracchus and Caesar? Why do you think so?

## 5-5  |  APPIAN OF ALEXANDRIA, *The Civil Wars* (ca. 100 C.E.)

Land reform was at the heart of the first major political crisis brought about by expansion. The wars of conquest had a profoundly destabilizing effect on the Italian countryside. Increasingly, small family farms gave way to enormous estates, owned by Roman elites and run, for the most part, with slave labor. The displaced farmers migrated to the cities, where they joined a rapidly growing population of urban poor. When Tiberius Gracchus, a Roman aristocrat, took up their cause in 133 B.C.E. and began to push for land reform in the Senate, his political enemies assassinated him. As you read Appian of Alexandria's account of Tiberius's rise and fall, consider the relationship between social division and political conflict in the late Roman Republic. How did issues of economic inequality lead to political upheaval?

The Romans, as they subdued the Italian nations successively in war, seized a part of their lands and built towns there, or established their own colonies in those already existing, and used them in place of garrisons. Of the land acquired by war they assigned the cultivated part forthwith to settlers, or leased or sold it. Since they had no leisure as yet to allot the part which then lay desolated by war (this was generally the greater part), they made proclamation that in the meantime those who

From Appian of Alexandria, *The Roman History of Appian of Alexandria*, vol. 2, trans. Horace White (New York: Macmillan Company, 1899), pp. 5–14.

were willing to work it might do so for a share of the yearly crops—a tenth of the grain and a fifth of the fruit. From those who kept flocks was required a share of the animals, both oxen and small cattle. They did these things in order to multiply the Italian race, which they considered the most laborious of peoples, so that they might have plenty of allies at home. But the very opposite thing happened; for the rich, getting possession of the greater part of the undistributed lands, and being emboldened by the lapse of time to believe that they would never be dispossessed, and adding to their holdings the small farms of their poor neighbors, partly by purchase and partly by force, came to cultivate vast tracts instead of single estates, using for this purpose slaves as laborers and herdsmen, lest free laborers should be drawn from agriculture into the army. The ownership of slaves itself brought them great gain from the multitude of their progeny, who increased because they were exempt from military service. Thus the powerful ones became enormously rich and the race of slaves multiplied throughout the country, while the Italian people dwindled in numbers and strength, being oppressed by penury, taxes, and military service. If they had any respite from these evils they passed their time in idleness, because the land was held by the rich, who employed slaves instead of freemen as cultivators.

For these reasons the [Roman] people became troubled lest they should no longer have sufficient allies of the Italian stock, and lest the government itself should be endangered by such a vast number of slaves. . . . At length Tiberius Sempronius Gracchus, an illustrious man, eager for glory, a most powerful speaker, and for these reasons well known to all, delivered an eloquent discourse, while serving as tribune, concerning the Italian race, lamenting that a people so valiant in war, and blood relations to the Romans, were declining little by little in pauperism and paucity of numbers without any hope of remedy. He inveighed against the multitude of slaves as useless in war and never faithful to their masters, and adduced the recent calamity brought upon the masters by their slaves in Sicily,[1] where the demands of agriculture had greatly increased the number of the latter; recalling also the war waged against them by the Romans, which was neither easy nor short, but long-protracted and full of vicissitudes and dangers. After speaking thus he again brought forward the law, providing that nobody should hold more than 500 jugera[2] of the public domain. But he added a provision to the former law, that the sons of the present occupiers might each hold one-half of that amount, and that the remainder should be divided among the poor. . . .

This was extremely disturbing to the rich because, . . . they could no longer disregard the law as they had done before; nor could they buy the allotments of others, because Gracchus had provided against this by forbidding sales. They collected together in groups, and made lamentation, and accused the poor of appropriating the results of their tillage, their vineyards, and their dwellings. Some said that they had paid the price of the land to their neighbors. Were they to lose the money with the land? Others said that the graves of their ancestors were in the ground, which had been allotted to them in the

---

[1]**recent calamity . . . Sicily**: A slave revolt was under way in Sicily at this time.
[2]**jugera**: Plural of *jugerum*. A jugerum is approximately two-thirds of an acre.

division of their fathers' estates. Others said that their wives' dowries had
been expended on the estates, or that the land had been given to their own
daughters as dowry. Money-lenders could show loans made on this security. All kinds of wailing and expressions of indignation were heard at once.
On the other side were heard the lamentations of the poor — that they had
been reduced from competence to extreme penury, and from that to child-
lessness, because they were unable to rear their offspring. They recounted
the military services they had rendered, by which this very land had been
acquired, and were angry that they should be robbed of their share of the
common property. They reproached the rich for employing slaves, who were
always faithless and ill-tempered and for that reason unserviceable in war,
instead of freemen, citizens, and soldiers. While these classes were lamenting
and indulging in mutual accusations, a great number of others, composed of
colonists, or inhabitants of the free towns, or persons otherwise interested
in the lands and who were under like apprehensions, flocked in and took
sides with their respective factions. Emboldened by numbers and exasper-
ated against each other they attached themselves to turbulent crowds, and
waited for the voting on the new law, some trying to prevent its enactment
by all means, and others supporting it in every possible way. . . .

What Gracchus had in his mind in proposing the measure was not wealth,
but an increase of efficient population. Inspired greatly by the usefulness of
the work, and believing that nothing more advantageous or admirable could
ever happen to Italy, he took no account of the difficulties surrounding it.
When the time for voting came he advanced many other arguments at considerable length and also asked them whether it was not just to divide among
the common people what belonged to them in common; whether a citizen
was not worthy of more consideration at all times than a slave; whether a
man who served in the army was not more useful than one who did not;
and whether one who had a share in the country was not more likely to be
devoted to the public interests. He did not dwell long on this comparison
between freemen and slaves, which he considered degrading, but proceeded
at once to a review of their hopes and fears for the country, saying that the
Romans had acquired most of their territory by conquest, and that they had
hopes of occupying the rest of the habitable world, but now the question of
greatest hazard was, whether they should gain the rest by having plenty of
brave men, or whether, through their weakness and mutual jealousy, their
enemies should take away what they already possessed. After exaggerating
the glory and riches on the one side and the danger and fear on the other, he
admonished the rich to take heed, and said that for the realization of these
hopes they ought to bestow this very land as a free gift, if necessary, on men
who would rear children, and not, by contending about small things, over-
look larger ones; especially since they were receiving an ample compensation
for labor expended in the undisputed title to 500 jugera each of free land, in
a high state of cultivation, without cost, and half as much more for each son
of those who had sons. After saying much more to the same purport and

exciting the poor, as well as others who were moved by reason rather than by the desire for gain, he ordered the scribe to read the proposed law. . . .

[Eventually the law is passed, but only after great difficulty.]

Gracchus became immensely popular by reason of the law and was escorted home by the multitude as though he were the founder, not of a single city or race, but of all the nations of Italy. After this the victorious party returned to the fields from which they had come to attend to this business. The defeated ones remained in the city and talked the matter over, feeling bitterly, and saying that as soon as Gracchus should become a private citizen he would be sorry that he had done despite[3] to the sacred and inviolable office of tribune, and had opened such a fountain of discord in Italy.

[Tension between the wealthy landowners and Gracchus's supporters eventually leads to violence.]

When [the landowners' faction] arrived at the temple and advanced against the partisans of Gracchus they yielded to the reputation of a foremost citizen, for they saw the Senate following with him. The latter wrested clubs out of the hands of the Gracchans themselves, or with fragments of broken benches or other apparatus that had been brought for the use of the assembly, began beating them, and pursued them. . . . In the tumult many of the Gracchans perished, and Gracchus himself was caught near a temple, and was slain at the door close by the statues of the kings. All the bodies were thrown by night into the Tiber. . . .

On the subject of the murder of Gracchus the city was divided between sorrow and joy. Some mourned for themselves and for him, and deplored the present condition of things, believing that the commonwealth no longer existed, but had been supplanted by force and violence. Others considered that everything had turned out for them exactly as they wished.

## READING QUESTIONS

1. What specific problems were created by the acquisition of the Italian lands?
2. What were the provisions of the new law?
3. What reasons did the landowners give for opposing the law?
4. What does this episode reveal about the strengths and weaknesses of the Roman government?

---

[3]**done despite**: Insulted or shown contempt for.

## 5-6   |   PLUTARCH, *On Julius Caesar, a Man of Unlimited Ambition* (ca. 44 B.C.E.)

By 44 B.C.E., Rome had suffered generations of civil war, and Caesar had become dictator for life. Throughout his political career, Caesar and his family had allied themselves with the interests of the common people, and he was generally well-liked among the Roman populace. This did not mean, however, that he was without powerful enemies or that his popularity was guaranteed. Caesar's "unlimited ambition" had been a key ingredient in his rise to power, but his enemies used this ambition to drive a wedge between him and the Roman people. In this excerpt from Plutarch's (ca. 46–120 C.E.) *Life of Caesar*, Plutarch describes the political fallout of an attempt to have Caesar named king. As you read it, pay particular attention to the way Caesar and his enemies sought to turn public opinion to their advantage.

But that which brought upon him the most apparent and mortal hatred was his desire of being king; which gave the common people the first occasion to quarrel with him, and proved the most specious pretence to those who had been his secret enemies all along. Those who would have procured him that title gave it out that it was foretold in the Sibyls' books[1] that the Romans should conquer the Parthians when they fought against them under the conduct of a king, but not before. And one day, as Caesar was coming down from Alba to Rome, some were so bold as to salute him by the name of king; but he, finding the people disrelish it, seemed to resent it himself, and said his name was Caesar, not king. Upon this there was a general silence, and he passed on looking not very well pleased or contented. Another time, when the senate had conferred on him some extravagant honors, he chanced to receive the message as he was sitting on the rostra,[2] where, though the consuls[3] and praetors[4] themselves waited on him, attended by the whole body of the senate, he did not rise, but behaved himself to them as if they had been private men, and told them his honors wanted rather to be retrenched than increased. This treatment offended not only the senate, but the commonalty too, as if they thought the affront upon the senate equally reflected upon the whole republic; so that all who could decently leave him went off, looking much discomposed. Caesar, perceiving the false step he had made, immediately retired home; and laying his throat bare, told his friends that he was ready to offer this to any one who would give the stroke. But afterwards he made the malady from which he suffered [epilepsy] the excuse for his sitting, saying that those who are attacked by it lose their presence of mind if they talk much standing; that they presently grow giddy, fall into convulsions, and quite lose

---

From A. H. Clough, trans., *Plutarch's Lives*, vol. 4 (Boston: Little, Brown and Company, 1859), pp. 316–320.

[1]**Sibyls' books**: Prophetic writings, widely read in ancient Rome.
[2]**rostra**: Platform from which politicians often addressed the Roman people.
[3]**consuls**: Highest elected officials in the republic. Two served each year.
[4]**praetors**: Magistrates.

their reason. But this was not the reality, for he would willingly have stood up to the senate, had not Cornelius Balbus, one of his friends, or rather flatterers, hindered him. "Will you not remember," said he, "you are Caesar, and claim the honor which is due to your merit?"

He gave a fresh occasion of resentment by his affront to the tribunes. The Lupercalia were then celebrated, a feast at the first institution belonging, as some writers say, to the shepherds, and having some connection with the Arcadian Lycae. Many young noblemen and magistrates run up and down the city with their upper garments off, striking all they meet with thongs of hide, by way of sport; and many women, even of the highest rank, place themselves in the way, and hold out their hands to the lash, as boys in a school do to the master, out of a belief that it procures an easy labor to those who are with child, and makes those conceive who are barren. Caesar, dressed in a triumphal robe, seated himself in a golden chair at the rostra to view this ceremony. Antony, as consul, was one of those who ran this course, and when he came into the forum, and the people made way for him, he went up and reached to Caesar a diadem wreathed with laurel. Upon this there was a shout, but only a slight one, made by the few who were planted there for that purpose; but when Caesar refused it, there was universal applause. Upon the second offer, very few, and upon the second refusal, all again applauded. Caesar finding it would not take, rose up, and ordered the crown to be carried into the capitol. Caesar's statues were afterwards found with royal diadems on their heads. Flavius and Marullus, two tribunes of the people, went presently and pulled them off, and having apprehended those who first saluted Caesar as king committed them to prison. The people followed them with acclamations, and called them by the name of Brutus,[5] because Brutus was the first who ended the succession of kings, and transferred the power which before was lodged in one man into the hands of the senate and people. Caesar so far resented this, that he displaced Marullus and Flavius; and in urging his charges against them, at the same time ridiculed the people, by himself giving the men more than once the names of Bruti and Cumaei.[6]

This made the multitude turn their thoughts to Marcus Brutus, who, by his father's side, was thought to be descended from that first Brutus, and by his mother's side from the Servilii, another noble family, being besides nephew and son-in-law to Cato.[7] But the honors and favors he had received from Caesar took off the edge from the desires he might himself have felt for overthrowing the new monarchy. For he had not only been pardoned himself after Pompey's defeat at Pharsalia, and had procured the same grace for many of his friends, but was one in whom Caesar had a particular confidence. He had at that time the most honorable praetorship for the year, and was named for the consulship four years

---

[5]**Brutus**: A reference to Marcus Brutus's ancestor, who had been instrumental in the Roman rebellion against Etruscan domination in the fifth century B.C.E. See Document 5-1.

[6]**Bruti and Cumaei**: In Latin, the word *brutus* (plural: *bruti*) means stupid, though it can also refer to the family that descends from the Brutus who opposed the last Tarquin king. *Cumaei* refers to the people from Cumae, who were considered dull and boring.

[7]**Cato**: Senator known for his strict adherence to tradition.

after, being preferred before Cassius, his competitor. Upon the question as to the choice, Caesar, it is related, said that Cassius had the fairer pretensions, but that he could not pass by Brutus. Nor would he afterwards listen to some who spoke against Brutus, when the conspiracy against him was already afoot, but laying his hand on his body, said to the informers, "Brutus will wait for this skin of mine," intimating that he was worthy to bear rule on account of his virtue, but would not be base and ungrateful to gain it. Those who desired a change, and looked on him as the only, or at least the most proper, person to effect it, did not venture to speak with him; but in the night-time laid papers about his chair of state, where he used to sit and determine causes, with such sentences in them as, "You are asleep, Brutus," "You are no longer Brutus." Cassius, when he perceived his ambition a little raised upon this, was more instant than before to work him yet further, having himself a private grudge against Caesar for some reasons that we have mentioned in the "Life of Brutus." Nor was Caesar without suspicions of him, and said once to his friends, "What do you think Cassius is aiming at? I don't like him, he looks so pale." And when it was told him that Antony and Dolabella[8] were in a plot against him, he said he did not fear such fat, luxurious men, but rather the pale, lean fellows, meaning Cassius and Brutus.

### READING QUESTIONS

1. Which segments of the Roman population wanted Caesar to become king, and why?

2. What were the motives of the conspirators against Caesar?

3. Why did Caesar have to be so careful about his actions in public? What does this tell you about the nature of Roman politics?

4. What made Marcus Brutus such a potentially valuable ally for Caesar and, at the same time, such a potentially dangerous enemy?

## ▪ COMPARATIVE AND DISCUSSION QUESTIONS ▪

1. What connections can you make between the social and political problems of republican Rome and Rome's rapid territorial expansion? What light do the documents in this chapter shed on this question?

2. What do the documents in this chapter reveal about how Romans thought about their ancestors? What do they reveal about other Roman values, or what they considered to be important aspects of their cultural behavior?

---

[8]**Dolabella**: A general.

3. The Brutus who took part in the assassination of Caesar was a descendant of the Brutus who gave the speech in the first document. How does this illuminate the ways in which the conspirators may have thought of themselves?

4. Compare and contrast Gracchus and Caesar. Are their methods or goals in any way alike? What is similar and different about the problems faced by the republic during Gracchus's life and during Caesar's? How does each man deal with these problems?

5. Consider Caesar's behavior in the Senate, as illustrated in Document 5-6, alongside the behavior of Alexander the Great as described in Document 4-1. What political message did each man wish to send through manners and behavior?

# 6

# The Roman Empire
## 27 B.C.E.–284 C.E.

The documents in this chapter help to illustrate the complex process of cultural exchange that accompanied the expansion and institutionalization of the Roman Empire. As the empire grew, its rulers gradually decided to extend the benefits of citizenship to select non-Romans. This process was completed in 212 C.E., when citizenship was granted to all free men in the empire. As they incorporated new peoples into the empire, Romans did not simply impose their culture on others; they allowed for a fusion of traditions. This tolerance, however, had limits. So long as local populations were willing to acknowledge the imperial cult and participate in public ceremonies affirming their loyalty to the empire, the Romans were content to leave local cultural and religious traditions alone. If, however, those beliefs and traditions seemed to undermine a population's loyalty to the empire, the Romans were inclined to see them in a very different light. Thus, the Romans persecuted the Jews of Judaea, not because their beliefs were different from those of the Romans, but because they resisted Roman rule and that resistance often had religious underpinnings. Similarly, the overt rejection of pagan religion by early Christians made them potential rebels and subversives in the eyes of many Romans, and they thus became the targets of sporadic persecution, particularly in times of general political and social unrest.

# 6-1   |   Romans and Barbarians
## TACITUS, *Germania* (ca. 100 C.E.)

Tacitus (ca. 56–117 C.E.), the greatest Roman historian, wrote at a time when Rome had reached the zenith of its power. In addition to his works on imperial politics, the *Annals* and the *Histories*, Tacitus wrote a study of the Germanic tribes who lived beyond the borders of the empire. In his studies of Roman politics, he described abundant examples of corruption and tyranny, but among the Germanic tribes he found a good deal to admire. As you read the document, think about the possible connections between Tacitus's critique of Roman politics and his admiration of the Germanic tribes. In what ways might his description of the Germanic tribes constitute an indirect criticism of his own society?

The land may vary a certain amount in its appearance, but in general it either bristles with forests or festers with marshes. It is wetter on the side facing the Gauls, windier opposite Noricum and Pannonia.[1] It is fertile for sown crops but will not grow fruit trees. It is rich in livestock, but these are mostly undersized. Even on their foreheads the cattle lack their proper distinction and glory. The people take pride in their quantity, for their cattle are their sole, greatly prized wealth.

Silver and gold have been denied them by the gods, whether as a sign of favor or of anger I cannot say. . . .

Their kings they choose for their noble birth, their army commanders for their valor. Even the kings do not have absolute or unrestricted power, and their commanders lead by example rather than by issuing orders, gaining respect if they are energetic, if they stand out, if they are on the front of the line. Executions, imprisonment, even floggings, are allowed to no one other than the priests, and are not carried out as a punishment or on the orders of the commander, but as it were at the behest of the deity whom they believe to be present as they wage war. They actually bring with them into battle certain images and symbols taken from the sacred groves.

It is a particular incitement to valor that their squadrons and wedges are not formed at random or by chance mustering but are composed of families and kinship groups. They have their nearest and dearest close by, as well, so that they can hear the shrieks of their women and the crying of their children. For each man these are the most sacred witnesses, their praise is the most highly valued. It is to their mothers and their wives, who do not shrink from examining their cuts, that they go with their wounds. They also bring food and words of encouragement to the men as they fight. It is recorded that some armies that were already wavering and on the point of collapse have been rallied by women pleading steadfastly, blocking their path with bared breasts, and reminding their men how

---

From Tacitus, *Agricola and Germania*, trans. Anthony R. Birley (Oxford: Oxford University Press, 1999), pp. 39–50.

[1]**Noricum and Pannonia**: What is today Austria, Hungary, and Croatia.

near they themselves are to being taken captive. This they fear by a long way more desperately for their women than for themselves. . . . They even believe that there is something holy and an element of the prophetic in women, hence they neither scorn their advice nor ignore their predictions. . . .

On minor matters only the chiefs decide, on major questions the whole community. But even cases where the decision lies with the commons are considered in advance by the chiefs. Except when there is some chance or sudden happening, they assemble on fixed days, either just before the new moon or just after the full moon. This they reckon to be the most auspicious starting point for transacting business. Indeed, they do not reckon time by days, as we do, but by nights. All their decisions, all their agreements, are made in this way: night is seen as ushering in the day.

Their freedom of spirit involves a drawback, in that they do not assemble all at the same time or as if commanded, but take two or three days over it, hanging back. When the assembled crowd is ready, they take their seats, carrying arms. Silence is commanded by the priests, who have on these occasions the right to enforce obedience. Then the king or the chiefs are heard, in accordance with each one's age, nobility, military distinction, or eloquence. The power of persuasion counts for more than the right to give orders. If a proposal displeases them, they shout out their dissent. If they approve, they clash their spears. Showing approval with weapons is the most honorable way to express assent.

One may also bring in an accusation in the assembly, including a capital charge. The penalty varies according to the crime. Traitors and deserters are hanged on trees. Cowards, those who will not fight, . . . are plunged into a boggy mire. . . .

They transact no business, public or private, except under arms. But it is their practice that no one may bear arms until the community has recognized him as fit to use them. Then in the assembly itself either one of the chiefs or his own father or his kinsmen present the young man with shield and spear. . . .

When they are not waging war they occupy a little of their time in hunting but a good deal is spent without occupation: they devote themselves to sleeping and eating. . . .

It is well known that none of the German peoples live in cities, and that they cannot even bear to live in adjoining houses. They dwell apart from one another, scattered about, wherever a spring, a plain, or a wood attracts them. They do not lay out their villages in our style, with buildings joined and connected together. Each of them leaves an open space around his house, either as a protection against the risk of fire, or because they lack skill in building. They do not use stones or bricks. They employ timber for all purposes, roughly cut, for they are not concerned to achieve a pleasant external appearance. . . .

The marriage code is strict there, and there is no aspect of their morality that deserves higher praise. They are almost the only barbarians who are content with a single wife, except for a very few, who are not motivated by sexual appetite — it is, rather, that they are courted with numerous offers of marriage on account of their noble rank. The dowry is not brought by the wife to the husband but by the husband to the wife. . . . They live a life of sheltered chastity, uncorrupted by the temptations of public shows or the excitements of banquets. Men and women alike know nothing of clandestine letters. Considering the great size of the population, adultery is very rare. The penalty for it is instant and left to the husband. He cuts off her hair, strips her naked in the presence of her kinsmen, and flogs her all through the village. They have no mercy on a woman who prostitutes her chastity. . . . [A wife] must love not so much the husband himself as their marriage. To limit the number of their children or to kill one of the later-born is regarded as a crime. Good morality is more effective there than good laws elsewhere.

In every household the children grow up, naked and dirty, to that size of limb and stature which we admire in them. Each mother breastfeeds her own child and does not hand them over to maids or nurses. . . . The young men are slow to mate, and reach manhood with unimpaired vigor. Nor are the virgins hurried into marriage. Being as old and as tall as the men, they are equal to their mates in age and strength, and the children inherit the robustness of their parents. . . .

It is an obligation to take over the father's or kinsman's feuds and friendships. But feuds do not go on with no reconciliation. In fact, even homicide can be atoned for with a fixed number of cattle or sheep. The whole family receives this compensation. This is an advantage for the community, since feuds are rather dangerous where freedom exists. . . .

The practice of lending out capital and stretching it out into interest is unknown: ignorance is a surer protection than any prohibition. Lands are occupied by the whole people to be cultivated, the quantity determined by the number of cultivators. They then divide the lands out among themselves according to rank. The great extent of the land makes the division easy. They plough different fields every year and there is still spare land available.

### READING QUESTIONS

1. According to Tacitus, why do the Germans fight with their families close by? What does this reveal about Germanic society?

2. Compare Germanic values, as described by Tacitus, to traditional Roman values. What might explain the similarities?

3. What connections might Tacitus have made between Germanic government and that of the Roman Republic?

4. What lessons might Tacitus have hoped his fellow Romans would learn from his description of the Germanic tribes?

## 6-2 | A Roman Seeks the Aid of an Egyptian Goddess

### APULEIUS, *The Golden Ass: The Veneration of Isis* (ca. 170 C.E.)

Cultural exchange between the Romans and their subject peoples was not a one-way street. Just as subject peoples adopted the imperial cult and other aspects of Roman religion and culture, the Romans were influenced by the traditions and beliefs of the peoples they conquered. The mystery religions that emerged during the Hellenistic period (see Chapter 4), such as the cult of the Egyptian goddess Isis, gained enormous popularity among the Romans. Participants believed that the god or goddess of the cult took a direct interest in their lives, and many such religions centered on the idea that devotees would be rewarded with some form of eternal life. In this excerpt from *The Golden Ass* by Apuleius (ah-puh-LAY-us), a young man, Lucius, has been turned into a donkey and calls on Isis for assistance. As you read it, think about what light this sheds on cultural fusion and exchange under the Roman Empire.

About the first watch of the night I awoke in sudden terror and saw the full orb of the moon just rising from the waves; exceeding bright it was and of unwonted splendor. All about me was the silent mystery of the dark night. I knew that the supreme goddess was now in the [fullness] of her power and that the lives of men were governed by her providence; I knew that not only all cattle and creatures of the wild, but even things inanimate were given new life by her divine splendor and the power of her godhead. . . . I resolved to address my prayers to the august vision of the goddess now present in power, and straightway shaking off sluggish slumber nimbly arose . . . and thus made I my supplication to the all-powerful goddess, my face bathed in tears:

Queen of heaven, whether you be Ceres,[1] the kindly mother from whom in the beginning spring the fruits of earth, . . . or be you Venus the heavenly one, who at the first beginning of things did unite the diversity of the sexes in the power of Love that is born of you, . . . or be you Phoebus's sister,[2] who with gentle healing brings relief to women in travail and has reared such multitudes, . . . or be you Proserpine,[3] to whom men render shuddering reverence with howls by night, . . . by whatever name, by whatever rite, in whatever semblance man may invoke you, do you now aid me in my utter woe. . . . Take from me the foul semblance of a four-footed beast, restore me to the sight of those I love, restore to me the Lucius that I knew. . . .

Thus had I outpoured my supplication and added thereto much woeful wailing, when once more slumber was shed about me on that same couch of

---

From Apuleius, *The Metamorphoses: or Golden Ass of Apuleius of Madaura*, vol. 2, trans. Harold Edgeworth Butler (Oxford: Clarendon Press, 1910), pp. 126–132. Text modernized by Amy R. Caldwell.

[1]**Ceres**: Roman agricultural goddess.
[2]**Phoebus's sister**: Artemis, Greek goddess of fertility, childbirth, and the hunt.
[3]**Proserpine**: Roman goddess of springtime.

sand and overcame my fainting soul. Yet scarce had I closed my eyes in sleep, [when the goddess appeared and spoke to me]. . . .

"Lo, Lucius, I am come, moved by your supplication, I, nature's mother, mistress of all the elements, the first-begotten offspring of the ages, of deities mightiest, queen of the dead, first of heaven's denizens, in whose aspect are blended the aspects of all gods and goddesses. With my rod I rule the shining heights of heaven, the health-giving breezes of the sea, the mournful silence of the underworld. The whole earth worships my godhead, one and individual, under many a changing shape, with varied rites and by many diverse names. There the Phrygians,[4] first-born of men, call me the mother of the gods; . . . there the Athenians, sprung from the soil they till, know me as Cecropian Minerva;[5] . . . Cretans, Diana of the hunter's net;[6] . . . Others call me Juno,[7] others Bellona,[8] others Hecate,[9] . . . and the Egyptians mighty in ancient lore, honor me with my peculiar rites and call me by my true name, Isis the Queen. I am come in pity for your woes. I am come propitious and strong to aid. . . . You must await [my] festival with heart untroubled and profane thoughts banished far from you. For the priest who shall assist in the celebration of the procession, forewarned by me, will bear . . . in his right hand a wreath of roses. Then delay not, but brush aside the crowds and lightly join my procession, relying on my goodwill. Draw nigh and gently, as though you wouldst kiss the priest's hand, pluck the roses and put off from you straightway the hide of that vile beast, that hath ever been hateful to me. And shrink not from any of these things as too hard for you. . . . At my bidding the people that throng you about will part and leave clear a path for you. Nor amid those merry sights and those gay ceremonies will any one shudder at that foul aspect you wear, nor will any interpret to your shame your sudden change of shape nor make malign accusation against you. But you must remember surely and keep hidden in your inmost soul this — that the rest of your life's course, to the term of your last breath, is dedicated to me. Nor is it unjust that you should, so long as you shalt live, owe all your life to her who brought you back to mankind. But you shalt live blessed, you shalt live crowned with glory beneath my protection, and when your life is run and you go down to the nether world, there also in that nether hemisphere you shall see me shining through the darkness of Acheron[10] and reigning in the inmost halls of Styx;[11] and you shall dwell in the Elysian fields,[12] and continually make offering of worship to me, and I will smile on you."

---

[4]**Phrygians**: People from Anatolia, the central region in the modern Republic of Turkey.

[5]**Minerva**: Roman equivalent of Athena, the Greek goddess of wisdom.

[6]**Diana of the hunter's net**: Roman goddess of virginity and the hunt.

[7]**Juno**: Queen of the Roman gods.

[8]**Bellona**: Roman goddess of warfare.

[9]**Hecate**: Goddess of magic and witchcraft.

[10]**Acheron**: One of five rivers in the Greek underworld.

[11]**Styx**: One of five rivers in the Greek underworld.

[12]**Elysian fields**: Home in the afterlife for those who lived a virtuous life.

## READING QUESTIONS

1. How does Lucius describe Isis? How does she describe herself?
2. What benefits does Isis offer her followers in this life? What about the afterlife?
3. What importance should we attach to the claim that Isis has appeared in many different places in many different guises?
4. How would you explain the appeal of mystery religions like the cult of Isis? What did such religions offer that more traditional religions did not?

## SOURCES IN CONVERSATION

# Jews, Christians, and the Hebrew Law

Jesus's teachings were essentially Jewish. They grew out of Jewish religious and moral traditions and centered on a Jewish conception of God. For Christianity to spread and grow, however, it would need to reach beyond its roots, shedding, or at the very least reinterpreting, aspects of Judaism in the process. Paul of Tarsus, the most important early Christian evangelist, clearly understood this imperative. Through his interpretation of the Christian message, Paul sought to draw a clear distinction between Christians, who were bound to Jesus by their faith, and Jews, who were subject to the Law — that is, the obligations and restrictions imposed on all Jews as part of their covenant with Yahweh.

### READ AND COMPARE

1. How are these two documents different in their approaches to the Law?
2. What do those differences reveal about how Christianity changed over time?

## 6-3 | *The Gospel According to Matthew: The Sermon on the Mount* (28 C.E.)

The Sermon on the Mount is perhaps the best-known summary of Jesus's moral teachings. The themes in this sermon appear throughout the Gospels of the New Testament. In it, Jesus builds on fundamental Jewish moral and religious obligations but reinterprets them for his audience, taking particular care to explain the relationship between his teachings and the law. As you read the sermon, think about how a largely Jewish audience might have responded to Jesus's words. Would they have seen the sermon as a departure from conventional Judaism? If so, in what ways?

From Matthew 5.

Now when he saw the crowds, he went up on a mountainside and sat down. His disciples came to him, and he began to teach them saying:

"Blessed are the poor in spirit, for theirs is the kingdom of heaven.

"Blessed are those who mourn, for they will be comforted.

"Blessed are the meek, for they will inherit the earth.

"Blessed are those who hunger and thirst for righteousness, for they will be filled.

"Blessed are the merciful, for they will be shown mercy.

"Blessed are the pure in heart, for they will see God.

"Blessed are the peacemakers, for they will be called sons of God.

"Blessed are those who are persecuted because of righteousness, for theirs is the kingdom of heaven.

"Blessed are you when people insult you, persecute you and falsely say all kinds of evil against you because of me. Rejoice and be glad, because great is your reward in heaven, for in the same way they persecuted the prophets who were before you.

"You are the salt of the earth. But if the salt loses its saltiness, how can it be made salty again? It is no longer good for anything, except to be thrown out and trampled by men.

"You are the light of the world. A city on a hill cannot be hidden. Neither do people light a lamp and put it under a bowl. Instead they put it on its stand, and it gives light to everyone in the house. In the same way, let your light shine before men, that they may see your good deeds and praise your Father in heaven.

"Do not think that I have come to abolish the Law or the Prophets; I have not come to abolish them but to fulfill them. I tell you the truth, until heaven and earth disappear, not the smallest letter, not the least stroke of a pen, will by any means disappear from the Law until everything is accomplished. Anyone who breaks one of the least of these commandments and teaches others to do the same will be called least in the kingdom of heaven, but whoever practices and teaches these commands will be called great in the kingdom of heaven. For I tell you that unless your righteousness surpasses that of the Pharisees and the teachers of the law, you will certainly not enter the kingdom of heaven.

"You have heard that it was said to the people long ago, 'Do not murder, and anyone who murders will be subject to judgment.' But I tell you that anyone who is angry with his brother will be subject to judgment. Again, anyone who says to his brother, 'Raca,'[1] is answerable to the Sanhedrin.[2] But anyone who says, 'You fool!' will be in danger of the fire of hell.

"Therefore, if you are offering your gift at the altar and there remember that your brother has something against you, leave your gift there in front of the altar. First go and be reconciled to your brother; then come and offer your gift.

---

[1]**Raca**: Aramaic for "worthless person."
[2]**Sanhedrin**: A Jewish judicial body.

"Settle matters quickly with your adversary who is taking you to court. Do it while you are still with him on the way, or he may hand you over to the judge, and the judge may hand you over to the officer, and you may be thrown into prison. I tell you the truth, you will not get out until you have paid the last penny.

"You have heard that it was said, 'Do not commit adultery.' But I tell you that anyone who looks at a woman lustfully has already committed adultery with her in his heart. If your right eye causes you to sin, gouge it out and throw it away. It is better for you to lose one part of your body than for your whole body to be thrown into hell. And if your right hand causes you to sin, cut it off and throw it away. It is better for you to lose one part of your body than for your whole body to go into hell.

"It has been said, 'Anyone who divorces his wife must give her a certificate of divorce.' But I tell you that anyone who divorces his wife, except for marital unfaithfulness, causes her to become an adulteress, and anyone who marries the divorced woman commits adultery.

"Again, you have heard that it was said to the people long ago, 'Do not break your oath, but keep the oaths you have made to the Lord.' But I tell you, Do not swear at all: either by heaven, for it is God's throne; or by the earth, for it is his footstool; or by Jerusalem, for it is the city of the Great King. And do not swear by your head, for you cannot make even one hair white or black. Simply let your 'Yes' be 'Yes,' and your 'No,' 'No'; anything beyond this comes from the evil one.

"You have heard that it was said, 'Eye for eye, and tooth for tooth.' But I tell you, Do not resist an evil person. If someone strikes you on the right cheek, turn to him the other also. And if someone wants to sue you and take your tunic, let him have your cloak as well. If someone forces you to go one mile, go with him two miles. Give to the one who asks you, and do not turn away from the one who wants to borrow from you.

"You have heard that it was said, 'Love your neighbor and hate your enemy.' But I tell you: Love your enemies and pray for those who persecute you, that you may be sons of your Father in heaven. He causes his sun to rise on the evil and the good, and sends rain on the righteous and the unrighteous. If you love those who love you, what reward will you get? Are not even the tax collectors doing that? And if you greet only your brothers, what are you doing more than others? Do not even pagans do that? Be perfect, therefore, as your heavenly Father is perfect."

### READING QUESTIONS

1. What similarities and differences do you see between the Sermon on the Mount and the Ten Commandments (see Document 2-2)?

2. What connection did Jesus draw between his message and the law? What did he mean when he said he had not "come to abolish the Law or the Prophets . . . but to fulfill them"?

3. What evidence, if any, does the sermon provide that Jesus might have intended his message for both Jews and non-Jews?

# 6-4 | PAUL OF TARSUS, *Epistle to the Romans* (ca. 57 c.e.)

Paul's efforts to spread the Christian message took him all over the Roman Empire. While on his travels, he wrote letters to a variety of individuals and groups, offering advice and religious instruction. These letters were copied and circulated among Christian communities, thereby shaping the Christian consensus on the meaning of Jesus's message. In his letter or epistle to the people of Rome, Paul offers what is considered to be one of the most important expressions of central Christian doctrine. He makes a connection between the "law," which was central in the Jewish tradition, and faith that Jesus would intercede to absolve the sins of human beings and thus allow them to attain salvation. He also makes it very clear that both Jews and gentiles (non-Jews) have access to salvation if they follow the teachings of Jesus. As you read the epistle, focus on Paul's arguments about the law and the concept of faith and how he clarifies Jesus's message about the connection between the two.

But glory, honor, and peace go to every man who does good, to the Jew first, and also to the Greek. For there is no partiality with God. For as many as have sinned without the law will also perish without the law. As many as have sinned under the law will be judged by the law. For it isn't the hearers of the law who are righteous before God, but the doers of the law will be justified (for when Gentiles who don't have the law do by nature the things of the law, these, not having the law, are a law to themselves, in that they show the work of the law written in their hearts, their conscience testifying with them, and their thoughts among themselves accusing or else excusing them) in the day when God will judge the secrets of men, according to my Good News, by Jesus Christ.

Indeed you bear the name of a Jew, rest on the law, glory in God, know his will, and approve the things that are excellent, being instructed out of the law, and are confident that you yourself are a guide of the blind, a light to those who are in darkness, a corrector of the foolish, a teacher of babies, having in the law the form of knowledge and of the truth. You therefore who teach another, don't you teach yourself? You who preach that a man shouldn't steal, do you steal? You who say a man shouldn't commit adultery, do you commit adultery? You who abhor idols, do you rob temples? You who glory in the law, do you dishonor God by disobeying the law? For "the name of God is blasphemed among the Gentiles because of you," just as it is written. For circumcision indeed profits, if you are a doer of the law, but if you are a transgressor of the law, your circumcision has become uncircumcision. If therefore the uncircumcised keep the ordinances of the law, won't his uncircumcision be accounted as circumcision? Won't the uncircumcision which is by nature, if it fulfills the law, judge you, who with the letter and circumcision are a transgressor of the law? For he is not a Jew who is one outwardly, neither is that circumcision which is outward in the flesh; but he is a Jew who is one inwardly, and circumcision is that of the heart, in the spirit not in the letter; whose praise is not from men, but from God.

From Romans 2, 3.

Then what advantage does the Jew have? Or what is the profit of circum-cision? Much in every way! Because first of all, they were entrusted with the revelations of God. For what if some were without faith? Will their lack of faith nullify the faithfulness of God? May it never be! Yes, let God be found true, but every man a liar. As it is written,

"that you might be justified in your words,
and might prevail when you come into judgment."

But if our unrighteousness commends the righteousness of God, what will we say? Is God unrighteous who inflicts wrath? I speak like men do. May it never be! For then how will God judge the world? For if the truth of God through my lie abounded to his glory, why am I also still judged as a sinner? Why not (as we are slanderously reported, and as some affirm that we say), "Let's do evil, that good may come?" Those who say so are justly condemned.

What then? Are we better than they? No, in no way. For we previously warned both Jews and Greeks that they are all under sin. As it is written,

"There is no one righteous;
no, not one.
There is no one who understands.
There is no one who seeks after God.
They have all turned away.
They have together become unprofitable.
There is no one who does good,
no, not so much as one."
"Their throat is an open tomb.
With their tongues they have used deceit."
"The poison of vipers is under their lips."
"Their mouth is full of cursing and bitterness."
"Their feet are swift to shed blood.
Destruction and misery are in their ways.
The way of peace, they haven't known."
"There is no fear of God before their eyes."

Now we know that whatever things the law says, it speaks to those who are under the law, that every mouth may be closed, and all the world may be brought under the judgment of God. Because by the works of the law, no flesh will be justified in his sight; for through the law comes the knowledge of sin.

But now apart from the law, a righteousness of God has been revealed, being testified by the law and the prophets; even the righteousness of God through faith in Jesus Christ to all and on all those who believe. For there is no distinction, for all have sinned, and fall short of the glory of God; being justified freely by his grace through the redemption that is in Christ Jesus; whom God sent to be an atoning sacrifice, through faith in his blood, for a demonstration of his righteousness through the passing over of prior sins, in God's forbearance;

to demonstrate his righteousness at this present time; that he might himself be just, and the justifier of him who has faith in Jesus.

Where then is the boasting? It is excluded. By what kind of law? Of works? No, but by a law of faith. We maintain therefore that a man is justified by faith apart from the works of the law. Or is God the God of Jews only? Isn't he the God of Gentiles also? Yes, of Gentiles also, since indeed there is one God who will justify the circumcised by faith, and the uncircumcised through faith.

Do we then nullify the law through faith? May it never be! No, we establish the law.

### READING QUESTIONS

1. How does Paul explain the privileged role of the Jews in the new faith of Christianity, and how does he make the case that it is available to Gentiles (non-Jews) as well?

2. Why does Paul say that faith in the Gospel of Jesus is essential in addition to the law?

3. How did Paul's interpretation of the importance of Jesus's life and teachings help transform Christianity from an outgrowth of Judaism into a distinct and universal religion?

## 6-5 | Anti-Christian Sentiment

### *The Alexamenos Graffito* (ca. 100 C.E.)

Graffiti was a common sight in Roman cities, and historians have learned much about daily Roman life from the examples they have found. This image was found carved into the wall of a police barracks. The caption, written in Greek, reads, "Alexamenos worships [his] god." The picture shows Jesus, with the head of a donkey, being crucified. The man next to the cross, probably meant to be Alexamenos, lifts an arm in worship. This posture with one arm raised was common among Roman mystery cults. At the time, it was widely rumored that Christians worshipped a god with a donkey's head.

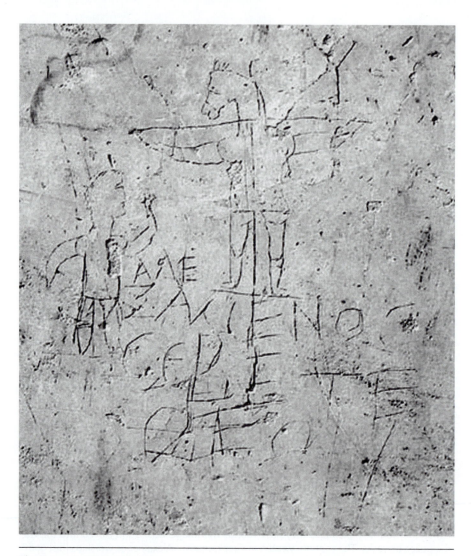

The Picture Art Collection/Alamy

### READING QUESTIONS

1. Who is being mocked in this image? Why?
2. How well does the person who created this image understand Christianity? What does that reveal about the relationship between Romans and Christians at this time?

## ■ COMPARATIVE AND DISCUSSION QUESTIONS ■

1. How would you characterize the Roman attitude toward other cultures? How do the documents in this chapter inform your response?

2. Consider the Sermon on the Mount and the Veneration of Isis. What aspects of each might have appealed to a Roman looking for an alternative to more conventional religious beliefs and practice?

3. What challenges might the early Christians have faced as they sought to spread their message to the wider Roman population? What clues do the Sermon on the Mount, the Epistle to the Romans, and the Alexamenos Graffito offer in this context?

# 7

# Late Antiquity
## 250–600

Late antiquity saw the division and collapse of the Roman Empire and
the emergence of two distinct heirs to its legacy: the Roman Catholic
West and the Orthodox Byzantine Empire. After a series of disasters in
the fifth century, the last Roman emperor in the West was deposed in
476. The society that evolved in the wake of imperial collapse was built
on a blend of Greco-Roman, Germanic, and Christian elements. It was
far more fragmented than its Roman predecessor, both politically and
economically, with local elites claiming considerable autonomy and
economic activity focused primarily on local needs. In this context,
the Roman Catholic Church served as a unifying element, acting as the
protector of the classical cultural legacy, working with secular elites to
establish political and social order, and providing a shared set of values
and beliefs. The eastern half of the empire, which would come to be
known as the Byzantine Empire, retained considerable strength and
would last, in various forms, for another thousand years. Here, ties to the
classical past were stronger, urban life and regional commerce remained
vibrant, and the imperial power structure remained largely intact, a fact
that contributed to the subordination of the Orthodox Church to the
Byzantine state. The documents in this chapter provide insight into these
two societies, offering glimpses of the forces that shaped their increasingly
divergent development.

## 7-1 | Church and State in Late Antiquity

### SAINT AMBROSE OF MILAN, *Emperor Theodosius Brought to Heel* (390)

Emperor Theodosius I (347–395) played an important role in the Christianization of the Roman Empire. In 380 he made Nicene Christianity the official religion of the empire and later carried out a campaign of suppression and persecution designed to stamp out religious dissent. If Theodosius believed that in so doing he had subordinated the church to the state, however, he was much mistaken. Bishop Ambrose of Milan's (ca. 339–397) decision to bar Theodosius from church services until he had truly repented for the massacre of seven thousand people in the Greek city of Thessalonica offers clear evidence of church leaders' determination to maintain their autonomy. As you read Ambrose's letter to Theodosius, consider the implications of Ambrose's decision to cast out of the church the man who had made Christianity Rome's official religion. What does the letter tell you about Ambrose's understanding of the relationship between church and state?

I have written these things, indeed, not to confound you, but that the example of these kings might induce you to put away this sin from your kingdom, which you will accomplish by humiliating your soul to God. You are a man and temptation has come to you; confess it. Sin is not put away except by tears and penitence. Neither an angel can do it nor an archangel; the Lord himself, who alone can say, "I am with you," does not forgive us if we have sinned except we be penitent.

I persuade, I beg, I exhort, I admonish; because it is a grief to me that you who were an example of unusual piety, who were the very personification of clemency, who would not allow guilty individuals to be brought into danger, that you do not grieve at the death of so many innocent persons. Although you have fought battles most successfully, although in other things also you are worthy of praise, yet the crown of all your work was always piety. This the devil envied you, since it was your ever present possession. Conquer him while as yet you have wherewith you may conquer. Do not add another sin to your sin, that you may practice what it has injured many to practice.

I, indeed, though in all other things a debtor to your kindness which I can never be ungrateful for, which kindness surpassed that of many emperors and was equaled by the kindness of one only, I, I say, have no cause for a charge of contumacy [resistance to authority] against you, but I have a cause for fear; I dare not offer the sacrifice if you will to be present. Is that which is not allowed after shedding the blood of one innocent person to be allowed after shedding the blood of many? I do not think so.

From *Translations and Reprints from the Original Sources of European History*, vol. 4 (Philadelphia: University of Pennsylvania Press, 1897), pp. 23–24.

## READING QUESTIONS

1. How would you describe the tone of Ambrose's letter? How does this tone fit the actual content of the letter?

2. What limits on imperial power are implied by the letter? How do you imagine Theodosius responded to it?

3. Ambrose escaped punishment for this letter; why was the emperor reluctant to punish Ambrose for daring to criticize him?

## 7-2    |    Rules for Monastic Living

### SAINT BENEDICT OF NURSIA, *The Rule of Saint Benedict* (529)

Benedict of Nursia (ca. 480–543) was perhaps the single most important figure in the history of Western monasticism. The rules he established for his monastery at Monte Casino, Italy, were widely copied and had a lasting impact on the organization of Roman Catholic religious life. Their success is explained, in part, by the careful balance they established between activity and spiritual reflection and by their suitability for men from all walks of life. Their facilitation of self-sufficient, sustainable communities, a crucial factor in the uncertain and fragmented world of late antiquity, also contributed to their success. As you read this excerpt from the *Rule*, ask yourself why the lifestyle described was appealing to so many people.

Concerning the daily manual labor. Idleness is the enemy of the soul. And therefore, at fixed times, the brothers ought to be occupied in manual labor; and again, at fixed times, in sacred reading. Therefore we believe that, according to this disposition, both seasons ought to be arranged; so that, from Easter until the Calends of October,[1] going out early, from the first until the fourth hour they shall do what labor may be necessary. Moreover, from the fourth hour until about the sixth, they shall be free for reading. After the meal of the sixth hour, moreover, rising from table, they shall rest in their beds with all silence; or, perchance, he that wishes to read may so read to himself that he do not disturb another. And the nona [the second meal] shall be gone through with more moderately about the middle of the eighth hour; and again they shall work at what is to be done until Vespers.[2] But, if the exigency or poverty of the place demands that they be occupied by themselves in picking fruits, they shall not be dismayed: for then they are truly monks if they live by the labors of their hands; as did also our fathers and the apostles. Let all things be done with moderation, however, on account of the faint-hearted. . . . [There follows a slightly different schedule for the winter

From E. F. Henderson, ed., *Select Historical Documents of the Middle Ages* (London: G. Bell, 1892), pp. 297–298.

[1]**Calends of October**: October 1.
[2]**Vespers**: Evening prayers.

months from October to Easter.] But in the days of Lent,[3] from dawn until the third full hour, they shall be free for their readings; and, until the tenth full hour, they shall do the labor that is enjoined on them. In which days of Lent they shall all receive separate books from the library; which they shall read entirely through in order. These books are to be given out on the first day of Lent. Above all there shall certainly be appointed one or two elders, who shall go round the monastery at the hours in which the brothers are engaged in reading, and see to it that no troublesome brother chance to be found who is open to idleness and trifling, and is not intent on his reading; being not only of no use to himself, but also stirring up others. If such a one — may it not happen — be found, he shall be admonished once and a second time. If he do not amend, he shall be subject under the Rule to such punishment that the others may have fear. . . . On feeble or delicate brothers such a labor or art is to be imposed, that they shall neither be idle, nor shall they be so oppressed by the violence of labor as to be driven to take flight. Their weakness is to be taken into consideration by the abbot.

### READING QUESTIONS

1. How did the monks spend their days? What activities dominated their waking hours?

2. What might explain the *Rule*'s emphasis on work? What practical value did work have? What spiritual value might Benedict have assigned to it?

3. What light does the *Rule* shed on the role of the church in the preservation of literary culture?

## 7-3 | Contrasting the Works of God with Those of Men
### SAINT AUGUSTINE, *City of God: The Two Cities* (413–426)

Saint Augustine (354–430), bishop of Hippo Regius in what is now Algeria, was the most influential church father in the West. He lived in challenging times. In 410, Rome was sacked by Alaric the Visigoth. By this time, Christianity was the official religion of the empire, but pagan religion was still influential, especially in the countryside and among some of the upper classes. Many pagans claimed that Rome had fallen because Christianity had turned people away from the old gods who had once protected the city. In this passage from the *City of God*, Augustine responds to this charge by making a distinction between the city of God, which is eternal, and the earthly city, which, like all human creations, is ephemeral.

---

From Rev. Marcus Dods, ed., *The City of God* (Edinburgh: T. & T. Clark, 1888), 1:1–2, 2:47–48.

[3]**Lent**: The season of fasting before Easter.

The glorious city of God is my theme in this work, which you, my dearest son Marcellinus,[1] suggested, and which is due to you by my promise. I have undertaken its defense against those who prefer their own gods to the Founder of this city, — a city surpassingly glorious, whether we view it as it still lives by faith in this fleeting course of time, and sojourns as a stranger in the midst of the ungodly, or as it shall dwell in the fixed stability of its eternal seat, which it now with patience waits for, expecting until "righteousness shall return unto judgment," and it obtain, by virtue of its excellence, final victory and perfect peace. A great work this, and an arduous; but God is my helper. For I am aware what ability is requisite to persuade the proud how great is the virtue of humility, which raises us, not by a quite human arrogance, but by a divine grace, above all earthly dignities that totter on this shifting scene. For the King and Founder of this city of which we speak, has in Scripture uttered to His people a dictum of the divine law in these words: "God resisteth the proud, but giveth grace unto the humble." But this, which is God's prerogative, the inflated ambition of a proud spirit also affects, and dearly loves that this be numbered among its attributes, to "Show pity to the humbled soul, And crush the sons of pride." And therefore, as the plan of this work we have undertaken requires, and as occasion offers, we must speak also of the earthly city, which, though it be mistress of the nations, is itself ruled by its lust of rule. . . .

Accordingly, two cities have been formed by two loves: the earthly by the love of self, even to the contempt of God; the heavenly by the love of God, even to the contempt of self. The former, in a word, glories in itself, the latter in the Lord. For the one seeks glory from men; but the greatest glory of the other is God, the witness of conscience. The one lifts up its head in its own glory; the other says to its God, "Thou art my glory, and the lifter up of mine head." In the one, the princes and the nations it subdues are ruled by the love of ruling; in the other, the princes and the subjects serve one another in love, the latter obeying, while the former take thought for all. The one delights in its own strength, represented in the persons of its rulers; the other says to its God, "I will love Thee, O Lord, my strength." And therefore the wise men of the one city, living according to man, have sought for profit to their own bodies or souls, or both, and those who have known God "glorified Him not as God, neither were thankful, but became vain in their imaginations, and their foolish heart was darkened; professing themselves to be wise," — that is, glorying in their own wisdom, and being possessed by pride, — "they became fools, and changed the glory of the incorruptible God into an image made like to corruptible man, and to birds, and four-footed beasts, and creeping things." For they were either leaders or followers of the people in adoring images, "and worshipped and served the creature more than the Creator, who is blessed for ever." But in the other city there is no human wisdom, but only godliness, which offers due worship to the true God, and looks for its reward in the society of the saints, of holy angels as well as holy men, "that God may be all in all."

---

[1]**Marcellinus**: Marcellinus of Carthage (d. 413), a friend of Augustine.

## READING QUESTIONS

1. How did Augustine characterize each city? What values and priorities gave rise to each?

2. What does Augustine's description of the two cities suggest about his views on the relationship between Christians and pagans?

3. Why might Augustine's writings have been comforting to his audience? How might the writings have helped his audience cope with the difficulties and challenges of late antiquity?

# 7-4 | Converting the Germanic Tribes to Catholicism
## GREGORY OF TOURS, *History of the Franks* (593–594)

Converting the Germanic tribes of Europe to Christianity was no easy task for the clergy of the Catholic Church. Clovis, a chieftain of the fifth and sixth centuries, united all the Frankish tribes and came to control significant territory as the first king of what eventually became France. He also converted to Catholicism and was baptized in 508. In the following story, Bishop Gregory of Tours recounts the events that convinced the great leader to become a Christian. As you read, note the elements of the story that would make sense to the martial sensibilities of Germanic tribespeople.

At this time the King was yet in the errors of his idolatry [and went to war] with the Alemanni, since he wished to render them tributary. Long was the battle, many were slain on one side or the other, for the Franks fought to win glory and renown, the Alemanni to save life and freedom. When the King at length saw the slaughter of his people and the boldness of his foes, he had greater expectation of disaster than of victory. He looked up to heaven humbly, and spoke thus, "Most mighty God, whom my queen Clothilde worships and adores with heart and soul, I pledge Thee perpetual service unto Thy faith, if only Thou givest me now the victory over mine enemies."

Instantly when he had said this, his men were filled with burning valor, and a great fear smote his enemies, so that they turned the back and fled the battle; and victory remained with the King and with the Franks. The king of the Alemanni was slain; and as for the Alemanni, seeing themselves discomfited, and that their king had fallen, they yielded themselves to Clovis and his Franks and became his tributaries.

The King returned after this victory into Frankland. . . . The Queen, who was wondrously overjoyed at the conversion of her lord, went at once to St. Remi, at that time archbishop of the city, . . . he said he would put to the test and try the hearts and wills of his chieftains and lesser people; for he would convert them more easily if they were converted by pleasant means and by mild words, than if they were driven to it by force; and this method seemed best to St. Remi.

From William Stearns Davis, *Readings in Ancient History: Illustrative Excerpts from the Sources*, vol. 2: *Rome and the West* (Boston: Allyn and Bacon, 1913), pp. 332–334.

The folk and the chieftains were assembled by the command of the King. He arose in the midst of them, and spoke to this effect:

"Lords of the Franks, it seems to me highly profitable that ye should know first of all what are those gods which ye worship. For we are certain of their falsity; and we come right freely into the knowledge of Him who is the true God. Know of a surety that this same God which I preach to you has given victory over your enemies in the recent battle against the Alemanni. Lift therefore your hearts in just hope; and ask the Sovran Defender, that He give to you all, that which ye desire—that He save our souls and give us victory over our enemies."

When the King full of faith had thus preached to and admonished his people, one and all banished from their hearts all unbelief, and recognized their Creator. . . .

After having made his profession of the orthodox faith, the King is plunged thrice in the waters of baptism. . . . [Two sisters of the King and] 3000 fighting men of the Franks and a great number of women and children were likewise baptized.

### READING QUESTIONS

1. What do you think convinced Clovis and his people to embrace Catholicism, and why was it effective given their cultural values? What other famous story of a great leader's conversion to Christianity is very similar?

2. What made it easier for the king to convince his people to become Catholic?

3. Besides his personal salvation, how could Clovis's new faith have helped him consolidate his rule? In what ways might it have made his task more difficult?

### SOURCES IN CONVERSATION

# The Rebirth of the Roman Empire in the East

The Roman Empire did not fall in 476. The last emperor to reside in the city of Rome may have been deposed in that year, but the empire, now centered on Constantinople, lived on in the East. At the same time that centralized government, long-distance trade and commerce, and urban life were in sharp decline in the West, the greatest of the Byzantine emperors, Justinian I (482–565), was busy expanding and consolidating imperial power and authority, carrying out monumental building projects, and reforming the Roman legal system. The following documents provide two very different views of Justinian and his policies. In the first, an excerpt from *The Institutes of Justinian,* Justinian explains the importance of his reform and codification of Roman law. In the second, an excerpt from *The Secret History* of Procopius of Caesarea, a Byzantine scholar and aristocrat paints a decidedly unflattering picture of the emperor. As you read the documents, think about the motives of each author. What role did Justinian assign himself in Byzantine government? What might explain the intensity of Procopius's dislike and distrust of the emperor?

## READ AND COMPARE

1. How do these two documents differ in their description of Byzantine society and government during Justinian's time?

2. What do you think each of the authors intended to accomplish with his message? How successful do you think they were at doing so?

## 7-5 | EMPEROR JUSTINIAN, *The Institutes of Justinian* (529–533)

By the time Justinian became emperor, Roman law was a confused jumble of traditions dating back centuries. Justinian set his legal experts to work systematically organizing the various laws into one code, the *Corpus Juris Civilis*. In so doing, he not only put his own government on a stronger legal foundation, but he also preserved Roman law for future generations. It was his work that made possible the reintroduction of Roman law in the West centuries later. In the introduction to the *Institutes*, a handbook of civil law designed for students that was part of the *Corpus*, Justinian placed his legal reforms in the context of Roman imperial renewal. As you read the introduction, consider Justinian's political motives for carrying out the project. How did the reform of Roman law contribute to the concentration of power in the hands of the emperor?

The imperial majesty should be not only made glorious by arms, but also strengthened by laws, that, alike in time of peace and in time of war, the state may be well governed, and that the emperor may not only be victorious in the field of battle, but also may by every legal means repel the iniquities of men who abuse the laws, and may at once religiously uphold justice and triumph over his conquered enemies.

By our incessant labors and great care, with the blessing of God, we have attained this double end. The barbarian nations reduced under our yoke know our efforts in war; to which also Africa and very many other provinces bear witness, which, after so long an interval, have been restored to the dominion of Rome and our empire, by our victories gained through the favor of heaven. All nations moreover are governed by laws which we have already either promulgated or compiled.

When we had arranged and brought into perfect harmony the hitherto confused mass of imperial constitutions, we then extended our care to the vast volumes of ancient law; and, sailing as it were across the mid-ocean, have now completed, through the favor of heaven, a work that once seemed beyond hope.

From Thomas Collett Sandars, trans. and ed., *The Institutes of Justinian* (New York: Longman's, Green, and Co., 1917), pp. 1–7.

When by the blessing of God this task was accomplished, we summoned the most eminent . . . professors of law, all of whom have on many occasions proved to us their ability, legal knowledge, and obedience to our orders; and we have specially charged them to compose, under our authority and advice, Institutes, so that you may no more learn the first elements of law from old and erroneous sources, but apprehend them by the clear light of imperial wisdom; and that your minds and ears may receive nothing that is useless or misplaced, but only what obtains in actual practice. So that, whereas, formerly, the junior students could scarcely, after three years' study, read the imperial constitutions, you may now commence your studies by reading them, you who have been thought worthy of an honor and a happiness so great as that the first and last lessons in the knowledge of the law should issue for you from the mouth of the emperor. . . .

In these [*Institutes*] a brief exposition is given of the ancient laws, and of those also which, overshadowed by disuse, have been again brought to light by our imperial authority.

These four books of Institutes thus compiled, from all the Institutes left us by the ancients, and chiefly from the commentaries of our Gaius,[1] both in his Institutes, and in his work on daily affairs, and also from many other commentaries, were presented to us by the three learned men we have above named. We have read and examined them and have accorded to them all the force of our constitutions.

Receive, therefore, with eagerness, and study with cheerful diligence, these our laws, and show yourselves persons of such learning that you may conceive the flattering hope of yourselves being able, when your course of legal study is completed, to govern our empire in the different portions that may be entrusted to your care. . . .

The term justice, in its most extended sense, was taken by the Roman jurists to include all the commands laid upon men that they are bound to fulfill, both the commands of morality and of law. . . .

The maxims of law are these: to live honestly, to hurt no one, to give every one his due.

### READING QUESTIONS

1. Why does Justinian want to see the laws put together in a systematic way?

2. How does a single, unified code of law benefit the people? How might it benefit the emperor?

3. Why is the concept of justice important to the law?

---

[1]**Gaius**: Gaius the Jurist (ca. 130–180), a Roman lawyer who wrote the *Institutes*, a textbook on Roman law.

## 7-6 | PROCOPIUS OF CAESAREA, *The Secret History* (ca. 550)

Procopius of Caesarea was not a neutral observer of events. He believed that his society was on the verge of collapse and that Justinian bore considerable responsibility for the imminent catastrophe. Far from seeing the emperor as a valiant reformer, Procopius saw him as a subversive force, a man whose blind ambition and criminal disregard for the consequences of his actions led him to promote policies that were antithetical to good social order and the long-term health of the empire. As you read this excerpt from *The Secret History*, published only after Procopius's death, pay particular attention to the connections Procopius made between the emperor's personal vices and what Procopius saw as the decay of Byzantine society. What does his attack on Justinian tell us about Procopius's own social and political views?

Everything was done at the wrong time, and nothing that was established was allowed to continue. To prevent my narrative being interminable, I will merely mention a few instances, and pass over the remainder in silence. In the first place, Justinian neither possessed in himself the appearance of Imperial dignity, nor demanded that it should be respected by others, but imitated the barbarians in language, appearance, and ideas. When he had to issue an Imperial decree, he did not entrust it to the Quaestor[1] in the usual way, but for the most part delivered it himself by word of mouth, although he spoke his own language like a foreigner; or else he left it in the hands of one of those by whom he was surrounded, so that those who had been injured by such resolutions did not know to whom to apply.

Those [secretaries] who . . . had from very ancient times fulfilled the duty of writing the secret dispatches of the Emperor, were no longer allowed to retain their privileges; for he himself wrote them nearly all, even the sentences of the municipal magistrates, no one throughout the Roman world being permitted to administer justice with a free hand. He took everything upon himself with unreasoning arrogance, and so managed cases that were to be decided, that, after he had heard one of the litigants, he immediately pronounced his verdict and obliged them to submit to it, acting in accordance with no law or principle of justice, but being evidently overpowered by shameful greed. For the Emperor was not ashamed to take bribes, since his avarice had deprived him of all feelings of shame. It frequently happened that the decrees of the Senate and the edicts of the Emperor were opposed to each other; for the Senate was as it were but an empty shadow, without the power of giving its vote or of keeping up its dignity; it was assembled merely for form's sake and in order to keep up an ancient custom, for none of its members were allowed to utter a single word. But the Emperor and his consort[2] took upon themselves the consideration of questions that were to be discussed, and whatever resolutions they came to between

---

From *Procopius: Literally and Completely Translated from the Greek for the First Time* (Athens: Athenian Society, 1896), pp. 116–121.

[1]**Quaestor**: An imperial official, usually in charge of finances.
[2]**consort**: Theodora.

themselves prevailed. If he whose cause had been victorious had any doubt as to the legality of his success, all he had to do was to make a present of gold to the Emperor, who immediately promulgated a law contrary to all those formerly in force. If, again, anyone else desired the revival of the law that had been repealed, the autocrat did not disdain to revoke the existing order of things and to reestablish it. There was nothing stable in his authority, but the balance of justice inclined to one side or the other, according to the weight of gold in either scale. In the market-place there were buildings under the management of palace officials, where traffic was carried on, not only in judicial, but also in legislative decisions. The officers called "Referendars" [or mediators] found it difficult to present the requests of petitioners to the Emperor, and still more difficult to bring before the council in the usual manner the answer proper to be made to each of them; but, gathering together from all quarters worthless and false testimony, they deceived Justinian, who was naturally a fit subject for deception, by fallacious reports and misleading statements. Then, immediately going out to the contending parties, without acquainting them with the conversation that had taken place, they extorted from them as much money as they required, without anyone venturing to oppose them.

Even the soldiers of the Praetorian guard,[3] whose duty it was to attend the judges in the court of the palace, forced from them whatsoever judgments they pleased. All, so to speak, abandoned their own sphere of duty, and followed the paths that pleased them, however difficult or untrodden they had previously been. Everything was out of gear; offices were degraded, not even their names being preserved. In a word, the Empire resembled a queen over boys at play.

### READING QUESTIONS

1. What personal characteristics did Procopius assign to Justinian? What connections did he make between those characteristics and his effectiveness as a ruler?

2. What kind of person might Procopius have seen as the ideal emperor? How would such a person have differed from Justinian?

3. What clues does the document offer about the kind of government and society that Procopius might have favored?

---

[3]**Praetorian guard**: The soldiers assigned to protect the emperor and court officials.

## ■ COMPARATIVE AND DISCUSSION QUESTIONS ■

1. What contributions did Ambrose, Benedict, and Augustine make to the development of the Roman Catholic Church? What commitments and objectives might all three have shared?

2. How do both Saint Benedict and Saint Augustine respond to potential or real critiques of the Catholic Church and clergy in their documents? What critiques do they respond to, and what solutions or answers do they provide? Which do you think is more effective in responding to critiques, and why do you think so?

3. Did Ambrose and Procopius criticize their emperors for similar reasons? If not, what was different about their tactics and motives? Which do you think was able to accomplish more with his critique, and why do you think so?

# 8

# Europe in the Early Middle Ages
## 600–1000

The period between 600 and 1000 witnessed the emergence of powerful new empires centered in Europe and the Middle East. In both cases, expansion and conquest were justified, at least in part, on religious grounds. At the time of Muhammad's death in 632, Islam was largely confined to the Arabian peninsula, but the caliphs who followed him led a series of aggressive military campaigns, creating a vast Muslim empire that stretched all the way to the Iberian Peninsula. In western Europe, the spread of Roman Catholicism was intertwined with political consolidation. In the eighth and ninth centuries, Charlemagne, king of the Franks, conquered an empire that included much of western and central Europe. Although a large part of this new empire was already Christian, Charlemagne forcibly converted pagans, most notably the Saxons, as he incorporated new territories. While Charlemagne's empire was short-lived, disintegrating rapidly in the century following his death, it had a lasting impact on European political, social, and cultural development. The documents in this chapter explore these new empires, giving particular attention to the relationship between conquest and conversion in Charlemagne's Europe.

# 8-1 | A Muslim Describes the Conquest of Spain

## IBN ABD-EL-HAKEM, *The Conquest of Spain* (ca. 870)

Ibn Abd-el-Hakem, an Egyptian from a prominent family of legal scholars, wrote his history of the conquest of Spain more than a century after the actual events. As the oldest of such histories written by an Islamic scholar, it was frequently cited by later Muslim historians. The events he describes are a combination of myth and fact. In the following excerpt, he discusses the events that led to the defeat of Roderic, a Visigothic king, by Tarik ibn Ziyad, the Muslim commander who led the conquest of Visigothic Spain. After the conquest, the Muslims in Spain — the land they called al-Andalus — built a kingdom known as a center of culture and the arts that lasted for centuries. As you read the excerpt, consider how distrust and misunderstanding shaped interactions between Muslims and Visigoths.

The governor of the straits between this district [Tangiers] and Andalus was a foreigner called Ilyan, Lord of Septa. He was also the governor of a town called Alchadra, situated on the same side of the straits of Andalus as Tangiers. Ilyan was a subject of Roderic, the Lord of Andalus [i.e., king of Spain], who used to reside in Toledo. Tarik put himself in communication with Ilyan, and treated him kindly, until they made peace with each other. Ilyan had sent one of his daughters to Roderic, the Lord of Andalus, for her improvement and education; but she became pregnant by him. Ilyan having heard of this, said, I see for him no other punishment or recompense, than that I should bring the Arabs against him. He sent to Tarik, saying, I will bring you to Andalus. . . . But Tarik said I cannot trust you until you send me a hostage. So he sent his two daughters, having no other children. Tarik allowed them to remain in Tlemsen, guarding them closely. After that Tarik went to Ilyan who was in Septa on the straits. The latter rejoicing at his coming, said, I will bring you to Andalus. But there was a mountain called the mountain of Tarik between the two landing-places, that is, between Septa and Andalus. When the evening came, Ilyan brought him the vessels, in which he made him embark for that landing-place, where he concealed himself during the day, and in the evening sent back the vessels to bring over the rest of his companions. So they embarked for the landing-place, none of them being left behind: whereas the people of Andalus did not observe them, thinking that the vessels crossing and recrossing were similar to the trading vessels which for their benefit plied backwards and forwards. Tarik was in the last division which went across. He proceeded to his companions, Ilyan together with the merchants that were with him being left behind in Alchadra, in order that he might the better encourage his companions and countrymen. The news of Tarik and of those who were with him, as well as of the place where they were, reached the people of Andalus. Tarik, going along with his companions, marched over a bridge of mountains to a town called Cartagena. . . .

From Ibn Abd-el-Hakem, *History of the Conquest of Spain*, trans. John Harris Jones (Goettingen: Dietrich, 1858), pp. 18–20. Text modernized by Amy R. Caldwell.

When the Muslims settled [on an island near Andalus], they found no other inhabitants there, than vinedressers.[1] They made them prisoners. After that they took one of the vinedressers, slaughtered him, cut him in pieces, and boiled him, while the rest of his companions looked on. They had also boiled meat in other cauldrons. When the meat was cooked, they threw away the flesh of that man which they had boiled; no one knowing that it was thrown away: and they ate the meat which they had boiled, while the rest of the vinedressers were spectators. These did not doubt but that the Muslims ate the flesh of their companion; the rest being afterwards sent away informed the people of Andalus that the Muslims feed on human flesh, acquainting them with what had been done to the vinedresser.

When Tarik landed, soldiers from Cordova came to meet him; and seeing the small number of his companions they despised him on that account. They then fought. The battle with Tarik was severe. They were routed, and he did not cease from the slaughter of them till they reached the town of Cordova. When Roderic heard of this, he came to their rescue from Toledo. . . . They fought a severe battle; but God, mighty and great, killed Roderic and his companions.

### READING QUESTIONS

1. According to this account, what provoked the invasion of Roderic's kingdom? Do you find this explanation of the decision to invade Spain convincing? Why or why not?

2. What might explain Tarik's demand for hostages from his would-be ally Ilyan?

3. What might Muslim readers have made of the episode of pretended cannibalism? What is the episode meant to suggest about the Muslim soldiers? About the Visigothic inhabitants of Spain?

4. What role, if any, did religion play in Ibn Abd-el-Hakem's account of the conquest?

## 8-2 | An Arab Account of the Frankish Defense of Gaul

### ANONYMOUS ARAB SOURCE, *The Battle of Poitiers* (ca. 732)

After the initial conquest of Spain by Muslim forces early in the eighth century, an expeditionary force continued into Frankish territory and was defeated by Frankish forces led by Charles Martel. The defeat marked the end of Muslim incursions across the Pyrenees and allowed the Franks and Martel to build a powerful kingdom, which peaked under his grandson Charlemagne. There are numerous Catholic accounts of the battle, but the following is one from an unknown Arab chronicler that provides a counterpoint to the Christian point of view. This excerpt picks up after a string of Muslim victories.

From Edward Creasy, *The Fifteen Decisive Battles of the World: From Marathon to Waterloo* (New York: Harper & Brothers, 1862), pp. 177–178.

[1]**vinedressers**: People who cultivate grapevines.

Abderrahman[2] drove them back; and the men of Abderrahman were puffed up in spirit by their repeated successes, and they were full of trust in the valor and the practice in war of their emir. So the Moslems smote their enemies, and passed the River Garonne, and laid waste the country, and took captives without number. And that army went through all places like a desolating storm. Prosperity made these warriors insatiable. At the passage of the river, Abderrahman overthrew the count,[3] and the count retired into his stronghold, but the Moslems fought against it, and entered it by force and slew the count; for everything gave way to their cimeters,[4] which were the robbers of lives. All the nations of the Franks trembled at that terrible army, and they betook them to their king Caldus,[5] and told him of the havoc made by the Moslem horsemen, and how they rode at their will through all the land of Narbonne, Toulouse, and Bordeaux, and they told the king of the death of their count. Then the king bade them be of good cheer, and offered to aid them. And in the 114th year[6] he mounted his horse, and he took with him a host that could not be numbered, and went against the Moslems. And he came upon them at the great city of Tours. And Abderrahman and other prudent cavaliers saw the disorder of the Moslem troops, who were loaded with spoil; but they did not venture to displease the soldiers by ordering them to abandon every thing except their arms and war-horses. And Abderrahman trusted in the valor of his soldiers, and in the good fortune which had ever attended him. But such defect of discipline is always fatal to armies. So Abderrahman and his host attacked Tours to gain still more spoil, and they fought against it so fiercely that they stormed the city almost before the eyes of the army that came to save it; and the fury and the cruelty of the Moslems toward the inhabitants of the city was like the fury and cruelty of raging tigers. It was manifest that God's chastisement was sure to follow such excesses; and Fortune thereupon turned her back upon the Moslems.

Near the River Owar[7] the two great hosts of the two languages and the two creeds were set in array against each other. The hearts of Abderrahman, his captains, and his men, were filled with wrath and pride, and they were the first to begin the fight. The Moslem horsemen dashed fierce and frequent forward against the battalions of the Franks, who resisted manfully, and many fell dead on either side, until the going down of the sun. Night parted the two armies; but in the gray of the morning the Moslems returned to the battle. Their cavaliers had soon hewn their way into the centre of the Christian host. But many of the Moslems were fearful for the safety of the spoil which they had stored in their tents, and a false cry arose in their ranks that some of the enemy were

---

[2]**Abderrahman**: Abd-ar-Rahman, the Muslim governor of Córdoba.

[3]**count**: Count Odo of Aquitaine, also known as Duke Odo.

[4]**cimeters**: Scimitars; curved swords used by the Muslim forces.

[5]**king Caldus**: Charles Martel, mayor of the Palace of Austrasia, a powerful statesman and military leader who basically ruled the territory of Francia from 718 to 741 C.E.

[6]**114th year**: This refers to 114 years after the hijra, or the migration of the Muslim community from Mecca to Medina in 622 C.E.

[7]**River Owar**: Possibly the Loire River.

plundering the camp; whereupon several squadrons of the Moslem horsemen rode off to protect their tents. But it seemed as if they fled; and all the host was troubled. And while Abderrahman strove to check their tumult, and to lead them back to battle, the warriors of the Franks came around him, and he was pierced through with many spears, so that he died. Then all the host fled before the enemy, and many died in the fight. This deadly defeat of the Moslems, and the loss of the great leader and good cavalier Abderrahman, took place in the hundred and fifteenth year.

### READING QUESTIONS

1. Does this account seem to portray the actions of the Muslim forces in a positive or negative light? How so?

2. How does religion enter into the explanation of the victory of the Franks? Does there appear to be a moral to the way the story is told?

3. This battle is considered crucial to the history of Christian Europe, while Muslim historians treat it as more of an aside. Why did the two cultures weigh its significance so differently?

### SOURCES IN CONVERSATION

# Conquest and Conversion

The adoption of Nicene Christianity as the official religion of the Roman Empire in 380 was only a first step in the Christianization of Europe. Not only were the majority of Europeans still pagans in 380, but a significant number of the Germanic peoples who had converted were Arians, Christians who rejected the Nicene Creed and, by extension, the authority of the Roman Catholic Church. The spread of Roman Catholicism throughout Europe would take centuries to accomplish, requiring a massive effort by both secular and religious leaders. At times, the process of conversion was relatively peaceful, accomplished, at least in part, through the persuasive powers of Catholic missionaries. In many cases, however, forced conversion followed conquest, with the spread of Roman Catholicism serving as a central justification for territorial expansion and the subjugation of non-Catholic populations. As you read the following documents, reflect on the role of force in the spread of Roman Catholicism. Would the conversion of western Europe have been possible without some degree of coercion? How did the expansion of Roman Catholicism serve the interests of both the church and secular rulers?

### READ AND COMPARE

1. How does each document incorporate concepts of violence into Christian conversion and dominance?

2. Do you think Willibald's or Charlemagne's tactics would be more successful (in theory) in securing authentic conversions? Why do you think so?

## 8-3 | WILLIBALD, *Saint Boniface Destroys the Oak of Thor* (ca. 750)

Saint Boniface (680–754) is known as the apostle of the Germans. He was born in England, an early center of European Christianity, and was commissioned by Pope Gregory II to spread the Gospel and reorganize the church in what is now Germany. In this excerpt from the monk Willibald's (ca. 700–787) account of Boniface's missionary activities, Boniface overcomes the remaining pagan resistance in Hesse by challenging the pagan god Thor to strike him down in punishment for his destruction of Thor's sacred oak tree. When Thor fails to act, the completion of the conversion of the local population quickly follows. As you read the document, be sure to note the alliance between Boniface and his early German converts. What role did these converts play in Boniface's success?

Many of the people of Hesse were converted [by Boniface] to the Catholic faith and confirmed by the grace of the spirit: and they received the laying on of hands. But some there were, not yet strong of soul, who refused to accept wholly the teachings of the true faith. Some men sacrificed secretly, some even openly, to trees and springs. Some secretly practiced divining, soothsaying, and incantations, and some openly. But others, who were of sounder mind, cast aside all heathen profanation and did none of these things; and it was with the advice and consent of these men that Boniface sought to fell a certain tree of great size, at Geismar, and called, in the ancient speech of the region, the oak of Jove [i.e., Thor].

The man of God was surrounded by the servants of God. When he would cut down the tree, behold a great throng of pagans who were there cursed him bitterly among themselves because he was the enemy of their gods. And when he had cut into the trunk a little way, a breeze sent by God stirred overhead, and suddenly the branching top of the tree was broken off, and the oak in all its huge bulk fell to the ground. And it was broken into four parts, as if by the divine will, so that the trunk was divided into four huge sections without any effort of the brethren who stood by. When the pagans who had cursed did see this, they left off cursing and, believing, blessed God. Then the most holy priest took counsel with the brethren: and he built from the wood of the tree an oratory [a chapel or place of prayer], and dedicated it to the holy apostle Peter.

From James Harvey Robinson, ed., *Readings in European History*, vol. 1 (Boston: Ginn, 1904), pp. 106–107.

## READING QUESTIONS

1. How did Willibald characterize pagan religion? Why might the pagans have felt it necessary to keep their religious practices secret?

2. What light does the account shed on the importance of early converts to the church's ultimate success?

3. What might explain Boniface's decision to use the wood from the tree to build a chapel?

## 8-4  |  CHARLEMAGNE, *Capitulary for Saxony* (ca. 775–790)

Charlemagne's conquest of the Saxons was a long and brutal affair. Claiming a divine obligation to bring Christianity to the peoples of northwestern Germany, Charlemagne carried out a thirty-year campaign of conquest characterized by bloody battles, mass executions and deportations, and the forced conversion of local populations. As the conquest moved forward, Charlemagne imposed a form of martial law on the Saxons, condemning to death anyone who continued to engage in pagan practices. As you read this excerpt from the *Capitulary for Saxony*, pay particular attention to the laws regarding the establishment of the church in Saxony. What does the capitulary, or collection of decrees, tell you about the motives behind Charlemagne's alliance with the church? What did the church gain? What did Charlemagne gain?

1. It was pleasing to all that the churches of Christ, which are now being built in Saxony and consecrated to God, should not have less, but greater and more illustrious honor, than the fanes[1] of the idols had had.

2. If any one shall have fled to a church for refuge, let no one presume to expel him from the church by violence, but he shall be left in peace until he shall be brought to the judicial assemblage; and on account of the honor due to God and the saints, and the reverence due to the church itself, let his life and all his members be granted to him. Moreover, let him plead his cause as best he can and he shall be judged; and so let him be led to the presence of the lord king, and the latter shall send him where it shall have seemed fitting to his clemency.

3. If any one shall have entered a church by violence and shall have carried off anything in it by force or theft, or shall have burned the church itself, let him be punished by death.

4. If any one, out of contempt for Christianity, shall have despised the holy Lenten fast and shall have eaten flesh, let him be punished by death. But, nevertheless, let it be taken into consideration by a priest, lest perchance any one from necessity has been led to eat flesh.

5. If any one shall have killed a bishop or priest or deacon, let him likewise be punished capitally.

---

*Capitulary for Saxony*. Republished with permission of McGraw-Hill Higher Education from *The Middle Ages, Volume I: Sources of Medieval History*, 3rd Edition, edited by Brian Tierney (1978); permission conveyed through Copyright Clearance Center, Inc.

[1]**fanes**: Temples or shrines.

6. If any one deceived by the devil shall have believed, after the manner of the pagans, that any man or woman is a witch and eats men, and on this account shall have burned the person, or shall have given the person's flesh to others to eat, or shall have eaten it himself, let him be punished by a capital sentence.

7. If any one, in accordance with pagan rites, shall have caused the body of a dead man to be burned and shall have reduced his bones to ashes, let him be punished capitally.

8. If any one of the race of the Saxons hereafter concealed among them shall have wished to hide himself unbaptized, and shall have scorned to come to baptism and shall have wished to remain a pagan, let him be punished by death.

9. If any one shall have sacrificed a man to the devil, and after the manner of the pagans shall have presented him as a victim to the demons, let him be punished by death.

10. If any one shall have formed a conspiracy with the pagans against the Christians, or shall have wished to join with them in opposition to the Christians, let him be punished by death; and whoever shall have consented to this same fraudulently against the king and the Christian people, let him be punished by death.

11. If any one shall have shown himself unfaithful to the lord king, let him be punished with a capital sentence.

12. If any one shall have ravished the daughter of his lord, let him be punished by death.

13. If any one shall have killed his lord or lady, let him be punished in a like manner.

14. If, indeed, for these mortal crimes secretly committed any one shall have fled of his own accord to a priest, and after confession shall have wished to do penance, let him be freed by the testimony of the priest from death.

15. Concerning the lesser chapter all have consented. To each church let the parishioners present a house and two mansi of land, and for each one hundred and twenty men, noble and free, and likewise liti [freedmen], let them give to the same church a manservant and a maid-servant.

16. And this has been pleasing, Christ being propitious, that whencesoever any receipts shall have come into the treasury, either for a breach of the peace or for any penalty of any kind, and in all income pertaining to the king, a tithe shall be rendered to the churches and priests.

17. Likewise, in accordance with the mandate of God, we command that all shall give a tithe of their property and labor to the churches and priests; let the nobles as well as the freemen, and likewise the liti, according to that which God shall have given to each Christian, return a part to God.

18. That on the Lord's day no meetings and public judicial assemblages shall be held, unless perchance in a case of great necessity or when war compels it, but all shall go to the church to hear the word of God, and shall be free for prayers or good works. Likewise, also, on the especial festivals they shall devote themselves to God and to the services of the church, and shall refrain from secular assemblies.

19. Likewise, it has been pleasing to insert in these decrees that all infants shall be baptized within a year; and we have decreed this, that if any one shall have despised to bring his infant to baptism within the course of a year, without

the advice or permission of the priest, if he is a noble he shall pay 120 solidi to the treasury, if a freeman 60, if a litus 30.

20. If any shall have made a prohibited or illegal marriage, if a noble 60 solidi, if a freeman 30, if a litus 15.

21. If any one shall have made a vow at springs or trees or groves, or shall have made any offerings after the manner of the heathen and shall have partaken of a repast in honor of the demons, if he shall be a noble 60 solidi, if a freeman 30, if a litus 15. If, indeed they have not the means of paying at once, they shall be given into the service of the church until the solidi are paid.

22. We command that the bodies of Saxon Christians shall be carried to the church cemeteries and not to the mounds of the pagans.

23. We have ordered that diviners and soothsayers shall be given to the church and priests. . . .

33. Concerning perjuries, let it be according to the law of the Saxons.

34. We have forbidden that all the Saxons shall hold public assemblies in general, unless perchance our *missus*[2] shall have caused them to come together in accordance with our command; but each count shall hold judicial assemblies and administer justice in his jurisdiction. And this shall be cared for by the priests, lest it be done otherwise.

### READING QUESTIONS

1. What practices were to be punished with death?

2. What provisions in the laws were meant to prevent future uprisings?

3. Why might Charlemagne have thought it so important to build churches throughout Saxony? How were such churches to be paid for and supported?

4. Is it fair to describe Charlemagne's Saxon wars as "religious wars"? Why or why not?

## 8-5  |  Instructions for Royal Envoys

### CHARLEMAGNE, *General Capitulary for the Missi* (802)

It was one thing for Charlemagne to claim absolute authority as emperor. It was quite another to translate that claim into reality. By the standards of modern government, Charlemagne's resources were meager. He had no standing army, no police force, and no legion of loyal administrators to enforce his will. Moreover, travel was slow and dangerous in the early Middle Ages, making communication between Charlemagne

*General Capitulary for the Missi.* Republished with permission of McGraw-Hill Higher Education from *The Middle Ages, Volume I: Sources of Medieval History*, 3rd Edition, edited by Brian Tierney (1978); permission conveyed through Copyright Clearance Center, Inc.

[2]*missus*: Imperial envoys.

and local elites difficult and, at times, impossible. In an effort to overcome these challenges, Charlemagne appointed envoys called *missi dominici*, "agents of the lord king," to check up on local conditions and to make sure that Charlemagne's wishes were known and obeyed. As you read Charlemagne's instructions for envoys, consider what they tell us about Charlemagne's conception of "good government." What connections did he seek to make between local recognition of his authority on the one hand, and justice, morality, and prosperity on the other?

First chapter. Concerning the embassy sent out by the lord emperor. Therefore, the most serene and most Christian lord emperor Charles has chosen from his nobles the wisest and most prudent men, both archbishops and some of the other bishops also, and venerable abbots and pious laymen, and has sent them throughout his whole kingdom, and through them by all the following chapters has allowed men to live in accordance with the correct law. Moreover, where anything which is not right and just has been enacted in the law, he has ordered them to inquire into this most diligently and to inform him of it; he desires, God granting, to reform it. And let no one, through his cleverness or astuteness, dare to oppose or thwart the written law, as many are wont to do, or the judicial sentence passed upon him, or to do injury to the churches of God or the poor or the widows or the wards or any Christian. But all shall live entirely in accordance with God's precept, justly and under a just rule, and each one shall be admonished to live in harmony with his fellows in his business or profession; the canonical clergy ought to observe in every respect a canonical life without heeding base gain, nuns ought to keep diligent watch over their lives, laymen and the secular clergy ought rightly to observe their laws without malicious fraud, and all ought to live in mutual charity and perfect peace. And let the *missi* themselves make a diligent investigation whenever any man claims that an injustice has been done to him by any one, just as they desire to deserve the grace of omnipotent God and to keep their fidelity promised to Him, so that entirely in all cases everywhere, in accordance with the will and fear of God, they shall administer the law fully and justly in the case of the holy churches of God and of the poor, of wards and widows and of the whole people. And if there shall be anything of such a nature that they, together with the provincial counts, are not able of themselves to correct it and to do justice concerning it, they shall, without any ambiguity, refer this, together with their reports, to the judgment of the emperor; and the straight path of justice shall not be impeded by any one on account of flattery or gifts from any one, or on account of any relationship, or from fear of the powerful.

2. Concerning the fidelity to be promised to the lord emperor. And he commanded that every man in his whole kingdom, whether ecclesiastic or layman, and each one according to his vow and occupation, should now promise to him as emperor the fidelity which he had previously promised to him as king; and all of those who had not yet made that promise should do likewise, down to those who were twelve years old. And that it shall be announced to all in public, so that each one might know, how great and how many things are comprehended in that oath; not merely, as many have thought hitherto, fidelity to the lord emperor as regards his life, and not introducing any enemy

into his kingdom out of enmity, and not consenting to or concealing another's faithlessness to him; but that all may know that this oath contains in itself this meaning:

3. First, that each one voluntarily shall strive, in accordance with his knowledge and ability, to live wholly in the holy service of God in accordance with the precept of God and in accordance with his own promise, because the lord emperor is unable to give to all individually the necessary care and discipline.

4. Secondly, that no man, either through perjury or any other wile or fraud, on account of the flattery or gift of any one, shall refuse to give back or dare to abstract or conceal a serf of the lord emperor or a district or land or anything that belongs to him; and that no one shall presume, through perjury or other wile, to conceal or abstract his fugitive fiscaline serfs[1] who unjustly and fraudulently say that they are free.

5. That no one shall presume to rob or do any injury fraudulently to the churches of God or widows or orphans or pilgrims; for the lord emperor himself, after God and His saints, has constituted himself their protector and defender.

6. That no one shall dare to lay waste a benefice[2] of the lord emperor, or to make it his own property.

7. That no one shall presume to neglect a summons to war from the lord emperor; and that no one of the counts shall be so presumptuous as to dare to dismiss thence any one of those who owe military service, either on account of relationship or flattery or gifts from any one.

8. That no one shall presume to impede at all in any way a ban or command of the lord emperor, or to dally with his work or to impede or to lessen or in any way to act contrary to his will or commands. And that no one shall dare to neglect to pay his dues or tax.

9. That no one, for any reason, shall make a practice in court of defending another unjustly, either from any desire of gain when the cause is weak, or by impeding a just judgment by his skill in reasoning, or by a desire of oppressing when the cause is weak. But each one shall answer for his own cause or tax or debt unless any one is infirm or ignorant of pleading; for these the *missi* or the chiefs who are in the court or the judge who knows the case in question shall plead before the court; or if it is necessary, such a person may be allowed as is acceptable to all and knows the case well; but this shall be done wholly according to the convenience of the chiefs or *missi* who are present. But in every case it shall be done in accordance with justice and the law; and that no one shall have the power to impede justice by a gift, reward, or any kind of evil flattery or from any hindrance of relationship. And that no one shall unjustly consent to another in anything, but that with all zeal and goodwill all shall be prepared to carry out justice.

For all the above mentioned ought to be observed by the imperial oath.

10. That bishops and priests shall live according to the canons and shall teach others to do the same.

---

[1]**fiscaline serfs**: Serfs belonging to Charlemagne's royal estates.
[2]**benefice**: A landed estate.

11. That bishops, abbots, abbesses, who are in charge of others, with the greatest veneration shall strive to surpass their subjects in this diligence and shall not oppress their subjects with a harsh rule or tyranny, but with sincere love shall carefully guard the flock committed to them with mercy and charity or by the examples of good works.

12. That abbots shall live where the monks are and wholly with the monks, in accordance with the rule, and shall diligently learn and observe the canons; the abbesses shall do the same. . . .

17. Moreover, that the monks shall live firmly and strictly in accordance with the rule, because we know that any one whose goodwill is lukewarm is displeasing to God, as John bears witness in the Apocalypse: "I would that thou wert cold or hot. So then, because thou art lukewarm, and neither cold nor hot, I will spue thee out of my mouth." Let them in no way usurp to themselves secular business. They shall not have leave to go outside of their monastery at all, unless compelled by a very great necessity; but nevertheless the bishops, in whose diocese they shall be, shall take care in every way that they do not get accustomed to wandering outside of the monastery. . . .

Let them entirely shun drunkenness and feasting, because it is known to all that from these men are especially polluted by lust. For a most pernicious rumor has come to our ears that many in the monasteries have already been detected in fornication and in abomination and uncleanness. It especially saddens and disturbs us that it can be said, without a great mistake, that some of the monks are understood to be sodomites, so that whereas the greatest hope of salvation to all Christians is believed to arise from the life and chastity of the monks, damage has been incurred instead. . . . Certainly, if any such report shall have come to our ears in the future, we shall inflict such a penalty, not only on the guilty but also on those who have consented to such deeds, that no Christian who shall have heard of it will ever dare in the future to perpetrate such acts. . . .

23. The priests shall carefully watch over the clerks whom they have with them, that the latter live according to the canons; that they are not given to vain sports or worldly convivialities or songs or luxuries; but that they live chastely and healthfully. . . .

25. That counts and *centenarii*[3] shall compel all to do justice in every respect, and shall have such assistants in their ministries as they can securely confide in, who will observe law and justice faithfully, who will oppress the poor in no manner, who will not dare under any pretext, on account of flattery or reward, to conceal thieves, robbers, murderers, adulterers, magicians, wizards or witches, and all sacrilegious men, but instead will give them up that they may be punished and chastised in accordance with the law, so that, God granting it, all of these evils may be removed from the Christian people.

26. That judges shall judge justly in accordance with the written law, and not according to their own will.

27. And we command that no one in our whole kingdom shall dare to deny hospitality to rich or poor or pilgrims, that is, no one shall deny shelter and fire

---

[3]*centenarii*: Principal officials of the counts.

and water to pilgrims traversing our country in God's name, or to anyone travelling for the love of God or for the safety of his own soul. If, moreover, any one shall wish to serve them farther, let him expect the best reward from God, who Himself said: "And whoso shall receive one such little child in my name, receiveth me"; and elsewhere: "I was a stranger and ye took me in."

28. Concerning embassies coming from the lord emperor. That the counts and *centenarii* shall provide most carefully, as they desire the grace of the lord emperor, for the *missi* who are sent out, so that they may go through their departments without any delay; and he commands to all everywhere that they ought to see to it that no delay is encountered anywhere, but they shall cause them to go on their way in all haste and shall provide for them in such a manner as our *missi* may direct. . . .

32. Murders, by which a multitude of the Christian people perishes, we command in every way to be shunned and to be forbidden; God Himself forbade to His followers hatred and enmity, much more murder. For in what manner does any one trust to placate God, who has killed his son nearest to him? In what manner truly does he, who has killed his brother, think that the Lord Christ will be propitious to him? It is a great and terrible danger also with God the Father and Christ, Lord of heaven and earth, to stir up enmities among men: it is possible to escape for some time by remaining concealed, but nevertheless by accident at some time he falls into the hands of his enemies; moreover, where is it possible to flee from God, to whom all secrets are manifest? By what rashness does any one think to escape His anger? Wherefore, lest the people committed to us to be ruled over should perish from this evil, we have taken care to shun this by every means of discipline; because he who shall not have dreaded the wrath of God, shall find us in no way propitious or to be placated; but we wish to inflict the most severe punishment upon any one who shall have dared to murder a man. Nevertheless, lest sin should also increase, in order that the greatest enmities may not arise among Christians, when by the persuasions of the devil murders happen, the criminal shall immediately hasten to make amends and with all celerity shall pay the fitting composition for the evil done to the relatives of the murdered man. And we forbid firmly, that the relatives of the murdered man shall dare in any way to continue their enmities on account of the evil done, or shall refuse to grant peace to him who asks it, but having given their pledges they shall receive the fitting composition and shall make a perpetual peace. . . . But if any one shall have scorned to make the fitting composition, he shall be deprived of his property until we shall render our decision. . . .

40. Lastly, therefore, we desire all our decrees to be known in our whole kingdom through our *missi* now sent out, either among the men of the church, bishops, abbots, priests, deacons, canons, all monks or nuns, so that each one in his ministry or profession may keep our ban or decree, or where it may be fitting to thank the citizens for their good will, or to furnish aid, or where there may be need still of correcting anything. Likewise also to the laymen and in all places everywhere, whether they concern the guardianship of the holy churches or of widows and orphans and the weaker; or the robbing of them; or the arrangements for the assembling of the army; or any other matters; how they are to

be obedient to our precept and will, or how they observe our ban, or how each one strives in all things to keep himself in the holy service of God; so that all these good things may be well done to the praise of omnipotent God, and we may return thanks where it is fitting. But where we believe there is anything unpunished, we shall so strive to correct it with all our zeal and will that with God's aid we may bring it to correction, both for our own eternal glory and that of all our faithful. Likewise we desire all the above to be fruitfully known by our counts or *centenarii*, our ministerials.

### READING QUESTIONS

1. What did Charlemagne expect from local elites? From priests, monks, and other church officials? What distinction, if any, did he make between his authority over secular elites and his authority over the clergy?

2. What connection did Charlemagne make between his law and God's law? How did he establish that connection in his instructions to the *missi*?

3. What might explain Charlemagne's effort to present himself as a good and Christian ruler? Why would that have been important to him?

## ▪ COMPARATIVE AND DISCUSSION QUESTIONS ▪

1. What information can be gleaned from the documents in this chapter about the relationship between the Roman Catholic Church and the Carolingians? What role did church officials play in the creation and government of Charlemagne's empire? What role did Charlemagne and the Franks play in the Christianization of Europe?

2. Compare and contrast "The Conquest of Spain" with "The Battle of Poitiers." How did cultural stereotypes and assumptions shape both documents?

3. How does Charlemagne's *Capitulary for Saxony* complicate the vision of Carolingian government presented in his *General Capitulary for the Missi*?

# 9

# State and Church
# in the High Middle Ages
## 1000–1300

In the High Middle Ages, monarchs across Europe embarked on a program of political centralization, concentrating power in their own hands while expanding the reach and effectiveness of royal administrative and legal institutions. This process did not move forward in the same way in every kingdom, however, and it was not universally successful. In France and England, a series of reforming monarchs laid the foundation for further centralization, even as local elites developed institutions designed to ensure their continued participation in royal decision making. In contrast, Otto I's efforts in Germany were ultimately undone by the fallout from the long struggle with the papacy for control of northern Italy. At the same time that European monarchs sought greater control over their kingdoms, reform-minded leaders of the Roman Catholic Church sought greater control over church officials. The tensions created by these mutually exclusive objectives exploded in the eleventh-century controversy over lay investiture — the appointment of church officials by secular rulers. Church and state were not always at war, however, and often found ways to work together to the benefit of both. When, in 1095, Pope Urban II called on Europe's secular leaders to join him in a crusade to reclaim the Holy Lands, they responded enthusiastically, sensing that their association with a holy cause could only serve to increase the scope and legitimacy of their power. This chapter's documents explore the conflict and cooperation that existed between nobles, monarchies, and the Catholic Church as each group attempted to secure power over the people of Europe; they also touch upon the impacts of those relationships for people that were not among the powerful elites of Europe.

## 9-1  |  William the Conqueror Surveys His Kingdom

### *Anglo-Saxon Chronicle: William the Conqueror and the* Domesday Book (1086)

In 1066, William, duke of Normandy, conquered England, claiming to be the legitimate heir to the throne. Twenty years later, in December 1085, William ordered a complete survey of the entire kingdom, the results of which came to be known as the *Domesday Book*. William's motives for initiating the project went far beyond mere curiosity. The *Domesday Book* was an instrument of power, a tool for maximizing royal revenues from taxation and from the king's estates. This description of the *Domesday Book* and of William is taken from the *Anglo-Saxon Chronicle*, a historical record begun long before the Norman Conquest and maintained by monastic scribes. As you read it, pay particular attention to what it reveals about the author's attitude toward Norman rule. What did the author admire about England's new rulers? What aspects of Norman rule did he find less appealing?

At Midwinter the king was at Gloucester with his "witan" [advisers], and there held his court five days; and afterwards the archbishop and clergy had a synod [ecclesiastical assembly] three days. There was Maurice chosen bishop of London, and William, of Norfolk, and Robert, of Cheshire. They were all the king's clerks. After this the king had a great council, and very deep speech with his "witan" about this land, how it was peopled, or by what men; then he sent his men over all England, into every shire, and caused to be ascertained how many hundred hides were in the shire, or what land the king himself had, and cattle within the land, or what dues he ought to have, in twelve months, from the shire. Also he caused to be written how much land his archbishops had, and his suffragan bishops,[1] and his abbots, and his earls: and—though I may narrate somewhat prolixly[2]—what or how much each man had who was a landholder in England, in land, or in cattle, and how much money it might be worth. So very narrowly he caused it to be traced out, that there was not one single hide, nor one yard of land, nor even—it is shame to tell, though it seemed to him no shame to do—an ox, nor a cow, nor a swine, left that was not set down in his writ.

King William, about whom we speak, was a very wise man, and very powerful, more dignified and strong than any of his predecessors were. He was mild to the good men who loved God, and beyond all measure severe to the men who gainsaid his will. . . . He was also very dignified; thrice every year he wore his crown, as oft as he was in England. At Easter he wore it in Winchester; at Pentecost, in Westminster; at Midwinter, in Gloucester. And then were with him all the great men over all England, archbishops and suffragan bishops, abbots and earls, thanes[3] and knights.

---

From James Harvey Robinson, ed., *Readings in European History,* vol. 1 (Boston: Ginn, 1904), pp. 229–231.

[1]**suffragan bishop**: Assistant to an archbishop, whose territory might be too large for one person to administer effectively.

[2]**prolixly**: In a wordy, verbose fashion.

[3]**thane**: Low-ranking feudal lord.

So also was he a very rigid and cruel man, so that no one durst do anything against his will. He had earls in bonds who had acted against his will; bishops he cast from their bishoprics, and abbots from their abbacies, and thanes into prison; and at last he spared not his own brother, named Odo: he was a very rich bishop in Normandy; at Bayeux was his episcopal see;[4] and he was the foremost man besides the king; and he had an earldom in England, and when the king was in Normandy, then was he the most powerful in this land: and him the king put in prison.

Among other good things is not to be forgotten the good peace that he made in this land; so that a man who had any confidence in himself might go over his realm, with his bosom full of gold, unhurt. Nor durst any man slay another man had he done ever so great evil to the other. He reigned over England, and by his sagacity so thoroughly surveyed it that there was not a hide of land within England that he knew not who had it, or what it was worth, and afterwards set it in his writ.

Brytland [Wales] was in his power, and therein he built castles, and completely ruled over that race of men. In like manner he also subjected Scotland to him by his great strength. The land of Normandy was naturally his, and over the country which is called Le Maine he reigned; and if he might yet have lived two years he would, by his valor, have won Ireland, and without any weapons.

Certainly in his time men had great hardship and very many injuries. Castles he caused to be made, and poor men to be greatly oppressed. The king was very rigid, and took from his subjects many a mark of gold, and more hundred pounds of silver, all which he took, by right and with great unright, from his people, for little need. He had fallen into covetousness, and altogether loved greediness.

He planted a great preserve for deer, and he laid down laws therewith, that whosoever should slay hart[5] or hind[6] should be blinded. He forbade the harts and also the boars to be killed. As greatly did he love the tall deer as if he were their father. He also ordained concerning the hares that they should go free. His great men bewailed it, and the poor men murmured thereat; but he was so obdurate that he recked not of the hatred of them all; but they must wholly follow the king's will if they would live, or have land, or property, or even his peace. Alas that any man should be so proud, so raise himself up, and account himself above all men! May the Almighty God show mercy to his soul, and grant him forgiveness of his sins!

---

[4]**episcopal see**: A bishop's official headquarters.
[5]**hart**: Male red deer.
[6]**hind**: Female red deer.

## READING QUESTIONS

1. How did the author characterize the *Domesday Book*? Did he approve of its creation? Why or why not?

2. What were William's principal faults and virtues? How did they support or detract from one another?

3. How well had William established peace after conquering England? Give specific examples to support your position.

## 9-2 | Placing Limits on Royal Power

### KING JOHN OF ENGLAND, *Magna Carta: The Great Charter of Liberties* (1215)

The English kings had extensive possessions in France and spent much of their resources trying to defend or expand these holdings. By 1215, King John—through a series of military defeats and poorly conducted alliances—had lost many of these French lands. In an effort to make up for his losses, John increased the pressure on his English subjects to provide him with revenue, often going beyond traditional levels of taxation and revenue extraction and, in some cases, beyond his subjects' ability to pay. John's fiscal policies and military failures produced a backlash among England's elite, and in 1215 his nobles forced him to issue a charter that would clearly define both the rights of subjects and the limits of royal power.

John, by the grace of God, king of England, lord of Ireland, duke of Normandy and Aquitaine, and count of Anjou, to the archbishops, bishops, abbots, earls, barons . . . [and] subjects, greeting. . . .

We have also granted to all free men of our kingdom, for us and our heirs forever, all the underwritten liberties, to be had and held by them and their heirs, of us and our heirs forever. . . .

No widow shall be compelled to marry, so long as she prefers to live without a husband, provided always that she gives security not to marry without our consent, if she holds [a fief] of us, or without the consent of her lord of whom she holds, if she holds of another. . . .

No scutage[1] or aid shall be imposed on our kingdom, unless by common counsel of our kingdom, except for ransoming our person, for making our eldest son a knight, and for once marrying our eldest daughter; and for these there shall not be levied more than a reasonable aid. . . .

Neither we nor our bailiffs shall take, for castles or for any other work of ours, wood which is not ours, against the will of the owner of that wood. . . .

We will not retain beyond one year and one day, the lands of those who have been convicted of felony, and the lands shall thereafter be handed over to the lords of the fiefs. . . .

From William Sharp McKechnie, *Magna Carta: A Commentary on the Great Charter of King John* (New York: Burt Franklin, 1914), pp. 186, 191, 220, 232, 336–337, 375, 395, 399, 431, 466–467.

[1]**scutage**: Payment in lieu of performing military service.

No freeman shall be taken or [and] imprisoned or disseised [dispossessed] or exiled or in any way destroyed, nor will we [attack] him nor send [people to attack] him, except by the lawful judgment of his peers or [and] by the law of the land.

To no one will we sell, to no one will we refuse or delay, right or justice.

All merchants shall have safe and secure exit from England, and entry to England, with the right to tarry there and to move about as well by land as by water. . . .

We will appoint justices, constables, sheriffs, or bailiffs only such as know the law of the kingdom and mean to observe it well. . . .

Since, moreover, for God and the amendment of our kingdom and for the better allaying of the quarrel that has arisen between us and our barons, we have granted all these concessions, desirous that they should enjoy them in complete and firm endurance for ever, we give and grant to them the underwritten security, namely, that the barons choose five-and-twenty barons of the kingdom, whomsoever they will, who shall be bound with all their might, to observe and hold, and cause to be observed, the peace and liberties we have granted and confirmed to them by this our present Charter.

### READING QUESTIONS

1. In what ways does the Magna Carta limit how the king can raise money?

2. How did the authors of the Magna Carta seek to reform the administration of justice?

3. Judging from these sections of the charter, who in the kingdom seemed to have the strongest grievances against the king? Use examples to support your claim.

## 9-3 | A Pope and an Emperor Compete for Power

### POPE GREGORY VII AND EMPEROR HENRY IV, *Mutual Recriminations: The Investiture Controversy Begins* (1076)

The investiture controversy centered on who had the right to appoint the officials of the Roman Catholic Church. In addition to being servants of the church, bishops and abbots were often great landowners. Because the clergy were the most extensive literate class, many royal or imperial officials were drawn from their ranks, and secular rulers sought to appoint men who were loyal to them. However, those who were trying to reform the church from within, like Pope Gregory VII, argued that reform would be impossible if church officials owed their positions to secular rulers. Henry VI responded to the following admonition from

*Pope Gregory: The Correspondence of Pope Gregory VII,* ed. and trans. Ephraim Emerton (Columbia University Press, 1932; rpt 1969), pp. 86–90. *Henry IV: Imperial Lives and Letters of the Eleventh Century,* trans. Theodor E. Mommsen and Karl F. Morrison (Columbia University Press, 1962; rpt 2000), pp. 150–151.

Gregory with two letters: a brief reply to Gregory himself and the inflammatory version featured below, the latter of which he circulated throughout Germany in hopes of gaining the support of the people.

## [Pope Gregory VII to Emperor Henry IV]

Gregory, bishop, servant of God's servants, to King Henry, greeting and the apostolic benediction—but with the understanding that he obeys the Apostolic See[1] as becomes a Christian king.

Considering and weighing carefully to how strict a judge we must render any account of the stewardship committed to us by St. Peter, prince of the Apostles, we have hesitated to send you the apostolic benediction, since you are reported to be in voluntary communication with men who are under the censure of the Apostolic See. . . . If this be true, you yourself know that you cannot receive the favor of God nor the apostolic blessing unless you shall first put away those excommunicated persons and force them to do penance and shall yourself obtain absolution and forgiveness for your sin by due repentance and satisfaction. Wherefore we counsel Your Excellency, if you feel yourself guilty in this matter, to make your confession at once to some pious bishop who, with our sanction, may impose upon you a penance suited to the offense, may absolve you and with your consent in writing may be free to send us a true report of the manner of your penance.

We marvel exceedingly that you have sent us so many devoted letters and displayed such humility by the spoken words of your legates, calling yourself a son of our Holy Mother Church and subject to us in the faith, singular in affection, a leader in devotion, commending yourself with every expression of gentleness and reverence, and yet in action showing yourself most bitterly hostile to the canons and apostolic decrees in those duties especially required by loyalty to the Church. . . . And now, heaping wounds upon wounds, you have handed over the sees of Fermo and Spoleto—if indeed a church may be given over by any human power—to persons entirely unknown to us, whereas it is not lawful to consecrate anyone except after probation and with due knowledge.

It would have been becoming to you, since you confess yourself to be a son of the Church, to give more respectful attention to the master of the Church, that is, to Peter, prince of the Apostles. To him, if you are of the Lord's flock, you have been committed for your pasture, since Christ said to him: "Peter, feed my sheep" (John 21:17), and again: "to thee are given the keys of Heaven, and whatsoever thou shalt bind on earth shall be bound in Heaven, and whatsoever thou shalt loose on earth shall be loosed in Heaven" (Matt. 16:9). Now, while we, unworthy sinner that we are, stand in his place of power, still whatever you send to us, whether in writing or by word of mouth, he himself receives, and while we read what is written or hear the voice of those who speak, he discerns with subtle insight from what spirit the message comes. Wherefore Your Highness

---

[1]**Apostolic See**: The papacy.

should beware lest any defect of will toward the Apostolic See be found in your words or in your messages. . . .

A synod[2] held at Rome during the current year, and over which Divine Providence willed us to preside, several of your subjects being present, we saw that the order of the Christian religion had long been greatly disturbed and its chief and proper function, the redemption of souls, had fallen low and through the wiles of the Devil had been trodden under foot. Startled by this danger and by the manifest ruin of the Lord's flock we returned to the teaching of the holy fathers, declaring no novelties nor any inventions of our own. . . .

Nevertheless, in order that these demands may not seem to you too burdensome or unfair we have sent word by your own liegemen not to be troubled by this reform of an evil practice but to send us prudent and pious [ambassadors] from your own people. If these can show in any reasonable way how we can moderate the decision of the holy fathers saving the honor of the eternal king and without peril to our own soul, we will condescend to hear their counsel. It would in fact have been the fair thing for you, even if you had not been so graciously admonished, to make reasonable inquiry of us in what respect we had offended you or assailed your honor, before you proceeded to violate the apostolic decrees. But how little you cared for our warnings or for doing right was shown by your later actions.

However, since the long-enduring patience of God summons you to improvement, we hope that with increase of understanding your heart and mind may be turned to obey the commands of God. We warn you with a father's love that you accept the rule of Christ, that you consider the peril of preferring your own honor to his, that you do not hamper by your actions the freedom of that church which he deigned to bind to himself as a bride by a divine union, but, that she may increase as greatly as possible, you will begin to lend to Almighty God and to St. Peter, by whom also your own glory may merit increase, the aid of your valor by faithful devotion.

### [Emperor Henry IV to Pope Gregory VII]

Henry, King not by usurpation, but by the pious ordination of God, to Hildebrand,[3] now not Pope, but false monk:

You have deserved such a salutation as this because of the confusion you have wrought; for you left untouched no order of the Church which you could make a sharer of confusion instead of honor, of malediction instead of benediction.

For to discuss a few outstanding points among many: Not only have you dared to touch the rectors of the holy Church—the archbishops, the bishops, and the priests, anointed of the Lord as they are—but you have trodden them under foot like slaves who know not what their lord may do. In crushing them you have gained for yourself acclaim from the mouth of the rabble. You have

---

[2]**synod**: Council of church officials.
[3]**Hildebrand**: Pope Gregory VII's given name.

judged that all these know nothing, while you alone know everything. In any case, you have sedulously[4] used this knowledge not for edification, but for destruction, so greatly that we may believe Saint Gregory, whose name you have arrogated to yourself, rightly made this prophesy of you when he said: "From the abundance of his subjects, the mind of the prelate is often exalted, and he thinks that he has more knowledge than anyone else, since he sees that he has more power than anyone else."

And we, indeed, bore with all these abuses, since we were eager to preserve the honor of the Apostolic See. But you construed our humility as fear, and so you were emboldened to rise up even against the royal power itself, granted to us by God. You dared to threaten to take the kingship away from us—as though we had received the kingship from you, as though kingship and empire were in your hand and not in the hand of God.

Our Lord, Jesus Christ, has called us to kingship, but has not called you to the priesthood. For you have risen by these steps: namely, by cunning, which the monastic profession abhors, to money; by money to favor; by favor to the sword. By the sword you have come to the throne of peace, and from the throne of peace you have destroyed the peace. You have armed subjects against their prelates; you who have not been called by God have taught that our bishops who have been called by God are to be spurned; you have usurped for laymen the bishops' ministry over the priests, with the result that these laymen depose and condemn the very men whom the laymen themselves received as teachers from the hand of God, through the imposition of the hands of bishops.

You have also touched me, one who, though unworthy, has been anointed to kingship among the anointed. This wrong you have done to me, although as the tradition of the holy Fathers has taught, I am to be judged by God alone and am not to be deposed for any crime unless—may it never happen—I should deviate from the Faith. For the prudence of the holy bishops entrusted the judgment and the deposition even of [the late Roman emperor] Julian the Apostate[5] not to themselves, but to God alone. The true pope Saint Peter also exclaims, "Fear God, honor the king." You, however, since you do not fear God, dishonor me, ordained of Him.

Wherefore, when Saint Paul gave no quarter to an angel from heaven if the angel should preach heterodoxy, he did not except you who are now teaching heterodoxy throughout the earth. For he says, "If anyone, either I or an angel from heaven, preach any other gospel unto you than that which we have preached unto you, let him be accursed." Descend, therefore, condemned by this anathema and by the common judgment of all our bishops and of ourself. Relinquish the Apostolic See which you have arrogated. Let another mount the throne of Saint Peter, another who will not cloak violence with religion but who will teach the pure doctrine of Saint Peter.

---

[4]**sedulously**: With great care and effort.

[5]**Julian the Apostate**: Last pagan Roman emperor (r. ca. 355–363), known for unsuccessfully trying to thwart the spread of Christianity within the empire.

I, Henry, King by the grace of God, together with all our bishops say to you: Descend! Descend!

### READING QUESTIONS

1. On what basis does Gregory claim the right to appoint church officials?
2. What authority does he claim to have over an emperor?
3. In what ways does the emperor claim that the pope was attacking both the church and imperial power?
4. How does Henry use both political and religious traditions to defend himself?

## 9-4   |   A Call for Crusade

### ROBERT THE MONK OF RHEIMS, *Urban II at the Council of Clermont* (ca. 1120)

The capture of Jerusalem by Seljuk Turks and the subsequent appeal by the Byzantine emperor for military support presented Pope Urban II with an opportunity to increase the prestige of the Roman Catholic Church. Assuming the mantel of leadership of all of Christendom, in 1095 Urban called on Europe's military elite to wage a holy war for the recapture of Jerusalem. The enthusiasm of the response to Urban's appeal illustrates the centrality of Christianity to medieval Europeans' sense of their own identity. As you read this account of Urban's call for holy war, ask yourself what might have prompted tens of thousands of European Christians to travel to distant lands to fight an enemy who posed no direct threat to them.

"Oh, race of Franks, race from across the mountains, race beloved and chosen by God,—as is clear from many of your works,—set apart from all other nations by the situation of your country as well as by your Catholic faith and the honor which you render to the holy Church: to you our discourse is addressed, and for you our exhortations are intended. We wish you to know what a grievous cause has led us to your country, for it is the imminent peril threatening you and all the faithful which has brought us hither.

"From the confines of Jerusalem and from the city of Constantinople a grievous report has gone forth and has repeatedly been brought to our ears; namely, that a race from the kingdom of the Persians, an accursed race, a race wholly alienated from God, 'a generation that set not their heart aright, and whose spirit was not steadfast with God,' has violently invaded the lands of those Christians and has depopulated them by pillage and fire. They have led away a part of the captives into their own country, and a part they have killed by cruel tortures. They have either destroyed the churches of God or appropriated them for the rites of their own religion. They destroy the altars, after having defiled them with their uncleanness. . . . The kingdom of the Greeks is now dismembered by

From James Harvey Robinson, ed., *Readings in European History*, vol. 1 (Boston: Ginn, 1904), pp. 312–315.

them and has been deprived of territory so vast in extent that it could not be traversed in two months' time.

"On whom, therefore, is the labor of avenging these wrongs and of recovering this territory incumbent, if not upon you,—you, upon whom, above all other nations, God has conferred remarkable glory in arms, great courage, bodily activity, and strength to humble the heads of those who resist you? Let the deeds of your ancestors encourage you and incite your minds to manly achievements:—the glory and greatness of King Charlemagne, and of his son Louis, and of your other monarchs, who have destroyed the kingdoms of the Turks and have extended the sway of the holy Church over lands previously pagan. Let the holy sepulcher of our Lord and Savior, which is possessed by the unclean nations, especially arouse you, and the holy places which are now treated with ignominy and irreverently polluted with the filth of the unclean. Oh, most valiant soldiers and descendants of invincible ancestors, do not degenerate, but recall the valor of your progenitors.

"But if you are hindered by love of children, parents, or wife, remember what the Lord says in the Gospel, 'He that loveth father or mother more than me is not worthy of me.' 'Every one that hath forsaken houses, or brethren, or sisters, or father, or mother, or wife, or children, or lands, for my name's sake, shall receive an hundredfold, and shall inherit everlasting life.' Let none of your possessions retain you, nor solicitude for your family affairs. For this land which you inhabit, shut in on all sides by the seas and surrounded by the mountain peaks, is too narrow for your large population; nor does it abound in wealth; and it furnishes scarcely food enough for its cultivators. Hence it is that you murder and devour one another, that you wage war, and that very many among you perish in intestine[1] strife.

"Let hatred therefore depart from among you, let your quarrels end, let wars cease, and let all dissensions and controversies slumber. Enter upon the road to the Holy Sepulcher; wrest that land from the wicked race, and subject it to yourselves. That land which, as the Scripture says, 'floweth with milk and honey' was given by God into the power of the children of Israel. Jerusalem is the center of the earth; the land is fruitful above all others, like another paradise of delights. This spot the Redeemer of mankind has made illustrious by his advent, has beautified by his sojourn, has consecrated by his passion, has redeemed by his death, has glorified by his burial.

"This royal city, however, situated at the center of the earth, is now held captive by the enemies of Christ and is subjected, by those who do not know God, to the worship of the heathen. She seeks, therefore, and desires to be liberated and ceases not to implore you to come to her aid. From you especially she asks succor, because, as we have already said, God has conferred upon you above all other nations great glory in arms. Accordingly, undertake this journey eagerly for the remission of your sins, with the assurance of the reward of imperishable glory in the kingdom of heaven."

---

[1]**intestine:** Internal to a state or a country.

When Pope Urban had urbanely said these and very many similar things, he so centered in one purpose the desires of all who were present that all cried out, "It is the will of God! It is the will of God!" When the venerable Roman pontiff heard that, with eyes uplifted to heaven, he gave thanks to God and, commanding silence with his hand, said:

"Most beloved brethren, to-day is manifest in you what the Lord says in the Gospel, 'Where two or three are gathered together in my name, there am I in the midst of them'; for unless God had been present in your spirits, all of you would not have uttered the same cry; since, although the cry issued from numerous mouths, yet the origin of the cry was one. Therefore I say to you that God, who implanted this in your breasts, has drawn it forth from you. Let that then be your war cry in combats, because it is given to you by God. When an armed attack is made upon the enemy, let this one cry be raised by all the soldiers of God: 'It is the will of God! It is the will of God!'"

### READING QUESTIONS

1. To whom did Urban II direct his call for a crusade? What values and traditions did he invoke in his effort to sway his intended audience?

2. How did Urban II present holy war as a potential solution for internal European problems?

3. In what ways were the Crusades an example of international cooperation? Why might the papacy have been particularly interested in claiming leadership in such a venture?

## SOURCES IN CONVERSATION

# The Response to Urban II's Call for Holy War

Urban II's call for holy war had a variety of unintended consequences. First, his message resonated well beyond the military elite. Pilgrimages had long been part of European religious culture, and for many the First Crusade fit into this established tradition. Across Europe, men and women from all walks of life joined "armies" led by charismatic preachers like Peter the Hermit, "took up the cross," and headed for Jerusalem. Second, while Urban called for war against an external enemy, Europeans expanded the scope of the holy war to include perceived internal threats. As bands of pilgrim-soldiers made their way toward their destination, anti-Jewish violence erupted in many of the communities they visited, sparked by the Crusaders' contention that success in the Holy Land depended on the "purification" of Christian Europe. As you read the documents below, which relate to these two aspects of the response to Urban's call for holy war, consider what they tell you about European religious culture in the Middle Ages. Why did so many Europeans find the call for a crusade compelling? Why did Europe's Jews become a target of the religious zeal the Crusades inspired?

### READ AND COMPARE

1. How do the descriptions of the Crusaders in these accounts differ? Why do you think they are so different, and what motivated each author to describe the Crusaders as they did?

## 9-5 | GUIBERT OF NOGENT/ANNA COMNENA, *Peter the Hermit and the "People's Crusade"* (ca. 1108–1148)

Peter the Hermit (d. 1115) was, perhaps, the most important leader of the "People's Crusade," a spontaneous effort by ordinary Europeans to join in the battle for Jerusalem. An itinerant preacher, Peter led a sizable group of followers to the Holy Land. In the end, the People's Crusade was an abject failure. Largely untrained and poorly led, its participants were obliterated by the well-trained, battle-tested Turks. Two documents related to Peter are included here. The first, written by the Benedictine monk Guibert of Nogent (ca. 1055–1124), offers a contemporaneous account of Peter's early activities. The second, written by Anna Comnena (1083–1153), daughter of the Byzantine emperor Alexius I, describes the calamitous end of Peter's expedition.

### Guibert of Nogent's Version

Therefore, while the princes, who felt the need of many expenses and great services from their attendants, made their preparations slowly and carefully; the common people who had little property, but were very numerous, joined a certain Peter the Hermit, and obeyed him as a master while these affairs were going on among us.

He was, if I am not mistaken, from the city of Amiens, and we have learned that he had lived as a hermit, dressed as a monk, somewhere in Upper Gaul. After he had departed from there—I do not know with what intention—we saw him going through the cities and towns under a pretense of preaching. He was surrounded by so great throngs of people, he received such enormous gifts, his holiness was lauded so highly, that no one within my memory has been held in such honor.

From Edward Peters, ed., *The First Crusade: The Chronicle of Fulcher and Other Source Materials,* 2d ed. (Philadelphia: University of Pennsylvania Press, 1998), pp. 103, 150–151.

He was very liberal in the distribution to the poor of what he had received. He restored prostitutes to their husbands with gifts. By his wonderful authority he restored everywhere peace and concord, in place of discord. For in whatever he did or said it seemed as if there was something divine, especially when the hairs were snatched from his mule for relics. We do not report this as true, but for the common people who love novelties. He wore a woolen shirt, and over it a mantle reaching to his ankles; his arms and feet were bare. He lived on wine and fish; he hardly ever, or never, ate bread.

## Anna Comnena's Version

[Just prior to the events described below, Peter and his army had been routed by the Turks. With his forces weakened, Peter was warned by Emperor Alexius I not to risk another engagement with the enemy. His decision to ignore the emperor's advice would prove disastrous.]

But relying on the multitude of those who followed him, Peter did not heed the warning and, after crossing the strait[1] pitched camp at a little town called *Helenopolis*.

But since there were also Normans in his army, estimated at about ten thousand men, these, separating themselves from the rest of the body, devastated the region lying around the city of Nicaea, rioting most cruelly in every way. For they tore some of the children apart, limb from limb and, piercing others through with wooden stakes, roasted them in fire; likewise, upon those advanced in years they inflicted every kind of torture. When those in the city saw this being done, they opened the gates and went out against them. As a result, a fierce battle took place, in which, since the Normans fought ferociously, the citizens were hurled back into the fortress. The Normans, after gathering up all the plunder, again returned to *Helenopolis*. There a quarrel arose between themselves and the other pilgrims who had not gone off with them, a thing which usually happens in an affair of this kind, envy inflaming the wrath of those left behind, and a riotous fight followed the quarrel. The fierce Normans again separated [from the others] and captured *Xerogord* on their way at the first attack.

When this was learned, the Sultan sent Elchanes against them with a suitable number of troops. When he reached them, he recaptured *Xerogord*, killed some of the Normans with the sword, and carried off the rest as captives, planning at the same time, also, an attack upon those who had remained with Kuku-Peter.[2] And he set ambushes at opportune places into which, when they left for Nicaea, they would unexpectedly fall and be killed. But knowing also of the avarice of the Gauls, he had summoned two men of bold spirit and ordered them to go to the camp of Kuku-Peter to announce that the Normans had captured Nicaea and were now sacking it to the utmost. This report, brought to the camp of Peter, excited all violently; for when the mention of plunder and riches was heard, they straightway set out in tumult on the road which leads to Nicaea, forgetful of their

---

[1]**strait**: The body of water separating Constantinople from Turkish-controlled territory.
[2]**Kuku-Peter**: Peter the Hermit.

military training and of observing discipline in going out to battle. For the Latins are not only most fond of riches, as we said above, but when they give themselves to raiding any region for plunder, are also no longer obedient to reason, or any other check. Accordingly, since they were neither keeping order nor forming into lines, they fell into the ambush of the Turks around *Draco* and were wretchedly cut to pieces. Indeed, so great a multitude of Gauls and Normans were cut down by the Ishmaelite sword that when the dead bodies of the killed, which were lying all about in the place, were brought together, they made a very great mound, or hill, or look-out place, lofty as a mountain, and occupying a space very conspicuous for its width and depth. So high did that mound of bones tower, that some barbarians of the same race as the killed later used the bones of the slain instead of stones in constructing a wall, thus making that fortress a sort of sepulchre for them. It stands to this day, an enclosure of walls built with mixed rocks and bones.

And thus, after all had been wiped out in the slaughter, Peter returned with only a few to *Helenopolis*. The Turks, in their desire to get him into their power, again beset him with an ambush. But when the Emperor heard of the whole affair and learned how great was the slaughter of men, he held it very wrong that Peter should also be taken. Immediately, therefore, he summoned Catacalon Constantine Euphorbenus, of whom mention has often been made in this history, and sent him with suitable forces on war-vessels across the sea as a succour to Peter. When the Turks saw him approach, they fled. . . .

### READING QUESTIONS

1. How would you characterize Guibert's opinion of Peter and his followers? What did he admire about them? How did he qualify his admiration?

2. What importance should we attach to the contrast Guibert drew between the preparations of the "princes" and the "common people" for the journey to Jerusalem?

3. According to Comnena, what led to the destruction of Peter's army?

4. What might explain the emperor's decision to save Peter? Why was Peter not held responsible for the violence in Nicaea?

## 9-6 | ANONYMOUS OF MAINZ, *The Slaughter of the Jews* (ca. 1096)

The Crusades were a catastrophe for Europe's Jews. As armies of Crusaders moved through Europe, they joined with local Christians in horrific attacks on Jewish communities. This account of anti-Jewish violence by an anonymous Jewish resident of Mainz, a German city in which more than one thousand Jews were killed, provides a sense of the ferocity of the attacks. As you read it, think about what it tells you about the position of Jews in medieval Europe. Why were they the targets of such intense hatred? What means of defense, if any, did they have against the hostility of their Christian neighbors?

From Robert Chazan, *European Jewry and the First Crusade* (Berkeley: University of California Press, 1987), pp. 225–228.

I shall begin the account of the former persecution. May the Lord protect us and all Israel from persecution.

It came to pass in the year one thousand twenty-eight after the destruction of the Temple[1] that this evil befell Israel. There first arose the princes and nobles and common folk in France, who took counsel and set plans to ascend and "to rise up like eagles" and to do battle and "to clear a way" for journeying to Jerusalem, the Holy City, and for reaching the sepulcher of the Crucified,[2] "a trampled corpse" "who cannot profit and cannot save for he is worthless." They said to one another: "Behold we travel to a distant land to do battle with the kings of that land. 'We take our souls in our hands' in order to kill and to subjugate all those kingdoms that do not believe in the Crucified. How much more so [should we kill and subjugate] the Jews, who killed and crucified him." They taunted us from every direction. They took counsel, ordering that either we turn to their abominable faith or they would destroy us "from infant to suckling." They—both princes and common folk—placed an evil sign upon their garments, a cross, and helmets upon their heads.

When the [Jewish] communities in France heard, they were seized by consternation, fear, and trembling. . . . They wrote letters and sent emissaries to all the [Jewish] communities along the Rhine River, [asking that they] fast and deprive themselves and seek mercy from [God "who] dwells on high," so that he deliver them [the Jews] from their [the Crusaders'] hands. When the letters reached the saintly ones who were in that land, they—those men of God, "the pillars of the universe," who were in Mainz—wrote in reply to France. Thus was it written in them [their letters]: "All the [Jewish] communities have decreed a fast. We have done our part. May God save us and save you from 'all distress and hardship.' We are greatly fearful for you. We, however, have less reason to fear [for ourselves], for we have heard not even a rumor [of such developments]." Indeed we did not hear that a decree had been issued and that "a sword was to afflict us mortally."

When the crusaders began to reach this land, they sought funds with which to purchase bread. We gave them, considering ourselves to be fulfilling the verse: "Serve the king of Babylon, and live." All this, however, was of no avail, for our sins brought it about that the burghers in every city to which the crusaders came were hostile to us, for their [the burghers'] hands were also with them [the Crusaders] to destroy vine and stock all along the way to Jerusalem.

It came to pass that, when the crusaders came, battalion after battalion, like the army of Sennacherib,[3] some of the princes in the empire said: "Why do we sit thus? Let us also go with them. For every man who sets forth on this journey and undertakes to ascend to the impure sepulcher dedicated to the Crucified will be assured paradise." Then the crusaders along with them [the princes] gathered from all the provinces until they became as numerous "as the sands of the sea," including both princes and common folk. They circulated a report. . . . "Anyone

---

[1]**Temple**: Second Temple of Jerusalem, destroyed by the Romans in 70 c.e.
[2]**sepulcher of the Crucified**: Tomb of Christ in Jerusalem.
[3]**Sennacherib**: An ancient Assyrian king.

who kills a single Jew will have all his sins absolved." Indeed there was a certain nobleman, Ditmar by name, who announced that he would not depart from this empire until he would kill one Jew—then he would depart. Now when the holy community in Mainz heard this, they decreed a fast. "They cried out mightily to the Lord" and they passed night and day in fasting. Likewise they recited dirges both morning and evening, both small and great. Nonetheless our God "did not turn away from his awesome wrath" against us. For the crusaders with their insignia came, with their standards before our houses. When they saw one of us, they ran after him and pierced him with a spear, to the point that we were afraid even to cross our thresholds. . . .

It came to pass on the tenth of Iyyar, on Sunday, "they plotted craftily against them." They took "a trampled corpse" of theirs, that had been buried thirty days previously and carried it through the city, saying: "Behold what the Jews have done to our comrade. They took a gentile and boiled him in water. They then poured the water into our wells in order to kill us." When the crusaders and burghers heard this, they cried out and gathered—all who bore and unsheathed [a sword], from great to small—saying: "Behold the time has come to avenge him who was crucified, whom their ancestors slew. Now let not 'a remnant or a residue' escape, even 'an infant or a suckling' in the cradle." They then came and struck those who had remained in their houses—comely young men and comely and lovely young women along with elders. All of them stretched forth their necks. Even manumitted serv-ingmen and serving-women were killed along with them for the sanctification of the Name which is awesome and sublime, . . . who rules above and below, who was and will be. Indeed the Lord of Hosts is his Name. He is crowned with the splendor of seventy-two names; he created the Torah nine hundred and seventy-four generations prior to the creation of the world. There were twenty-six generations from the creation of the world to Moses, the father of the prophets, through whom [God] gave the holy Torah. Moses came and wrote in it: "The Lord has affirmed this day that you are, as he promised you, his treasured people which shall observe all his commandments." For him and his Torah they were killed like oxen and were dragged through the mar-ket places and streets "like sheep to the slaughter" and lay naked, for they [the attackers] stripped them and left them naked.

### READING QUESTIONS

1. What explanation did the author offer for the attacks on Europe's Jews? How did he use Jewish history to help give context to the events he described?

2. What segments of European society did the author blame for the attacks?

3. What steps did Jewish communities take in response to the violence? What do those steps tell you about the connections between Jewish communities? About the options available to Jewish communities under assault?

## 9-7    |    A Muslim Historian Recounts the Crusades
### ALI IBN AL-ATHIR, *The Complete History* (1231)

Predictably, Muslim historians from the eleventh to thirteenth centuries presented the major events of the Crusades and Catholic invaders in a very different light than European chroniclers. The Muslim world was in the middle of an extended cultural and technological "golden age," and most Muslims of the period considered their own culture, cities, and religion to be superior to those of medieval Catholic Europe. Muslim states had controlled Jerusalem since the seventh century, and as it was considered holy to Jews, Christians, and Muslims alike, they welcomed Christian pilgrims and protected Christian sites before the eleventh century. Moreover, after the First Crusade resulted in the creation of the Crusader states in the Levant, Muslim leaders often cooperated with Catholic rulers in the region, and Muslim accounts during the period after the First Crusade reflected both positive and negative impressions of the "Franks," as they called them. In the following account, written by Muslim historian Ali Ibn al-Athir in 1231, the author contrasts the Catholic seizure of Jerusalem in 1099 with the retaking of the city in 1187 by the Muslim commander Saladin.

Jerusalem was taken . . . on the morning of Friday 22 sha'ban 492/15 July 1099. The population was put to the sword by the Franks,[1] who pillaged the area for a week. A band of Muslims barricaded themselves in the Tower of David and fought on for several days. They were granted their lives in return for surrendering. The Franks honored their word, and the group left by night. . . . In the Masjid al-Aqsa[2] the Franks slaughtered more than 70,000 people, among them a large number of Imams[3] and Muslim scholars, devout and ascetic men who had left their homelands to live lives of pious seclusion in the Holy Place. The Franks stripped the Dome of the Rock of more than forty silver candelabra, . . . and a great silver lamp as well as a hundred and fifty smaller silver candelabra and more than twenty gold ones, and a great deal more booty.

Refugees from Syria reached Baghdad in Ramadan[4]. . . . They told the Caliph's ministers a story that wrung their hearts and brought tears to their eyes. On Friday they went to the Cathedral Mosque and begged for help, weeping so that their hearers wept with them as they described the sufferings of the

---

From Francesco Gabrieli, *Arab Historians of the Crusades* (Oakland: University of California Press, 1984), pp. 6–7, 119.

[1]**Franks:** The term Muslim writers used universally for all Crusaders, regardless of their origins in Europe.

[2]**Masjid al-Aqsa:** Most prominent mosque (Muslim place of worship) in Jerusalem, the third-holiest site in Islam.

[3]**Imams:** Muslims that lead prayers.

[4]**Ramadan:** The sacred month of fasting in Islam that commemorates when the first revelations came to Muhammad.

Muslims in that Holy City: the men killed, the women and children taken prisoner, the homes pillaged. Because of the terrible hardships they had suffered, they were allowed to break the fast. It was the discord between the Muslim princes that enabled the Franks to overrun the country.

[Ibn al-Athir then describes how Jerusalem was retaken by the Muslims in 1187, led by the famous sultan of Syria and Egypt, Saladin.]

When the Franks saw how violently the Muslims were attacking, they grew desperate, and their leaders assembled to take counsel. They decided to ask for safe conduct out of the city and to hand Jerusalem over to Saladin. They sent a deputation of their lords and nobles to ask for terms, but when they spoke of it to Saladin he refused to grant their request. "We shall deal with you," he said. "Just as you dealt with the population of Jerusalem when you took it in 492/1099, with murder and enslavement and other such savageries!" The messengers returned empty handed. Then Balian ibn Barzan[5] asked for safe conduct for himself so that he might appear before Saladin to discuss developments. Consent was given, and he presented himself and once again began asking for a general amnesty in return for surrender. The sultan still refused his requests and entreaties to show mercy.

Finally, despairing of this approach, Balian said: "Know, O Sultan, that there are very many of us in this city, God alone knows how many. At the moment we are fighting half-heartedly in the hope of saving our lives, hoping to be spared by you as you have spared others; this is because of our horror of death and our love of life. But if we see that death is inevitable, then by God we shall kill our children and our wives, burn our possessions, so as not to leave you with a dinar or a drachma[6] or a single man or woman to enslave. When this is done, we shall pull down the Sanctuary of the Rock and the Masjid al-Aqsa and the other sacred, slaughtering the Muslim prisoners we hold—5,000 of them—and killing every horse and animal we possess. Then we shall come out to fight you like men fighting for their lives, when each man, before he falls dead, kills his equals, we shall die with honour, or win a noble victory!"

Then Saladin took counsel with his advisers, all of whom were in favour of his granting the assurances requested by the Franks, without forcing them to take extreme measures whose outcome could not be foreseen. "Let us consider them as being already our prisoners," they said, "and allow them to ransom themselves on terms agreed between us." The Sultan agreed to give the Franks

---

[5]**Balian ibn Barzan**: French aristocrat who lived in the Catholic-held Kingdom of Jerusalem.

[6]**dinar ... drachma**: Islamic and Greek currencies (respectively).

assurances of safety on the understanding that each man, rich and poor alike, should pay ten dinar, children of both sexes two dinar and women five dinar. All who paid this sum within forty days should go free, and those who had not paid at the end of the time should be enslaved. Balian ibn Barzan offered 30,000 dinar as ransom for the poor, which was accepted, and the city surrendered on Friday 27 rajab/2 October 1187, a memorable day on which the Muslim flags were hoisted over the walls of Jerusalem. . . .

The Grand Patriarch of the Franks left the city with the treasures from the Dome of the Rock, the Masjid al-Aqsa, the Church of the Resurrection and others, God alone knows the amount of treasure; he also took an equal quantity of money. Saladin made no difficulties, and when he was advised to sequestrate[7] the whole lot for Islam, replied that he would not go back on his word. He took only the ten dinar from him, and let him go, heavily escorted, to Tyre.

At the top of the cupola of the Dome of the Rock there was a great gilded cross. When the Muslims entered the city on the Friday, some of them climbed up to the top of the cupola to take down the cross. When they reached the top a great cry went up from the city and from outside the walls, the Muslims crying the Allah akbar in their joy, the Franks groaning in consternation and grief. So loud and piercing was the cry that the earth shook.

## READING QUESTIONS

1. How does this account compare with the rhetoric of Urban II at the Council of Clermont, as well as other Catholic and Byzantine accounts? Why do you think they are different?

2. Does this account seem to take sides, presenting the Muslims in a more favorable light? If not, offer examples of where it seems more complex.

3. Why did Saladin respond to appeals for mercy in the way that he did? What ideologies, moral understandings, or diplomatic norms shaped his response, and was he being primarily pragmatic, political, or religious when he let the Crusaders go?

---

[7]**sequestrate**: Take.

# ▪ COMPARATIVE AND DISCUSSION QUESTIONS ▪

1. What do the *Domesday Book* and the Magna Carta reveal about the strategies medieval monarchs used to expand their power? What do they tell you about the opposition to such efforts?

2. Compare and contrast the arguments on both sides of the investiture controversy. In your opinion, who had the stronger case? Why?

3. What light do the investiture controversy and the call for the First Crusade shed on the power of the medieval church? What do they tell you about the limits of that power?

4. What does the response to Urban II's call for a crusade reveal about the religious culture of medieval Europe?

5. If the Crusades were described exclusively as a "holy war" between Christians and Muslims, what evidence could you present that would refute that characterization?

# 10

# Life in Villages and Cities of the High Middle Ages
## 1000–1300

As Europe moved into a new millennium, much remained unchanged from previous centuries, at least on the surface. The vast majority of Europeans were engaged in agriculture, and most were unfree, laboring as serfs on land they did not own and could not leave. The military elite retained their position at the top of the social and political ladder. The church continued to play a central role in European culture, providing a unifying set of values and beliefs. Nonetheless, a decisive shift had taken place. As the invasions of the ninth century came to an end, a measure of stability and security returned to European society. This stability and the introduction of new agricultural technologies led to increased agricultural production and, with it, accelerating population growth. These developments, in turn, stimulated trade and the revival of urban life. As Europe's towns and cities grew, they became centers of wealth, power, and culture that traditional landed elites ignored at their peril. The documents included in this chapter explore these complicated and interrelated social, economic, and cultural changes, offering insight into the dynamic forces that shaped life in the High Middle Ages.

## 10-1 | Life on a Medieval Manor
### *Manorial Records of Bernehorne* (1307)

In the High Middle Ages, agricultural production took place on manors. Serfs were bound to a specific manor and required to work its land, dividing their time between raising crops for the lord of the manor and for their own consumption. In addition to their labor obligations, they were subject to a variety of fees and duties. Serfs were not slaves; individual serfs could not be sold, and serfs enjoyed certain recognized rights and protections. While it was certainly the case that lords had considerable power over the lives of their serfs, this power was limited by tradition and by obligations to their serfs. As you read the excerpt from the manorial records of Bernehorne, consider what it tells you about the power dynamics at work on a medieval manor. What limits existed on a lord's ability to use his land and its people as he saw fit?

Extent of the manor of Bernehorne, made on Wednesday following the feast of St. Gregory the pope, in the thirty-fifth year of the reign of King Edward, in the presence of Brother Thomas, keeper of Marley, John de la More, and Adam de Thruhlegh, clerks, on the oath of William de Gocecoumbe, Walter le Parker, Richard le Knyst, Richard the son of the latter, Andrew of Estone, Stephen Morsprich, Thomas Brembel, William of Swynham, John Pollard, Roger le Glede, John Syward, and John de Lillingewist, who say that there are all the following holdings: . . .

John Pollard holds a half acre in Aldithewisse and owes 18d. at the four terms, and owes for it relief and heriot.[1]

John Suthinton holds a house and 40 acres of land and owes 3s. 6d. at Easter and Michaelmas.[2]

William of Swynham holds 1 acre of meadow in the thicket of Swynham and owes 1d. at the feast of Michaelmas.

Ralph of Leybourne holds a cottage and 1 acre of land in Pinden and owes 3s. at Easter and Michaelmas, and attendance at the court in the manor every three weeks, also relief and heriot.

Richard Knyst of Swynham holds 2 acres and a half of land and owes yearly 4s.

William of Knelle holds 2 acres of land in Aldithewisse and owes yearly 4s. . . .

They say, moreover, that John of Cayworth holds a house and 30 acres of land, and owes yearly 2s. at Easter and Michaelmas; and he owes a cock and two hens at Christmas of the value of 4d.

And he ought to harrow for 2 days at the Lenten sowing with one man and his own horse and his own harrow, the value of the work being 4d.; and he is to

From James Harvey Robinson, ed., *Readings in European History*, abridged ed. (Boston: Ginn, 1906), pp. 181–184.

[1]**relief and heriot**: Payments owed to the lord when a serf died.
[2]**Michaelmas**: Feast honoring the Archangel Michael; celebrated on September 29.

receive from the lord on each day 3 meals, of the value of 5d., and then the lord will be at a loss of 1d. Thus his harrowing is of no value to the service of the lord.

And he ought to carry the manure of the lord for 2 days with 1 cart, with his own 2 oxen, the value of the work being 8d.; and he is to receive from the lord each day 3 meals as above. And thus the service is worth 3d.

And he shall find one man for 2 days, for mowing the meadow of the lord, who can mow, by estimation, 1 acre and a half, the value of the mowing of an acre being 6d.: the sum is therefore 9d. And he is to receive each day 3 meals of the value given above. And thus that mowing is worth 4d. . . .

And he ought to carry wood from the woods of the lord as far as the manor, for two days in summer, with a cart and 3 animals of his own, the value of the work being 9d. And he shall receive from the lord each day 3 meals of the price given above. And thus the work is worth 4d.

William of Cayworth holds a house and 30 acres of land and owes at Easter and Michaelmas 2s. rent. And he shall do all customs just as the aforesaid John of Cayworth.

William atte Grene holds a house and 30 acres of land and owes in all things the same as the said John. . . .

And it is to be noted that none of the above-named villeins[3] can give their daughters in marriage, nor cause their sons to be tonsured,[4] nor can they cut down timber growing on the lands they hold, without license of the bailiff or sergeant of the lord, and then for building purposes and not otherwise. And after the death of any one of the aforesaid villeins, the lord shall have as a heriot his best animal, if he had any; if, however, he have no living beast, the lord shall have no heriot, as they say. The sons or daughters of the aforesaid villeins shall give, for entrance into the holding after the death of their predecessors, as much as they give of rent per year.

### READING QUESTIONS

1. What did serfs owe their lord? What did he owe them?

2. What importance should we attach to the fact that the manorial obligations were written down? What purpose might written records such as these have served?

3. What should we make of the differences in wealth among agricultural workers revealed in this document? How might one such worker have come to control much more land than another?

---

[3]**villeins**: Serfs.
[4]**cause their sons to be tonsured**: Have their sons become monks.

## 10-2 | Medieval Workers

### *On Laborers: A Dialogue Between Teacher and Student* (ca. 1000)

The following document was likely used to teach students Latin. It also provides a short explanation of social relations — information useful for students who would later keep records or supervise workers. By 1000, especially in the countryside, various forms of unfree status had been imposed, although outright slavery was one of the less common forms. Serfs, for instance, could not be bought and sold as individuals, but they also could not leave their land, and their duties to their masters were carefully prescribed. When the land they worked passed to another owner, they acquired a new master.

TEACHER: What do your companions know?

STUDENT: They are plowmen, shepherds, oxherds, huntsmen, fishermen, falconers, merchants, cobblers, salt-makers, and bakers.

TEACHER: What sayest thou plowman? How do you do your work?

PLOWMAN: O my lord, I work very hard: I go out at dawn, driving the cattle to the field, and I yoke them to the plow. Nor is the weather so bad in winter that I dare to stay at home, for fear of my lord: but when the oxen are yoked, and the plowshare and coulter attached to the plow, I must plow one whole field a day, or more.

TEACHER: Have you any assistant?

PLOWMAN: I have a boy to drive the oxen with a goad, and he too is hoarse with cold and shouting.

TEACHER: What more do you do in a day?

PLOWMAN: Certainly I do more. I must fill the manger of the oxen with hay, and water them and carry out the dung.

TEACHER: Indeed, that is a great labor.

PLOWMAN: Even so, it is a great labor for I am not free.

TEACHER: What have you to say shepherd? Have you heavy work too?

SHEPHERD: I have indeed. In the grey dawn I drive my sheep to the pasture and I stand watch over them, in heat and cold, with my dogs, lest the wolves devour them. And I bring them back to the fold and milk them twice a day. And I move their fold; and I make cheese and butter, and I am faithful to my lord.

TEACHER: Oxherd, what work do you do?

OXHERD: O my lord, I work hard. When the plowman unyokes the oxen I lead them to the pasture and I stand all night guarding them against thieves. Then in the morning I hand them over to the plowman well fed and watered.

From Thomas Wright, ed., *Anglo-Saxon and Old English Vocabularies*, vol. 1 (London: Trubner, 1884), p. 88, reprinted in Roy C. Cave and Herbert H. Coulson, *A Source Book for Medieval Economic History* (New York: The Bruce Publishing Co., 1936; repr., New York: Biblo & Tannen, 1965), pp. 46–48. The text has been modernized by Jerome S. Arkenberg, California State University–Fullerton.

TEACHER: What is your craft?

FISHERMAN: I am a fisherman.

TEACHER: What do you obtain from your work?

FISHERMAN: Food and clothing and money.

TEACHER: How do you take the fish?

FISHERMAN: I get into a boat, and place my nets in the water, and I throw out my hook and lines, and whatever they take I keep.

TEACHER: What if the fish should be unclean?

FISHERMAN: I throw out the unclean fish and use the clean as food.

TEACHER: Where do you sell your fish?

FISHERMAN: In the town.

TEACHER: Who buys them?

FISHERMAN: The citizens. I cannot catch as much as I can sell.

TEACHER: What fish do you take?

FISHERMAN: Herring, salmon, porpoises, sturgeon, oysters, crabs, mussels, periwinkles, cockles, plaice, sole, lobsters, and the like.

TEACHER: Do you wish to capture a whale?

FISHERMAN: No.

TEACHER: Why?

FISHERMAN: Because it is a dangerous thing to capture a whale. It is safer for me to go to the river with my boat than to go with many ships hunting whales.

TEACHER: Why so?

FISHERMAN: Because I prefer to take a fish that I can kill rather than one which with a single blow can sink or kill not only me but also my companions.

TEACHER: Yet many people do capture whales and escape the danger, and they obtain a great price for what they do.

FISHERMAN: You speak the truth, but I do not dare because of my cowardice.

### READING QUESTIONS

1. What can you deduce about the social status of the various speakers?

2. What light does the document shed on the division of labor on a medieval manor?

3. In what ways does the work of the fisherman differ from that of the other speakers? What hints does the description of his activities provide about changes in the medieval economy?

# 10-3 | Life as a Medieval Guild Member
## *The Ordinances of London's Leatherworkers* (1346)

The revival of urban life was one of the most important developments of the High Middle Ages. Trade and towns grew in tandem, as increased trade brought new wealth to Europe's urban centers. That wealth stimulated urban population growth, which, in turn, produced increased demand for trade goods. In urban areas, merchants engaged in similar kinds of trade formed merchant guilds, and those who specialized in producing the same kind of products formed craft guilds. Guilds set wages and prices, controlled access to economic opportunity, decided what goods could or could not be produced, and regulated production methods and standards. To this sweeping economic power was added considerable political clout, as the same individuals who sat at the top of the guild hierarchy occupied the highest positions in town governance. As you read the guild regulations of London's leatherworkers, pay particular attention to the non-economic aspects of the regulations. What does the document tell you about the role of guilds in the social and cultural life of medieval towns?

In honor of God, of Our Lady, and of all Saints, and for the nurture of tranquillity [*sic*] and peace among the good folks the Megucers, called "*Whittawyers*,"[1] the folks of the same trade have, by assent of Richard Lacer, Mayor, and of the Aldermen [of London], ordained the points under-written.

In the first place, they have ordained that they will find a wax candle, to burn before Our Lady in the Church of All Hallows near London Wall. Also, that each person of the said trade shall put in the box such sum as he shall think fit, in aid of maintaining the said candle.

Also, if by chance any one of the said trade shall fall into poverty, whether through old age, or because he cannot labor or work, and have nothing with which to help himself; he shall have every week from the said box 7*d*. for his support if he be a man of good repute. And after his decease, if he have a wife, a woman of good repute, she shall have weekly for her support 7*d*. from the said box, so long as she shall behave herself well, and keep single.

And that no stranger shall work in the said trade, or keep house [for the same] in the city, if he be not an apprentice, or a man admitted to the franchise of the said city.

And that no one shall take the serving man of another to work with him, during his term, unless it be with the permission of his master.

And if any one of the said trade shall have work in his house that he cannot complete, or if for want of assistance such work shall be in danger of being lost, those of the said trade shall aid him, that so the said work be not lost.

---

From Alfred Edward Bland, Philip Anthony Brown, and Richard Henry Tawney, eds., *English Economic History: Select Documents* (New York: Macmillan, 1919), pp. 136–138.

[1]**Megucers, called "*Whittawyers*"**: Leatherworkers who specialized in turning leather white.

And if any one of the said trade shall depart this life, and have not where-withal to be buried, he shall be buried at the expense of their common box; and when any one of the said trade shall die, all those of the said trade shall go to the Vigil, and make offering on the [next day].

And if any serving-man shall conduct himself in any other manner than properly towards his master, and act rebelliously towards him, no one of the said trade shall set him to work, until he shall have made amends before the Mayor and Aldermen. . . .

And that no one of the said trade shall behave himself the more thought-lessly, in the way of speaking or acting amiss, by reason of the points aforesaid; and if any one shall do to the contrary thereof, he shall not follow the said trade until he shall have reasonably made amends.

And if any one of the said trade shall do to the contrary of any point of the Ordinances aforesaid, and be convicted thereof by good men of the said trade, he shall pay to the Chamber of the Guildhall of London, the first time 2s., the second time 40d., the third time half a mark, and the fourth time 10s., and shall forswear the trade.

Also, that the good folks of the same trade shall once in the year be assem-bled in a certain place, convenient thereto, there to choose two men of the most loyal and befitting of the said trade, to be overseers of work and all other things touching the trade, for that year, which persons shall be presented to the Mayor and Aldermen for the time being, and sworn before them diligently to enquire and make search, and loyally to present to the said Mayor and Aldermen such defaults as they shall find touching the said trade without sparing any one for friendship or for hatred, or in any other manner. And if any one of the said trade shall be found rebellious against the said overseers, so as not to let them prop-erly make their search and assay, as they ought to do; or if he shall absent him-self from the meeting aforesaid, without reasonable cause, after due warning by the said overseers, he shall pay to the Chamber, upon the first default, 40d.; and on the second like default, half a mark; and on the third, one mark; and on the fourth, 20s. and shall forswear the trade for ever.

Also, that if the overseers shall be found lax and negligent about their duty, or partial to any person, . . . maintaining him, or voluntarily permitting him [to continue] in his default, and shall not present him to the Mayor and Aldermen, as before stated, they are to incur the penalty aforesaid.

Also, that each year, at such assemblies of the good folks of the said trade, there shall be chosen overseers, as before stated. And if it shall be found that through laxity or negligence of the said governors such assemblies are not held, each of the said overseers is to incur the said penalty.

Also, that all skins falsely and deceitfully wrought in their trade, which the said overseers shall find on sale in the hands of any person, citizen or foreigner, within the franchise, shall be forfeited to the said Chamber, and the worker thereof amerced in manner aforesaid.

Also, that no one who has not been an apprentice, and has not finished his term of apprenticeship in the said trade shall be made free of the same trade; unless it be attested by the overseers for the time being or by four persons of the said trade, that such person is able, and sufficiently skilled to be made free of the same.

Also, that no one of the said trade shall induce the servant of another to work with him in the same trade, until he has made a proper fine with his first master, at the discretion of the said overseers, or of four reputable men of the said trade. And if any one shall do to the contrary thereof, or receive the serving workman of another to work with him during his term, without leave of the trade, he is to incur the said penalty.

### READING QUESTIONS

1. What material benefits does the guild provide to members?

2. Other than standardizing the quality of work, what other things does the guild do to ensure the members produce good work?

3. What connections does the document reveal between the guild and the London city government?

4. How does this document address and support the social hierarchy of cities? Whose interests does it appear to represent best?

## 10-4 | Medieval Clothing Laws

### THE COMMUNE OF FLORENCE, *A Sumptuary Law: Restrictions on Dress* (1373)

Medieval governments, both at the local and national level, exercised broad authority over economic activity. This authority was reflected in sumptuary laws, which taxed and regulated consumption — most often of clothing and ornamentation — in ways that were seen as conducive to the general well-being of the community. For example, in an effort to reinforce distinctions of social rank and status, a sumptuary law might reserve the use of luxury fabrics and materials for members of the nobility. Here, the Commune of Florence puts a sumptuary law to a different purpose: the enhancement of communal revenues. As you read the law, consider what it reveals about Florentine society.

It is well known to all that the worthy men, Benozzo di Francesco di Andrea . . . [and fifteen others] . . . have been selected to discover ways and means by which money will accrue to the Commune. . . . Considering the Commune's need for revenue to pay current expenses . . . they have enacted . . . the following:

First, all women and girls, whether married or not, whether betrothed or not, of whatever age, rank, and condition . . . who wear — or who wear in future — any gold, silver, pearls, precious stones, bells, ribbons of gold or silver, or cloth of silk brocade on their bodies or heads . . . for the ornamentation of their bodies . . . will

From Gene Brucker, *The Society of Renaissance Florence* (New York: Harper and Row, 1971), pp. 46–47.

be required to pay each year . . . the sum of 50 florins . . . to the treasurer of the gabelle[1] on contracts. . . . [The exceptions to this prohibition are] that every married woman may wear on her hand or hands as many as two rings. . . . And every married woman or girl who is betrothed may wear . . . a silver belt which does not exceed fourteen ounces in weight. . . .

So that the gabelle is not defrauded, and so that citizens—on account of clothing already made—are not forced to bear new expenditures, [the officials] have decreed that all dresses, gowns, coats, capes, and other items of clothing belonging to any women or girls above the age of ten years, which were made up to the present day and which are decorated in whatever manner, may be worn for ten years in the future without the payment of any gabelle.

## READING QUESTIONS

1. What was the principal reason for passing this sumptuary law?
2. In what ways did the sumptuary laws create a kind of income tax?
3. What does this law suggest about the tastes and consumption habits of medieval Florentines?

## SOURCES IN CONVERSATION

# Synthesizing Reason and Faith

During the medieval period, the disciplines of philosophy and theology intersected, and scholars wrestled with the contradictions between rational thought and faith in an unseeable, unknowable divine deity. To do this, they often referred to the ideas of the ancient Greek philosopher Aristotle, though they also often arrived at very different conclusions. In these documents, the great Andalusian Muslim scholar Ibn Rushd and the Catholic academic and theologian Thomas Aquinas attempt to rationally prove that God exists.

## READ AND COMPARE

1. How do these two great scholars argue for the existence of God? What is similar in their arguments, and what is different?
2. Which of their arguments do you find most convincing, and why?

---

[1]**treasurer of the gabelle**: Officer in the Florentine government responsible for collecting taxes.

## 10-5 | IBN RUSHD (AVERROES), *Religion and Philosophy* (ca. 1190)

Ibn Rushd, or Averroes to the European world, was a Muslim scholar from Spain who lived in the twelfth century. His distinguished career was impressive: besides serving as a judge and court physician, he wrote extensively about a staggering variety of academic subjects, including medicine, physics, Islamic law, languages, theology, mathematics, and astronomy. While he was a highly respected scholar, he also held very radical ideas, such as his argument that the physical universe had always existed, just as God had, and thus was not created by God. Additionally, he held that human intellect was not individualized, but was part of a collective entity shared by all people, and that people would not be resurrected in their physical bodies in the afterlife. The Christian theologian Thomas Aquinas later refuted these claims. As you read, consider how he combines the logical principles of the "Ancients" with the "Law" of Islam, or the Qu'ran itself.

We maintain that the business of philosophy is nothing other than to look into creation and to ponder over it in order to be guided to the Creator — in other words, to look into the meaning of existence. For the knowledge of creation leads to the cognizance of the Creator, through the knowledge of the created. The more perfect becomes the knowledge of creation, the more perfect becomes the knowledge of the Creator. The Law encourages and exhorts us to observe creation. Thus, it is clear that this is to be taken either as a religious injunction or as something approved by the Law. But the Law urges us to observe creation by means of reason and demands the knowledge thereof through reason. This is evident from different verses of the Quran. For example, the Quran says: "Wherefore take example from them, you who have eyes" [Qur'an 49.2]. That is a clear indication of the necessity of using the reasoning faculty, or rather both reason and religion, in the interpretation of things.

. . .

   Now, such is the case. All that is wanted in an enquiry into philosophical reasoning has already been perfectly examined by the Ancients. All that is required of us is that we should go back to their books and see what they have said in this connection. . . . For so long as one does not know its general character one cannot know the created, and so long as he does not know the created, he can have no knowledge of the Creator. . . . Imagine that the science of geometry and astronomy had become extinct in our day, and a single individual desired to find out by himself the magnitude of the heavenly bodies, their forms, and their distances from one another. Even though he were the most sagacious of men, it would be as impossible for him to ascertain the proportion of the sun and the earth and the magnitude of the other stars. It would only be attainable by aid of divine revelation, or something like it. If it be said to him that the sun is a hundred and fifty or sixty times as big as the earth, he would take it to be sheer madness on the part of the speaker, though it is an established fact in the science of astronomy, so that no one learned in that science will have any doubt about it.

. . .

From Mohammad Jamil-ur-Behman, *The Philosophy and Theology of Averroes* (Baroda: A. G. Widgery, 1921), p. 14.

All things have been made and created. This is quite clear in itself, in the case of animals and plants, as God has said "Verily the idols which you invoke, beside God, can never create a single fly, though they may all assemble for that purpose" [Qur'an 22.72]. We see an inorganic substance and then there is life in it. So we know for certain that there is an inventor and bestower of life, and He is God. Of the heavens we know by their movements, which never become slackened, that they work for our benefit by divine solicitude, and are subordinate to our welfare. Such an appointed and subordinate object is always created for some purpose. The second principle is that for every created thing there is a creator. So it is right to say from the two foregoing principles that for every existent thing there is an inventor. There are many arguments, according to the number of the created things, which can be advanced to prove this premise. Thus, it is necessary for one who wants to know God as He ought to be known to acquaint himself with the essence of things, so that he may get information about the creation of all things. . . . It is to this that God refers in the following verse "Or do they not contemplate the heaven and the earth, and the things which God has created?" [Qur'an 7.184]. And so a man who would follow the purpose of philosophy in investigating the existence of things, that is, would try to know the cause which led to its creation, and the purpose of it would know the argument of kindness most perfectly. These two arguments are those adopted by Law.

The verses of the Quran leading to a knowledge of the existence of God are dependent only on the two foregoing arguments. . . . These, when investigated, will be found to be of three kinds: either they are verses showing the "arguments of kindness," or those mentioning the "arguments of creation," or those which include both the kinds of arguments. The following verses may be taken as illustrating the argument of kindness. "Have we not made the earth for a bed, and the mountains for stakes to find the same? And have we not created you of two sexes; and appointed your sleep for rest; and made the night a garment to cover you; and destined the day to the gaining of your livelihood and built over you seven solid heavens; and placed therein a burning lamp? And do we not send down from the clouds pressing forth rain, water pouring down in abundance, that we may thereby produce corn, and herbs, and gardens planted thick with trees?" [Qur'an 77.6-16] and, "Blessed be He Who has placed the twelve signs in the heavens; has placed therein a lamp by day, and the moon which shines by night" [Qur'an 25.62] and again, "Let man consider his food" [Qur'an 80.24].

The following verses refer to the argument of invention, "Let man consider, therefore of what he is created. He is created of the seed poured forth, issuing from the loins, and the breast bones" [Qur'an 86.6]; and, "Do they not consider the camels, how they are created; the heaven, how it is raised; the mountains, how they are fixed; the earth how it is extended" [Qur'an 88.17]; and again "O man, a parable is propounded unto you; wherefore hearken unto it. Verily the idols which they invoke, besides God, can never create a single fly, though they may all assemble for the purpose" [Qur'an 22.72]. Then we may point to the story of Abraham, referred to in the following verse, "I direct my face unto Him Who has created heaven and earth; I am orthodox, and not of the idolaters" [Qur'an 6.79]. There may be quoted many verses referring to this argument. The verses comprising both the arguments are also many, for instance, "O men, of Mecca, serve your Lord, Who has created you, and those who have been before you: peradventure you will fear Him; Who has spread the earth as a bed for you, and the heaven as a covering, and has caused water to descend from heaven, and thereby produced fruits for your sustenance. Set not up, therefore, any equals unto God, against your own knowledge [Qur'an 2.19]. His words, "Who has created you, and those who have been before you," lead us to the argument of creation; while the words, "who has spread the earth" refer to the argument of divine solicitude for man. . . . Many verses of this kind comprise both the kinds of arguments.

This method is the right path by which God has invited men to a knowledge of His existence, and informed them of it through the intelligence which He has implanted in their nature. The following verse refers to this fixed and innate nature of man, "And when the Lord drew forth their posterity from the loins of the sons of Adam, and took them witness against themselves, Am I not your Lord? They answered, Yes, we do bear witness" [Qur'an 7.171]. So it is incumbent for one who intends to obey God, and follow the injunction of His Prophet, that he should adopt this method, thus making himself one of those learned men who bear witness to the divinity of God, with His own witness, and that of His angels, as He says, "God has borne witness, that there is no God but He, and the angels, and those who are endowed with wisdom profess the same; who execute righteousness; there is no God but He; the Mighty, the Wise" [Qur'an 3.16]. Among the arguments for both of themselves is the praise which God refers to in the following verse, "Neither is there anything which does not celebrate his praise; but you understand not their celebration thereof" [Qur'an 17.46].

It is evident from the above arguments for the existence of God that they are dependent upon two categories of reasoning. It is also clear that both of these methods are meant for particular people; that is, the learned. Now as to the method for the masses. The difference between the two lies only in details. The masses cannot understand the two above-mentioned arguments but only what they can grasp by their senses; while the learned men can go further and learn by reasoning also, besides learning by sense. . . . If this be so, then this is the method which is taught both by Law and by Nature. It is the method which was preached by the Prophet and the divine books. The learned men do not mention these two lines of reasoning to the masses, not because of their number, but because of a want of depth of learning on their part about the knowledge of a single thing only. The example of the common people, considering and pondering over the universe, is like a man who looks into a thing, the manufacture of which he does not know. For all that such a man can know about it is that it has been made, and that there must be a maker of it. But, on the other hand, the learned look into the universe, just as a man knowing the art would do; try to understand the real purpose of it. So it is quite clear that their knowledge about the Maker, as the maker of the universe, would be far better than that of the man who only knows it as made. The atheists, who deny the Creator altogether, are like men who can see and feel the created things, but would not acknowledge any Creator for them, but would attribute all to chance alone, and that they come into being by themselves.

. . .

If you look a little intently it will become clear to you, that in spite of the fact that the Law has not given illustration of those things for the common people, beyond which their imagination cannot go, it has also informed the learned men of the underlying meanings of those illustrations. So it is necessary to bear in mind the limits which the Law has set about the instruction of every class of men, and not to mix them together. For in this manner the purpose of the Law is multiplied. Hence it is that the Prophet has said, "We, the prophets, have been commanded to adapt ourselves to the conditions of the people, and address them according to their intelligence." He who tries to instruct all the people in the matter of religion, in one and the same way, is like a man who wants to make them alike in actions too, which is quite against apparent laws and reason.

### READING QUESTIONS

1. How does Ibn Rushd organize his arguments about the existence of God, or what are the two types of textual evidence that he cites from the Qu'ran?

2. What are the two main ways that humans can grasp the existence of God?

3. How does Ibn Rushd define and address social-class differences in this excerpt? Do you think Thomas Aquinas would agree with his arguments about the "common people"? Why or why not?

## 10-6 | SAINT THOMAS AQUINAS, *Summa Theologica: Proof of the Existence of God* (1268)

Thomas Aquinas (1225–1274) was one of the foremost theologians and philosophers of the Middle Ages. Born in Sicily, he traveled widely, taught at great universities in France and Germany, and was an adviser to popes and kings. A consummate scholastic, Aquinas applied ancient philosophical principles, particularly those of Aristotle, to Christian theology. Aquinas's mode of argument was very much a product of the medieval university system, an approach to education that emphasized the mastery of established Christian and classical authorities. As you read the document, focus on the way Aquinas drew on such authorities. What role did they play in his argument? To what degree is Aquinas's argument "original"?

### Article II. Whether the Existence of God Is Demonstrable

Let us proceed to the second point. It is objected (1) that the existence of God is not demonstrable: that God's existence is an article of faith, and that articles of faith are not demonstrable, because the office of demonstration is to prove, but faith pertains (only) to things that are not to be proven, as is evident from the Epistle to the Hebrews, 11. Hence that God's existence is not demonstrable.

From Oliver J. Thatcher, ed., *The Library of Original Sources*, vol. 4: *The Early Medieval World* (Milwaukee, Wisc.: University Research Extension Co., 1907), pp. 359–363.

Again, (2) that the subject matter of demonstration is that something exists, but in the case of God we cannot know what exists, but only what does not, as Damascenus[1] says (Of the Orthodox Faith, I., 4.). Hence that we cannot demonstrate God's existence.

Again, (3) that if God's existence is to be proved it must be from what He causes, and that what He effects is not sufficient for His supposed nature, since He is infinite, but the effects finite, and the finite is not proportional to the infinite. Since, therefore, a cause cannot be proved through an effect not proportional to itself, it is said that God's existence cannot be proved.

But against this argument the apostle says (Rom. I., 20), "The unseen things of God are visible through His manifest works." But this would not be so unless it were possible to demonstrate God's existence through His works. What ought to be understood concerning anything, is first of all, whether it exists.

*Conclusion. It is possible to demonstrate God's existence, although not a priori (by pure reason), yet a posteriori[2] from some work of His more surely known to us.*

In answer I must say that the proof is double. One is through the nature of a cause and is called *propter quid*: this is through the nature of preceding events simply. The other is through the nature of the effect, and is called *quia*, and is through the nature of preceding things as respects us. Since the effect is better known to us than the cause, we proceed from the effect to the knowledge of the cause. From any effect whatsoever it can be proved that a corresponding cause exists, if only the effects of it are sufficiently known to us, for since effects depend on causes, the effect being given, it is necessary that a preceding cause exists. Whence, that God exists, although this is not itself known to us, is provable through effects that are known to us.

To the first objection above, I reply, therefore, that God's existence, and those other things of this nature that can be known through natural reason concerning God, as is said in Rom. I., are not articles of faith, but preambles to these articles. So faith presupposes natural knowledge, so grace nature, and perfection a perfectible thing. Nothing prevents a thing that is in itself demonstrable and knowable, from being accepted as an article of faith by someone that does not accept the proof of it.

To the second objection, I reply that, since the cause is proven from the effect, one must use the effect in the place of a definition of the cause in demonstrating that the cause exists; and that this applies especially in the case of God, because for proving that anything exists, it is necessary to accept in this method what the name signifies, not however that anything exists, because the question *what it is* is secondary to the question *whether it exists at all*. The characteristics of God are drawn from His works as shall be shown hereafter, (Question XIII). Whence by proving that God exists through His works as shall be shown hereafter, (Question XIII). Whence by proving that God exists through His works, we are able by this very method to see what the name God signifies.

---

[1]**Damascenus**: John of Damascus (ca. 676–749), a Christian theologian.
[2]*a priori . . . a posteriori*: *A priori* refers to knowledge gained through logic and reasoning. *A posteriori* refers to knowledge gained from facts and observation.

To the third objection, I reply that, although a perfect knowledge of the cause cannot be had from inadequate effects, yet that from any effect manifest to us it can be shown that a cause does exist, as has been said. And thus from the works of God His existence can be proved, although we cannot in this way know Him perfectly in accordance with His own essence.

## Article III. Whether God Exists

Let us proceed to the third article. It is objected (1) that God does not exist, because if one of two contradictory things is infinite, the other will be totally destroyed; that it is implied in the name God that there is a certain infinite goodness: if then God existed, no evil would be found. But evil is found in the world; therefore it is objected that God does not exist.

Again, that what can be accomplished through a less number of principles will not be accomplished through more. It is objected that all things that appear on the earth can be accounted for through other principles, without supposing that God exists, since what is natural can be traced to a natural principle, and what proceeds from a proposition can be traced to the human reason or will. Therefore that there is no necessity to suppose that God exists. But as against this note what is said of the person of God (Exod. III., 14) *I am that I am.*

*Conclusion. There must be found in the nature of things one first immovable Being, a primary cause, necessarily existing, not created; existing the most widely, good, even the best possible; the first ruler through the intellect, and the ultimate end of all things, which is God.*

I answer that it can be proved in five ways that God exists. The first and plainest is the method that proceeds from the point of view of motion. It is certain and in accord with experience, that things on earth undergo change. Now, everything that is moved is moved by something; nothing, indeed, is changed, except it is changed to something which it is in potentiality. Moreover, anything moves in accordance with something actually existing; change itself, is nothing else than to bring forth something from potentiality into actuality. Now, nothing can be brought from potentiality to actual existence except through something actually existing: thus heat in action, as fire, makes fire-wood, which is hot in potentiality, to be hot actually, and through this process, changes itself. The same thing cannot at the same time be actually and potentially the same thing, but only in regard to different things. What is actually hot cannot be at the same time potentially hot, but it is possible for it at the same time to be potentially cold. It is impossible, then, that anything should be both mover and the thing moved, in regard to the same thing and in the same way, or that it should move itself. Everything, therefore, is moved by something else. If, then, that by which it is moved, is also moved, this must be moved by something still different, and this, again, by something else. But this process cannot go on to infinity because there would not be any first mover, nor, because of this fact, anything else in motion, as the succeeding things would not move except because of what is moved by the first mover, just as a stick is not moved except through what is moved from the hand. Therefore it is necessary to go back to some first mover, which is itself moved by nothing—and this all men know as God.

The second proof is from the nature of the efficient cause. We find in our experience that there is a chain of causes: nor is it found possible for anything to be the efficient cause of itself, since it would have to exist before itself, which is impossible. Nor in the case of efficient causes can the chain go back indefinitely, because in all chains of efficient causes, the first is the cause of the middle, and these of the last, whether they be one or many. If the cause is removed, the effect is removed. Hence if there is not a first cause, there will not be a last, nor a middle. But if the chain were to go back infinitely, there would be no first cause, and thus no ultimate effect, nor middle causes, which is admittedly false. Hence we must presuppose some first efficient cause—which all call God.

The third proof is taken from the natures of the merely possible and necessary. We find that certain things either may or may not exist, since they are found to come into being and be destroyed, and in consequence potentially, either existent or non-existent. But it is impossible for all things that are of this character to exist eternally, because what *may* not exist, at length *will* not. If, then, all things were merely possible (mere accidents), eventually nothing among things would exist. If this is true, even now there would be nothing, because what does not exist, does not take its beginning except through something that does exist. If then nothing existed, it would be impossible for anything to begin, and there would now be nothing existing, which is admittedly false. Hence not all things are mere accidents, but there must be one necessarily existing being. Now every necessary thing either has a cause of its necessary existence, or has not. In the case of necessary things that have a cause for their necessary existence, the chain of causes cannot go back infinitely, just as not in the case of efficient causes, as proved. Hence there must be presupposed something necessarily existing through its own nature, not having a cause elsewhere but being itself the cause of the necessary existence of other things—which all call God.

The fourth proof arises from the degrees that are found in things. For there is found a greater and a less degree of goodness, truth, nobility, and the like. But more or less are terms spoken of various things as they approach in diverse ways toward something that is the greatest, just as in the case of hotter (more hot) which approaches nearer the greatest heat. There exists therefore something that is the truest, and best, and most noble, and in consequence, the greatest being. For what are the greatest truths are the greatest beings, as is said in the Metaphysics Bk. II. 2. What moreover is the greatest in its way, in another way is the cause of all things of its own kind (or genus); thus fire, which is the greatest heat, is the cause of all heat, as is said in the same book (cf. Plato and Aristotle). Therefore there exists something that is the cause of the existence of all things and of the goodness and of every perfection whatsoever—and this we call God.

The fifth proof arises from the ordering of things for we see that some things which lack reason, such as natural bodies, are operated in accordance with a plan. It appears from this that they are operated always or the more frequently in this same way the closer they follow what is the Highest; whence it is clear that they do not arrive at the result by chance but because of a purpose. The things, moreover, that do not have intelligence do not tend toward a result unless directed by some one knowing and intelligent; just as an arrow is sent by an archer. Therefore there is something intelligent by which all natural things are arranged in accordance with a plan—and this we call God.

In response to the first objection, then, I reply what Augustine says; that since God is entirely good, He would permit evil to exist in His works only if He were so good and omnipotent that He might bring forth good even from the evil. It therefore pertains to the infinite goodness of God that he permits evil to exist and from this brings forth good.

My reply to the second objection is that since nature is ordered in accordance with some defined purpose by the direction of some superior agent, those things that spring from nature must be dependent upon God, just as upon a first cause. Likewise, what springs from a proposition must be traceable to some higher cause which is not the human reason or will, because this is changeable and defective and everything changeable and liable to non-existence is dependent upon some unchangeable first principle that is necessarily self-existent as has been shown.

### READING QUESTIONS

1. According to Aquinas, what objections might one have to the idea of the existence of God?

2. What are the five proofs, summarized in your own words?

3. Compare Aquinas with Aristotle (Document 3-6). What is similar about their work?

4. What importance should we attach to the fact that Aquinas used both classical and Christian authorities to support his argument?

## 10-7 | An Author Relates a Popular Religious Story

### JACQUES DE VITRY, *The Virgin Mary Saves a Monk and His Lover* (ca. 1200)

Ordinary medieval people were not passive participants in their religion. Their engagement with Christianity was not limited to kneeling mute and uncomprehending in church as a priest intoned the prescribed Latin words and phrases. Rather, medieval Christianity was an integral part of daily experience—something ordinary people helped shape, even as it influenced almost every aspect of their lives. The story of the Virgin Mary's intercession

From Dana Carleton Munro, ed., *Translations and Reprints from the Original Sources of European History*, vol. 2, series 4 (Philadelphia: History Department of the University of Pennsylvania, 1897), pp. 2–4.

on behalf of a monk and his lover, as told by the priest and scholar Jacques de Vitry (ca. 1160/70–1240), provides a sense of medieval popular religion. As you read it, think about the moral of the story. What attitudes and beliefs might de Vitry have hoped to inspire in his audience?

A certain very religious man told me that this happened in a place where he had been staying. A virtuous and pious matron came frequently to the church and served God most devoutly, day and night. Also a certain monk, the guardian and treasurer of the monastery, had a great reputation for piety, and truly he was devout. When, however, the two frequently conversed together in the church concerning religious matters, the devil, envying their virtue and reputation, tempted them very sorely, so that the spiritual love was changed to carnal. Accordingly they made an agreement and fixed upon a night in which the monk was to leave his monastery, taking the treasures of the church, and the matron was to leave her home, with a sum of money which she should secretly steal from her husband.

After they had fled, the monks on rising in the morning, saw that the receptacles were broken and the treasures of the church stolen; and not finding the monk, they quickly pursued him. Likewise the husband of the said woman, seeing his chest open and the money gone, pursued his wife. Overtaking the monk and the woman with the treasure and money, they brought them back and threw them into prison. Moreover so great was the scandal throughout the whole country and so much were all religious persons reviled that the damage from the infamy and scandal was far greater than from the sin itself.

Then the monk restored to his senses, began with many tears to pray to the blessed Virgin, whom from infancy he had always served, and never before had any such misfortune happened to him. Likewise the said matron began urgently to implore the aid of the blessed Virgin whom, constantly, day and night, she was accustomed to salute and to kneel in prayer before her image. At length, the blessed Virgin very irate, appeared and after she had upbraided them severely, she said, "I am able to obtain the remission of your sins from my son, but what can I do about such an awful scandal? For you have so befouled the name of religious persons before all the people, that in the future no one will trust them. This is an almost irremediable damage."

Nevertheless the pious Virgin, overcome by their prayers, summoned the demons, who had caused the deed, and enjoined upon them that, as they had caused the scandal to religion, they must bring the infamy to an end. Since, indeed, they were not able to resist her commands, after much anxiety and various conferences they found a way to remove the infamy. In the night they placed the monk in his church and repairing the broken receptacle as it was before, they placed the treasure in it. Also they closed and locked the chest which the matron had opened and replaced the money in it. And they set the woman in her room and in the place where she was accustomed to pray by night.

When, moreover, the monks found the treasure of their house and the monk, who was praying to God just as he had been accustomed to do; and the husband saw his wife and the treasure; and they found the money just as it had been before, they became stupefied and wondered. Rushing to the prison they saw the monk and the woman in fetters just as they had left them. For one of the demons was seen by them transformed into the likeness of a monk and another into the likeness of a woman. When all in the whole city had come together to see the miracle, the demons said in the hearing of all, "Let us go, for sufficiently have we deluded these people and caused them to think evil of religious persons." And, saying this, they suddenly disappeared. Moreover all threw themselves at the feet of the monk and of the woman and demanded pardon.

Behold how great infamy and scandal and how inestimable damage the devil would have wrought against religious persons, if the blessed Virgin had not aided them.

### READING QUESTIONS

1. What role did the Devil play in the story? What does this suggest about medieval ideas concerning sin and the Devil?

2. How did the Virgin Mary respond to the monk and the matron's prayers for help? What powers did she use to resolve the situation?

3. How did the Virgin Mary's actions reinforce the piety of the community at large?

4. What was the moral of the story?

## ▪ COMPARATIVE AND DISCUSSION QUESTIONS ▪

1. Compare and contrast the status of unfree persons as illustrated in the first two documents. What light do the documents shed on differences in wealth and status within Europe's unfree population?

2. How did town officials seek to shape the communities they governed and the relationship between those communities and the outside world?

3. What light do the *Summa Theologica* and the story of the Virgin Mary, the monk, and his lover shed on the nature of medieval Christianity? What do they, along with Ibn Rushd's *Religion and Philosophy*, tell you about the diversity of religious experience in the Middle Ages?

# 11

# The Later Middle Ages
## 1300–1450

Calamity followed calamity over the course of the fourteenth century. The High Middle Ages had been a period of slow but sustained population growth. That trend began to reverse itself at the beginning of the fourteenth century, when Europe's climate took a turn for the worse. As Europe grew colder and wetter, crop yields fell and famine followed. Thus, Europe's population was already weakened by malnutrition when plague struck in 1347, introduced into Europe through the same trade routes that had fueled the prosperity of the previous century. In the wake of the plague, peasant uprisings were frequent, as were uprisings of the urban poor. Between 1337 and 1453, the Hundred Years' War—in actuality a series of wars and civil wars—wreaked havoc on France. Finally, the papacy experienced a period of sharp decline in prestige and power, as the political rivalries of secular rulers led to schism within the church. The documents included in this chapter examine these catastrophes and their consequences. As you read the documents, think about the impact of war, disease, and religious strife on medieval social, religious, and political institutions. What changes in European society were made possible by the destruction of the fourteenth century?

## 11-1 | The Psychological and Emotional Impact of the Plague
### GIOVANNI BOCCACCIO, *The Decameron: The Plague Hits Florence* (ca. 1350)

The first wave of the Black Death began in the late 1340s. The disease spread rapidly, and contemporaries understood very little about it, although they did associate it with rats. The only effective countermeasures were quarantine and isolation. The infection, which

---

From *The Decameron, or Ten Days' Entertainment of Boccaccio* (Chicago: Stewart & Kidd Company, 1920), pp. xix–xxii.

spread along trade routes from Central Asia, killed some 75 million people. Even after the first incidence receded, plague returned to Europe in many subsequent outbreaks until the 1700s, with varying mortality rates. In this document, excerpted from his famous collection of novellas, the Italian writer Giovanni Boccaccio (JEE-oh-VAH-nee buh-CAH-chee-oh) details the chaos unleashed in Florence as a result of the plague.

In the year then of our Lord 1348, there happened at Florence, the finest city in all Italy, a most terrible plague; which, whether owing to the influence of the planets, or that it was sent from God as a just punishment for our sins, had broken out some years before in the Levant;[1] and after passing from place to place, and making incredible havoc all the way, had now reached the west; where, in spite of all the means that art and human foresight could suggest, such as keeping the city clear from filth, and excluding all suspected persons, notwithstanding frequent consultations what else was to be done; nor omitting prayers to God in frequent processions: in the spring of the forgoing year, it began to show itself in a sad and wonderful[2] manner; and, different from what it had been in the east, where bleeding from the nose is the fatal prognostic, here there appeared certain tumors in the groin, or under the armpits, some as big as a small apple, others as an egg; and afterwards purple spots in most parts of the body; in some cases large and but few in number, in others smaller and more numerous, both sorts the usual messengers of death. . . .

These accidents, and others of the like sort, occasioned various fears and devices amongst those people who survived, all tending to the same uncharitable and cruel end; which was to avoid the sick, and everything that had been near them, expecting by that means to save themselves. And some holding it best to live temperately, and to avoid excesses of all kinds, made parties, and shut themselves up from the rest of the world; eating and drinking moderately of the best, and diverting themselves with music, and such other entertainments as they might have within doors; never listening to anything from without, to make them uneasy. Others maintained free living to be a better preservative, and would balk no passion or appetite they wished to gratify, drinking and revelling incessantly from tavern to tavern, or in private houses; which were frequently found deserted by the owners, and therefore common to every one, yet avoiding, with all this irregularity, to come near the infected. And such at that time was the public distress, that the laws, human and divine, were not regarded; for the officers, to put them in force, being either dead, sick, or in want of persons to assist them, every one did just as he pleased. A third sort of people chose a method between these two: not confining themselves to rules of diet like the former, and yet avoiding the intemperance of the latter; but eating and drinking what their appetites required, they walked everywhere with odors and nosegays[3] to smell to; as holding it best to corroborate the brain: for they supposed the

---

[1]**the Levant**: The eastern Mediterranean.
[2]**wonderful**: Astonishing.
[3]**odors and nosegays**: Perfumes and small bunches of flowers.

whole atmosphere to be tainted with the stink of dead bodies, arising partly from the distemper itself, and partly from the fermenting of the medicines within them. Others of a more cruel disposition, as perhaps the more safe to themselves, declared that the only remedy was to avoid it: persuaded, therefore, of this, and taking care for themselves only, men and women in great numbers left the city, their houses, relations, and effects, and fled into the country; as if the wrath of God had been restrained to visit those only within the walls of the city. . . . I pass over the little regard that citizens and relations showed to each other; for their terror was such that a brother even fled from his brother, a wife from her husband, and, what is more uncommon, a parent from its own child.

### READING QUESTIONS

1. According to this account, how did civil order break down during the plague?

2. How does the narrator try to explain why the plague happened?

3. What are some of the things people thought might save them from the plague?

## 11-2 | A Town Chronicler Describes the Black Death
### AGNOLO DI TURA, *Sienese Chronicle* (1348–1351)

Densely populated and closely connected to the Mediterranean trade routes that brought the plague to Europe, Italian cities were among the hardest hit communities. Agnolo di Tura was the town chronicler for the Tuscan town of Siena when the Black Death struck in the spring of 1348. According to di Tura, more people died in Siena in the first few months following the arrival of plague than had died in the previous twenty years. As you read his account of the devastation, reflect on the impact of the plague on the town's ability to function. With more than half the population wiped out, how did the Sienese community keep from falling into anarchy?

The mortality, which was a thing horrible and cruel, began in Siena in the month of May [1348]. I do not know from where came this cruelty or these pitiless ways, which were painful to see and stupefied everyone. There are not words to describe how horrible these events have been and, in fact, whoever can say that they have not lived in utterly horrid conditions can truly consider themselves lucky. The infected die almost immediately. They swell beneath the armpits and in the groin, and fall over while talking. Fathers abandon their sons, wives their husbands, and one brother the other. In the end, everyone escapes and abandons anyone who might be infected. Moreover, it appears that this plague can be communicated through bad breath and even by just seeing one of the infected.

---

From John Aberth, *The Black Death: The Great Mortality of 1348–1350: A Brief History with Documents* (Boston: Bedford/St. Martin's, 2005), pp. 81–82.

In these ways, they die and no one can be found who would want to bury them, not even for money or in the name of friendship. Those who get infected in their own house, they remove them the best way they can and they bury them without the supervision of a priest. No one controls anything and they do not even ring the church bells anymore. Throughout Siena, giant pits are being excavated for the multitudes of the dead and the hundreds that die every night. The bodies are thrown into these mass graves and are covered bit by bit. When those ditches are full, new ditches are dug. So many have died that new pits have to be made every day.

And I, Agnolo di Tura, called the Fat, have buried five of my sons with my own hands. Yet still I do not steal from those who were poorly buried like the dogs that eat them and litter them about the city. There is no one who weeps for any of the dead, for instead everyone awaits their own impending death. So many have died that everyone believes it is the end of the world. Medicine and other cures do not work. In fact, the more medicine people are given the quicker they die. The leaders of the city have elected three citizens that have been given 1,000 florins for the expense of taking care of the homeless and for burying them. These conditions have been so horrible that I do not reflect as often as I used to about the situation. I have thought so much about these events that I cannot tell the stories any longer. This is how the people lived until September [1348], and it would be too much for me to write the whole story. One would find that in this period of time more people died than in twenty years or more. In Siena alone, 36,000 people have died. If you count the elderly and others, the number could be 52,000 in total. In all of the boroughs, the number could be as high as 30,000 more. So it can be seen that in total the death toll may be as high as 80,000. There are only about 10,000 people left in the city and those that live on are hopeless and in utter despair. They leave their homes and other things. Gold, silver, and copper lay scattered about. In the countryside, even more died, so many that farms and agricultural lands are left without people to work them. I cannot write about the cruelties that existed in the countryside: that wolves and other wild beasts eat the improperly buried and other horrors that are too difficult for anyone who would read this account. . . .

The city of Siena appeared uninhabited because almost no one was found there. The pestilence remained and everyone who survived celebrated his or her fate. Of the monks, priests, nuns, women, and others from the secular community, they didn't worry about their expenses or games. Everyone appeared to be rich because they had survived and regained value in life. Now, no one knows how to put their life back in order.

### READING QUESTIONS

1. How would you characterize di Tura's reaction to the plague?

2. What explanation, if any, did di Tura offer for the terrible events he described?

3. What signs of social breakdown did he note? What do they suggest about the full impact of the plague on late medieval life?

## 11-3 | Social and Economic Unrest in England

### *The Anonimalle Chronicle: The English Peasants' Revolt* (1381)

Agricultural labor was traditionally carried out by serfs, who were bound by tradition to fulfill their obligations to their lords. The high mortality rate of the plague, however, resulted in a labor shortage across Europe. Some peasants tried to act on this advantage and force the lords to end their serfdom. When their demands were not satisfied, peasants often rose up against their lords. In England in 1381, an unpopular tax on all adult males prompted thousands of peasants to revolt. As you read this account of the revolt, pay particular attention to the targets of the peasants' anger. What distinction did the rebels make between the nobility and the king?

And on that Thursday, the said feast of Corpus Christi, the King, being in the Tower [of London] very sad and sorry, mounted up into a little turret towards St. Catherine's, where were lying a great number of the commons, and had proclamation made to them that they all should go peaceably to their homes, and he would pardon them all manner of their trespasses. But all cried with one voice that they would not go before they had captured the traitors who lay in the Tower, nor until they had got charters to free them from all manner of serfdom, and had got certain other points which they wished to demand. And the King benevolently granted all, and made a clerk write a bill in their presence in these terms: "Richard, King of England and France, gives great thanks to his good commons, for that they have so great a desire to see and to keep their king, and grants them pardon for all manner of trespasses and misprisions and felonies done up to this hour, and wills and commands that every one should now return to his own home, and wills and commands that each should put his grievances in writing, and have them sent to him; and he will provide, with the aid of his loyal lords and his good council, such remedy as shall be profitable both to him and to them, and to all the kingdom." On this document he sealed his signet in presence of them all, and sent out the said bill by the hands of two of his knights to the folks before St. Catherine's. And he caused it to be read to them, and the knight who read it stood up on an old chair before the others so that all could hear. All this time the King was in the Tower in great distress of mind. And when the commons had heard the Bill, they said that this was nothing but trifles and mockery. Therefore they returned to London and had it cried around the City that all lawyers, and all the clerks of the Chancery and the Exchequer and every man who could write a brief or a letter should be beheaded, whenever they could be found. At this time they burnt several more houses in the City, and the King himself ascended to a high garret of the Tower and watched the fires. Then he came down again, and sent for the lords to have

From Charles Oman, *The Great Revolt of 1381* (Oxford: Clarendon Press, 1906), pp. 196–203.

their counsel, but they knew not how they should counsel him, and all were wondrous abashed. . . .

And by seven o'clock the King [went to meet the peasants]. And when he was come the commons all knelt down to him, saying "Welcome our Lord King Richard, if it pleases you, and we will not have any other king but you." And Wat Tighler [Wat Tyler], their leader and chief, prayed in the name of the commons that he would suffer them to take and deal with all the traitors against him and the law, and the King granted that they should have at their disposition all who were traitors, and could be proved to be traitors by process of law. The said Walter and the commons were carrying two banners, and many pennons and pennoncels,[1] while they made their petition to the King. And they required that for the future no man should be in serfdom, nor make any manner of homage or suit to any lord, but should give a rent of 4d. an acre for his land. They asked also that no one should serve any man except by his own good will, and on terms of regular covenant.

And at this time the King made the commons draw themselves out in two lines, and proclaimed to them that he would confirm and grant it that they should be free, and generally should have their will, and that they might go through all the realm of England and catch all traitors and bring them to him in safety, and then he would deal with them as the law demanded.

[Meanwhile, fighting between the nobles and peasants continues, and many lords lose their heads to the commoners.]

And when he was summoned, . . . Wat Tighler of Maidstone, he came to the King with great confidence, mounted on a little horse, that the commons might see him. And he dismounted, holding in his hand a dagger which he had taken from another man, and when he had dismounted he half bent his knee, and then took the King by the hand, and shook his arm forcibly and roughly, saying to him, "Brother, be of good comfort and joyful, for you shall have, in the fortnight that is to come, praise from the commons even more than you have yet had, and we shall be good companions." And the King said to Walter, "Why will you not go back to your own country?" But the other answered, with a great oath, that neither he nor his fellows would depart until they had got their charter such as they wished to have it, and had certain points rehearsed, and added to their charter which they wished to demand. And he said in a threatening fashion that the lords of the realm would rue it bitterly if these points were not settled to their pleasure. Then the King asked him what were the points which he wished to have

---

[1]**pennons and pennoncels:** Small banners attached to lances.

revised, and he should have them freely, without contradiction, written out and sealed. Thereupon the said Walter rehearsed the points which were to be demanded; and he asked that . . . there should be equality among all people save only the King, and that the goods of Holy Church should not remain in the hands of the religious, nor of parsons and vicars, and other churchmen; but that clergy already in possession should have a sufficient sustenance from the endowments, and the rest of the goods should be divided among the people of the parish.

[The king agrees to these terms, and after he leaves, the mayor of London captures Wat Tyler and kills him.]

### READING QUESTIONS

1. Who did the peasants blame for their troubles? Why?
2. What demands did the peasants make? What do these demands reveal about their social and political beliefs?
3. Is it plausible that the mayor of London would have Wat Tyler killed without the king's consent? What does this tell you about the king's true attitude toward the rebellion?

## 11-4 | Popular Religious Responses to the Plague
### *Flagellants in the Netherlands Town of Tournai* (1349)

Because European people and institutions were not equipped to prevent or treat the plague of the fourteenth century, and the Catholic Church itself could offer little solace or assistance to commoners, many people took matters into their own hands and attempted to do penance for the perceived sins of humanity by ritually whipping themselves to seek God's forgiveness. This extreme form of popular religion was memorialized in some of the artwork of the period, including this mid-fourteenth-century piece from the Netherlands.

Ann Ronan Pictures/Print Collector/Hulton Archive/Getty Images.

### READING QUESTIONS

1.  How did the flagellants' mode of dress aid their message and mission as they traveled around?

2.  What were the broad social consequences of this expression of popular religion for Catholics and people of other faiths? How did the flagellants' actions challenge traditional power structures and institutions in Europe, and how did the Catholic Church respond to their movement?

### SOURCES IN CONVERSATION

# Women and Power

Power politics in the late Middle Ages was a man's game. The medieval vision of government and society was profoundly patriarchal, and assumptions of male superiority shaped almost every aspect of medieval life. There were, however, women who were exceptions to the rule. For the most part, such women enjoyed the advantages of wealth and status. Less common were women, such as Catherine of Siena (1347–1380) and

Joan of Arc (ca. 1412–1431), who gained power through their reputation for holiness. Catherine, a nun of humble background who claimed to have experienced mystical visions, was an important participant in the religious and political debates of her day. Joan of Arc, a young woman from a small farming community, convinced many of France's leaders that God had chosen her to guide the French to victory in the Hundred Years' War.

### READ AND COMPARE

1. What made it possible for these two women to play such powerful roles?
2. What precedents helped legitimize their actions in male-dominated arenas?
3. What made their claims to divine authority more dangerous than they would have been for men?

## 11-5 | CATHERINE OF SIENA, *Letter to Gregory XI* (1372)

In the early 1300s, the papacy moved its capital to Avignon, inside French territory. Because the pope was the bishop of Rome, it seemed wrong to move the head of the church away from his rightful home—and to a place where he could be easily influenced by the French king. Many people blamed the Avignon papacy for the plague and warfare across Europe. Still more linked the Avignon papacy to a general decline in the reputation and prestige of the church. In the 1370s, Catherine joined the effort to persuade Pope Gregory XI to return to Rome. As you read her letter to the pope, consider how her gender and spiritual reputation might have influenced the pope's reaction to her message.

Alas, what confusion is this, to see those who ought to be a mirror of voluntary poverty, meek as lambs, distributing the possessions of Holy Church to the poor: and they appear in such luxury and state and pomp and worldly vanity, more than if they had turned them to the world a thousand times! Nay, many seculars put them to shame who live a good and holy life. . . . For ever since [the Church] has aimed more at temporal than at spiritual, things have gone from bad to worse. See therefore that God, in judgment, has allowed much persecution and tribulation to befall her. But comfort you, father, and fear not for anything that could happen, which God does to make her state perfect once more, in order that lambs may feed in that garden, and not wolves who devour the honor that should belong to God, which they steal and give to themselves. Comfort you in Christ sweet Jesus; for I hope that His aid will be near you, plenitude[1] of divine grace, aid and support divine in the way that I said before. Out of war you will attain greatest peace; out of persecution, greatest unity; not by human power, but by holy virtue, you will discomfit those visible demons, wicked men, and those invisible demons who never sleep around us.

From Vida D. Scudder, trans. and ed., *Catherine of Siena as Seen in Her Lives and Letters* (London: J. M. Dent, 1906), pp. 131–132.

[1]**plenitude**: Full supply.

But reflect, sweet father, that you could not do this easily unless you accomplished the other two things which precede the completion of the other: that is, your return to Rome and uplifting of the standard of the most holy Cross. Let not your holy desire fail on account of any scandal or rebellion of cities which you might see or hear; nay, let the flame of holy desire be more kindled to wish to do swiftly. Do not delay, then, your coming.

### READING QUESTIONS

1. What did Catherine want the pope to do, and why did she want him to do it?

2. According to Catherine, what happened to the church when the pope left Rome for Avignon?

3. What authority did Catherine have to make demands of the pope? How would you explain her prominence in the effort to persuade the pope to return to Rome?

## 11-6 | *The Debate over Joan of Arc's Clothes* (1429)

The public debate over Joan of Arc's status began almost as soon as she presented herself to the French court. Even after Joan had been accepted by the dauphin and joined the French in battle, supporters and opponents clashed over her claims to divine inspiration. In the spring of 1429, one of Joan's supporters circulated a treatise entitled *De mirabili victoria*. Later that same year, an anonymous member of the University of Paris countered with *De bono et malo spiritu*. One important point of contention between the two authors was Joan's decision to wear men's clothing. As you read the excerpts from these treatises, think about how female models and stereotypes shaped each author's argument.

### *De mirabili victoria*

Here follow three truths in justification of the wearing of male clothing by the Pucelle,[1] chosen while following her sheep.

I. The old law [of the Old Testament], prohibiting the woman from using the clothing of a man and the man from the clothing of a woman [Deuteronomy 22: 5], is purely judicial and does not carry any obligation under the new law [of the New Testament]. [This is] because it is a constant and necessary truth for salvation that the judicial precepts of the ancient law [Old Testament] are quashed and, as such, do not bind the new one, unless they have been instituted again and confirmed by superiors.

---

From Craig Taylor, trans. and ed., *Joan of Arc: La Pucelle* (Manchester, U.K.: Manchester University Press, 2006), pp. 82–83, 125–127.

[1]**the Pucelle**: The maid.

II. This law [of the Old Testament] included a moral dimension that must remain in all law. It can be expressed as a prohibition on indecent clothing both for the man and for the woman, [as this is] contrary to the requirement of virtue. This should affect all circumstances bound by law, so that the wise person will judge when, where, to whom and how it is appropriate, and in this way the rest. This [law of the Old Testament] on these things is not confined to that one situation.

III. This law [of the Old Testament], whether judicial or moral, does not condemn the wearing of the clothing of a man and a warrior by our Pucelle, manly and a warrior, whom God in heaven has chosen through certain signs as his standard-bearer for those fighting the enemies of justice and to raise up his friends, so that he might overthrow by the hand of a woman, a young girl [*puellaris*] and a virgin, the powerful weapons of iniquity, with the help of the angels. By her virginity, she is loved and known, according to St. Jerome; and this frequently appears in the histories of saints, such as Cecilia,[2] visibly with a crown of roses and lilies. On the other hand, through this she is safeguarded from the [consequences of the] cutting of her hair, which the Apostle prohibits from being seen on a woman.

Therefore may the iniquitious [*sic*] talk be put to an end and cease. For, when divine virtue operates, it establishes the means according to its aim; hence, it is not safe to disparage or to find fault, out of rash bravado, with those things which are from God, according to the Apostle.

Finally many details and examples from sacred and secular history could be added; for example those of Camilla and the Amazons,[3] and moreover in cases either of necessity or evident utility, or where approved by custom, or by the authority and dispensation of superiors. But these are sufficient for brevity and for the truth. The party having just cause should be on close guard unless, through disbelief and ingratitude, or some injustices, they might render the divine help useless, that has begun so patiently and miraculously; just as [happened] for Moses and the sons of Israel, after having received such divine promises, as we read contained [in the Scriptures]. For even if God does not change His advice, He does change his opinion according to what people deserve.

## De bono et malo spiritu

Regarding the preceding, I mean to deduce from canon law a small number of issues, in praise of all-mighty God, and in exaltation of the holy catholic faith.

And first, we have a duty to adhere firmly to the catholic faith, following the chapter Firmiter of the title *De Summa Trinitate*, without giving in any manner our approval to superstitious innovations, seeing that they engender discords, as one reads in the chapter Cum consuetudinis of the title *De consuetudine*.

Item, to give his support so easily to a young girl that was not known, without the support of a miracle or on the testimony of the holy scriptures, is to undermine this truth and this unchanging force of the catholic faith: wise men and canonists would not have any doubt about this. The proof is in the chapter Cum ex injuncto of the title *De hæreticis*.

---

[2]**Cecilia**: Catholic saint, martyred by the Romans in the second century C.E.
[3]**Camilla and the Amazons**: Examples of female warriors from classical mythology.

Item, if those who approve of the matter of this Pucelle say that she has been sent by God in an invisible, and in some sense inspired way, and that such an invisible mission is much more worthy than a visible mission, just as a divine mission is more worthy than a human mission, it is reasonable to reply to them that as this entirely inner mission escapes observation, it is not enough that someone claims purely and simply to be sent from God — this is the claim of all heretics — but it is necessary that he proves this invisible mission to us through a miraculous work or by a precise testimony drawn from the holy scripture. All this is demonstrated in the chapter cited above, Cum ex injuncto.

Item, as this Pucelle has not proved in any of these ways that she has been sent from God, there is no room to believe in her on her word, but there is room to proceed against her as if suspected of heresy.

Added to this, if she has really been sent from God, she would not take clothing prohibited by God and forbidden for women by canon law under penalty of anathema, according to the chapter Si qua mulier. . . .

Moreover, in the case where those who let themselves be deceived by this Pucelle attempt to excuse and to justify her clothing in consideration of the matter for which she was supposedly sent, such niceties are useless; these are rather those excuses of which the Psalmist speaks, that one searches for to excuse sins (Psalm 140: 4), and they accuse more than they excuse, as it says in chapter Quanto of the title *De consuetudine*. In this case, one might do lots of evil things under the appearance of good. And yet it is necessary to refrain not only from evil, but from all appearance of evil, as one reads in the chapter Cum ab omni of the title *De vita et honestate clericorum*.

Item, if a women [*sic*] could put on male clothing as she liked with impunity, women would have unrestrained opportunities to fornicate and to practice manly acts which are legally forbidden for them according to doctrine, etc., [as this is] against the canonical teaching contained in the chapter Nova quædam of the title *De pœnitentiis et remissionibus*.

Item, in general, all masculine duties are forbidden to women, for example, to preach, to teach, to bear arms, to absolve, to excommunicate, etc., as one sees in that chapter Nova quædam and in the Digest, in the [second] law of the title *De regulis juris*.

### READING QUESTIONS

1. On what grounds did the author of *De mirabili victoria* support Joan's insistence on wearing men's clothing?

2. Why did the author of *De bono et malo spiritu* believe that Joan's clothes supported his position that she was, in all likelihood, a heretic?

3. What do these treatises tell you about late medieval ideas about women's nature and their proper role in society?

■ **COMPARATIVE AND DISCUSSION QUESTIONS** ■

1. Consider the account of the English Peasants' Revolt and *Flagellants in the Netherlands Town of Tournai*. What light do they shed on disruption and challenges to institutions in late medieval Europe, as well as the eventual outcomes of those challenges?

2. What do the writings of Boccaccio and di Tura reveal about the range of reactions to the devastation produced by the Black Death?

3. What do Catherine and Joan have in common? What kind of power did they have, and how did they use it?

# 12

# European Society in the Age of the Renaissance
## 1350–1550

The Renaissance began in the Italian city-states in the fourteenth century and spread throughout Europe. Renaissance scholars, artists, and philosophers articulated a new vision of human possibility inspired by the classical past. Standing on the shoulders of the giants of Greco-Roman culture, they believed that their own society could match, or even exceed, the achievements of their ancestors. The commercial and political dynamism of the Italian city-states played a key role in fostering the Renaissance. Italian cities were primary beneficiaries of the commercial revival of the High Middle Ages, and competition, both within and between cities, spurred individuals and communities to pour their resources into cultural activity. Competition between city-states had a darker side, however, and often escalated into conflict; endemic warfare left Italy weak and divided. As you explore the sources, consider what the Renaissance meant to these authors and artists. How would they describe the movement in which they were participants? What hopes and fears did they have for their own society?

## 12-1 | An Italian Admirer of the Classical Past
### PETRARCH, *Letter to Livy* (1350)

Around 1350, Italian scholar and poet Francesco Petrarca, or Petrarch (1304–1374), proposed a new kind of education that centered on the study and emulation of the works of ancient Roman authors. In his view, this program would produce a generation

---

From Marco Emilio Cosenza, trans., *Petrarch's Letters to Classical Authors* (Chicago: University of Chicago Press, 1910), pp. 100–103.

of young men capable of achievements unmatched in Europe for a thousand years. Petrarch and his followers came to be known as humanists, and their intellectual agenda had a profound influence on the art and ideas of their age. We can sense the intensity of Petrarch's regard for classical culture in a letter addressed to the ancient Roman historian Livy. As you read it, consider what it tells you about the aspirations of Petrarch and his fellow humanists.

I should wish (if it were permitted from on high) either that I had been born in thine age or thou in ours; in the latter case our age itself, and in the former I personally should have been the better for it. I should surely have been one of those pilgrims who visited thee. For the sake of seeing thee I should have gone not merely to Rome, but indeed, from either Gaul or Spain I should have found my way to thee as far as India. . . . We know that thou didst write one hundred and forty-two books on Roman affairs. With what fervor, with what unflagging zeal must thou have labored; and of that entire number there are now extant scarcely thirty. . . . It is over these small remains that I toil whenever I wish to forget these regions, these times, and these customs. Often I am filled with bitter indignation against the morals of today, when men value nothing except gold and silver, and desire nothing except sensual, physical pleasures. If these are to be considered the goal of mankind, then not only the dumb beasts of the field, but even insensible and inert matter has a richer, a higher goal than that proposed to itself by thinking man. But of this elsewhere.

It is now fitter that I should render thee thanks, for many reasons indeed, but for this in especial: that thou didst so frequently cause me to forget the present evils, and transfer me to happier times. . . .

Pray greet in my behalf thy predecessors Polybius and Quintus Claudius and Valerius Antias, and all those whose glory thine own greater light has dimmed; and of the later historians, give greeting to Pliny the Younger, of Verona, a neighbor of thine, and also to thy former rival Crispus Sallustius. . . . Farewell forever, thou matchless historian!

*Written in the land of the living, in that part of Italy and in that city in which I am now living and where thou were once born and buried, . . . and in view of thy very tombstone; on the twenty-second of February, in the thirteen hundred and fiftieth year from the birth of Him whom thou wouldst have seen, or of whose birth thou couldst have heard, hadst thou lived a little longer.*

### READING QUESTIONS

1. Why did Petrarch admire Livy?
2. What implicit contrast did Petrarch draw between Livy's time and his own?
3. In what ways does Petrarch's wish to bring Livy into his world encapsulate the humanist program?

## 12-2 | Power Politics During the Italian Renaissance
### NICCOLÒ MACHIAVELLI, *The Prince* (1513)

Niccolò Machiavelli (nee-koh-LOH mah-key-ah-VEL-ee) (1469–1527) was a political philosopher and diplomat who had represented the Italian republic of Florence on numerous diplomatic missions. In 1512, when the powerful Medici family regained control of Florence, the anti-Medici Machiavelli was arrested and tortured. In 1513, he wrote *The Prince*, a guide to gaining and consolidating political power, and dedicated it to Lorenzo de Medici, perhaps as a way to curry favor with the new rulers. The cynicism of *The Prince* stands in stark contrast to the idealism exhibited in the excerpt from Petrarch included in this chapter. Here, Machiavelli argues that a willingness to engage in deception and violence is critical to a ruler's success.

Every one understands how praiseworthy it is in a prince to keep faith, and to live uprightly and not craftily. Nevertheless we see, from what has taken place in our own days, that princes who have set little store by their word, but have known how to overreach men by their cunning, have accomplished great things, and in the end got the better of those who trusted to honest dealing.

Be it known, then, that there are two ways of contending,—one in accordance with the laws, the other by force; the first of which is proper to men, the second to beasts. But since the first method is often ineffectual, it becomes necessary to resort to the second. A prince should, therefore, understand how to use well both the man and the beast. . . . But inasmuch as a prince should know how to use the beast's nature wisely, he ought of beasts to choose both the lion and the fox; for the lion cannot guard himself from the toils, nor the fox from wolves. He must therefore be a fox to discern toils, and a lion to drive off wolves.

To rely wholly on the lion is unwise; and for this reason a prudent prince neither can nor ought to keep his word when to keep it is hurtful to him and the causes which led him to pledge it are removed. If all men were good, this would not be good advice, but since they are dishonest and do not keep faith with you, you in return need not keep faith with them; and no prince was ever at a loss for plausible reasons to cloak a breach of faith. Of this numberless recent instances could be given, and it might be shown how many solemn treaties and engagements have been rendered inoperative and idle through want of faith among princes, and that he who has best known how to play the fox has had the best success.

It is necessary, indeed, to put a good color on this nature, and to be skilled in simulating and dissembling. But men are so simple, and governed so absolutely by their present needs, that he who wishes to deceive will never fail in finding willing dupes. One recent example I will not omit. Pope Alexander VI had no care or thought but how to deceive, and always found material to work on.

---

From Niccolò Machiavelli, *The Prince*, trans. N. H. Thomson, in James Harvey Robinson, ed., *Readings in European History*, vol. 2 (Boston: Ginn, 1906), pp. 10–13.

No man ever had a more effective manner of asseverating, or made promises with more solemn protestations, or observed them less. And yet, because he understood this side of human nature, his frauds always succeeded. . . .

In his efforts to aggrandize his son the duke [Cesare Borgia], Alexander VI had to face many difficulties, both immediate and remote. In the first place, he saw no way to make him ruler of any state which did not belong to the Church. Yet, if he sought to take for him a state of the Church, he knew that the duke of Milan and the Venetians would withhold their consent, Faenza and Rimini [towns in the province of Romagna] being already under the protection of the latter. Further, he saw that the forces of Italy, and those more especially of which he might have availed himself, were in the hands of men who had reason to fear his aggrandizement, — that is, of the Orsini, the Colonnesi [Roman noble families] and their followers. These, therefore, he could not trust. . . .

And since this part of his [Cesare Borgia's] conduct merits both attention and imitation, I shall not pass it over in silence. After the duke had taken Romagna, finding that it had been ruled by feeble lords, who thought more of plundering than of governing their subjects, — which gave them more cause for division than for union, so that the country was overrun with robbery, tumult, and every kind of outrage, — he judged it necessary, with a view to rendering it peaceful, and obedient to his authority, to provide it with a good government. Accordingly he set over it Messer Remiro d'Orco, a stern and prompt ruler, who, being entrusted with the fullest powers, in a very short time, and with much credit to himself, restored it to tranquility and order. But afterwards the duke, apprehending that such unlimited authority might become odious, decided that it was no longer needed, and established [at] the center of the province a civil tribunal, with an excellent president, in which every town was represented by its advocate. And knowing that past severities had generated ill feeling against himself, in order to purge the minds of the people and gain their good will, he sought to show them that any cruelty which had been done had not originated with him, but in the harsh disposition of this minister. Availing himself of the pretext which this afforded, he one morning caused Remiro to be beheaded, and exposed in the market place of Cesena with a block and bloody ax by his side. The barbarity of this spectacle at once astounded and satisfied the populace.

### READING QUESTIONS

1. Why must a prince be both a lion and a fox? What qualities do these animals represent?

2. What light does *The Prince* shed on the realities of Italian politics?

3. How might a Renaissance critic of Machiavelli have responded to his work? What objections might such a person have raised to *The Prince*? How might Machiavelli have countered his critics' arguments?

## 12-3 | A Description of the Ideal Courtier

### BALDASSARE CASTIGLIONE, *The Book of the Courtier* (1528)

Baldassare Castiglione (ball-duh-SAH-ray kahs-teel-YOH-nay) (1478–1529) was an Italian diplomat who spent many years traveling through the courts of Europe. Based on his experiences, he wrote *The Book of the Courtier* as a manual on the proper education, manners, dress, and skills of a companion to and defender of royalty. The book was written in the form of a conversation among some of the leading nobility in Italy and was a bestseller in its time. As you read this excerpt, think about the models upon which Castiglione might have drawn. To what extent does his courtier resemble the ideal medieval knight? To what extent does he seem to be a product of humanist education and training?

I wish then, that this Courtier of ours should be nobly born. I am of the opinion that the principal and true profession of the courtier ought to be that of arms;[1] which I would have him follow actively above all else, and be known among others as bold and strong, and loyal to whomsoever he serves. . . .

Therefore let the man we are seeking be very bold, stern, and always among the first, where the enemy are to be seen; and in every other place, gentle, modest, reserved, above all things avoiding ostentation and that impudent self-praise by which men ever excite hatred and disgust in all who hear him. . . .

And so I would have him well built and shapely of limb, and would have him show strength and lightness and suppleness, and know all bodily exercises that befit a man of war: whereof I think the first should be to handle every sort of weapon well on foot and on horse. . . .

There are also many other exercises, which although not immediately dependent upon arms, yet are closely connected therewith, and greatly foster manly sturdiness; and one of the chief among these seems to me to be the chase,[2] because it bears a certain likeness to war; and truly it is an amusement for great lords and befitting a man at court, and furthermore it is seen to have been much cultivated among the ancients. It is fitting also to know how to swim, to leap, to run, to throw stones, for besides the use that may be made of this in war, a man often has occasion to show what he can do in such matters; whence good esteem is to be won, especially with the multitude, who must be taken into account withal. Another admirable exercise, and one fitting a man at court, is the game of tennis, in which are well shown the disposition of the body. . . .

I think that the conversation, which the Courtier ought most to try in every way to make acceptable, is that which he holds with his prince; and although this word "conversation" implies a certain equality that seems impossible between a lord and his inferior, yet we will call it so for the moment. Therefore, besides

---

From Baldassare Castiglione, *The Book of the Courtier*, trans. Leonard Opdycke (New York: Charles Scribner's Sons, 1903), pp. 22, 26, 29, 31, 93–94.

[1]**arms**: Weaponry.
[2]**chase**: Hunting.

daily showing everyone that he possesses the worth we have already described, I would have the Courtier strive, with all the thoughts and forces of his mind, to love and almost adore the prince whom he serves, above every other thing, and mold his ways to his prince's liking. . . .

Moreover it is possible without flattery to obey and further the wishes of him we serve, for I am speaking of those wishes that are reasonable and right, or of those that in themselves are neither good nor evil, such as would be a liking for a play or devotion to one kind of exercise above another. And I would have the Courtier bend himself to this even if he be by nature alien to it, so that on seeing him his lord shall always feel that he will have something agreeable to say. . . . He will not be an idle or untruthful tattler, nor a boaster nor pointless flatterer, but modest and reserved, always and especially in public showing the reverence and respect which befit the servant towards the master.

### READING QUESTIONS

1. What are the characteristics of a good courtier? How would you explain the stress Castiglione places on military aptitude and training?

2. What role does the courtier play in royal government? How does he facilitate his master's success?

3. Would you describe Castiglione's courtier as a medieval or a Renaissance figure? Why?

## 12-4 | A Humanist Prescription for the Education of Princes

### DESIDERIUS ERASMUS, *The Education of a Christian Prince* (1516)

Desiderius Erasmus (1462–1536) of Rotterdam was the foremost northern humanist. A priest, theologian, and teacher, Erasmus placed humanist scholarship in the service of religious reform. His work combines a humanist's respect for reason and the value of the individual with an equally profound commitment to his faith. In this excerpt from *The Education of a Christian Prince*, Erasmus begins by discussing a classical metaphor for the relationship of the ruler to the state, and then uses this as a starting point for exploring the relationship between a Christian prince, his subjects, and God. As you read it, pay particular attention to the way in which he mixes classical and Christian concepts.

[R]emember this idea also, which was known and handed down by the pagan philosophers, that the rule of a prince over his people is no different from that of the mind over the body. The mind dominates the body because it knows more than the physical body, but it does so to the great advantage

From Desiderius Erasmus, *The Education of a Christian Prince*, trans. Lester K. Born (New York: Columbia University Press, 1936), pp. 175–178.

of the latter rather than to itself. The blessed fortune of the physical form is this rule of the mind. What the heart is in the body of a living creature, that the prince is in the state. If the heart is sound, it imparts life to the whole body, since it is the fountain of the blood and life spirit; but if it has been infected, it brings utter collapse to every part of the body. The heart is the last part of a living body to be broken down, and the very last traces of life are thought to survive in it. Consequently the prince should keep himself clean and undefiled from all corrupting folly whenever any such disease lays hold of the people. In a man it is the finely organized part (namely, the mind) that exercises the control. Likewise, in the mind it is its finest element, reason, that asserts itself. And God, who rules the universe, is the very essence of all things. Therefore, whosoever assumes the functions of rule in a state, as in a sort of great body, should excel all others in goodness, wisdom, and watchfulness. The prince should be superior to his officers in the same degree that they are to the common people. If there is any evil in the mind it springs from infection, and contact with the body, which is subject to the passions. Any good that the body possesses is drawn from the mind as from a fountain. How unbelievable it would be and how contrary to nature, if ills should spread from the mind down into the body, and the health of the body be corrupted by the vicious habits of the mind. It would be just as absurd for wars, seditious uprisings, profligate morals, debased laws, corrupt officials, and every similar curse to a state, to spring from the prince whose wisdom should lay the storms stirred up by the folly of the common folk. But we often see states (*civitates*), well established and flourishing under the diligent activity of the people, overthrown by mismanagement of the princes. How unlike a Christian it is to take pleasure in the title "Master," which many who were not in the fold of Christ have shunned; that which in their ambition they desire to be but do not want to be called because of the odium attached to the name. Yet will a Christian prince think it just in the eyes of God for him to be the same [sort of man] and be called "The Magnificent"? The emperor Augustus, even though he had gained the imperial throne through foul intrigue, considered it an insult to be called "Master;" and when this title was used by an actor before all the people, he showed his disapproval by his facial expression and his remarks, as if it were a term of reproach applied to tyrants. And shall the Christian prince not imitate this propriety of the pagan? If you are master of all your subjects, they must of necessity be your slaves. Then have a care that you do not fulfill the ancient proverb: "You have as many enemies as you have slaves."

Nature created all men equal, and slavery was superimposed on nature, which fact the laws of even the pagans recognized. Now stop and think how out of proportion it is for a Christian to usurp full power over other Christians, whom the laws did not design to be slaves, and whom Christ redeemed from all slavery. Recall the instance when Paul called Onesimus (who was born a slave) the brother of his former master Philemon, from the time of his baptism. How incongruous it is to consider them slaves whom Christ redeemed with the same blood [as He did you]; whom He declared free along with all others; whom He fostered with the same sacraments as He did you; whom He calls to the same heritage of immortality! And over them, who have the same Master as you, the Prince, Jesus Christ, will you impose the yoke of slavery?

There is only one Master of Christian men. Why, then, do those who assume His functions, prefer to take their pattern of government from anyone except Him, who alone is in all ways to be imitated? It is proper enough to gather from others whatever virtues they have; but in Him is the perfect example of all virtue and wisdom. This seems the [essence of] foolishness to those outside the faith, but to us, if we are really faithful, He is the goodness of God and the wisdom of God. Now I do not want you to think that this means that you should be a slave, not a ruler. On the contrary, it illustrates the finest way to rule, unless, of course, you think God is only a bondsman because He governs the whole universe without recompense, because everyone and everything has felt His kindness, although they give Him nothing in return, and unless the mind seems a slave because it looks out so zealously for the welfare of the body, which it does not need, or unless you think the eye is a slave to all the other parts of the body because it sees for them all. You may well consider this: if someone should turn all these men whom you call your own into swine and asses by the art of Circe,[1] would you not say your ruling power had been reduced to a lower level? I think you would. And yet you may exercise more authority over swine and asses than over men. You may treat them as you please, divide them off as you will, and even kill them. Surely he who has reduced his free subjects to slaves has put his power on a meaner level. The loftier the ideal to which you fashion your authority, the more magnificently and splendidly will you rule. Whoever protects the liberty and standing of your subjects is the one that helps your sovereign power. God gave the angels and men free will so that He would not be ruling over bondsmen, and so that He might glorify and add further grandeur to His kingdom. And who, now, would swell with pride because he rules over men cowed down by fear, like so many cattle?

### READING QUESTIONS

1. What metaphors does Erasmus use to describe the relationship of a prince to his people?

2. In Erasmus's view, what qualities should a Christian prince embody? Why?

3. Erasmus argues that the ideal Christian prince rules over a "free" people. How might he have explained this apparent contradiction? What similarities and differences do you see between his understanding of the meaning of freedom and your own?

---

[1]**Circe**: An enchantress who turned the legendary Greek hero Odysseus and his men into pigs.

## 12-5 | A Female Author Argues for the Education of Women

### CHRISTINE DE PIZAN, *The Book of the City of Ladies: Against Those Men Who Claim It Is Not Good for Women to Be Educated* (1404)

Christine de Pizan (ca. 1363–1434) may have been the first European woman to earn her living as a writer. The daughter of a Venetian nobleman and scholar, de Pizan grew up in the court of Charles V of France, where her father had accepted a position as royal astrologer and physician. There, de Pizan was given the opportunity to develop her intellectual interests and abilities. In 1390, when her husband died in an epidemic and left her with three children, de Pizan began her literary career. Her works were popular among the French nobility, and she even enjoyed the financial support of the French queen. At this time, humanists were divided in their opinions on the education of women. Some thought women were simply not capable of learning. Others thought a limited form of education in good morals was sufficient. De Pizan challenged both of these ideas, and some scholars now regard her as one of the first Western feminists.

I realize that women have accomplished many good things and that even if evil women have done evil, it seems to me, nevertheless, that the benefits accrued and still accruing because of good women—particularly the wise and literary ones and those educated in the natural sciences whom I mentioned above—outweigh the evil. Therefore, I am amazed by the opinion of some men who claim that they do not want their daughters, wives, or kinswomen to be educated because their mores would be ruined as a result.

Here you can clearly see that not all opinions of men are based on reason and that these men are wrong. For it must not be presumed that mores necessarily grow worse from knowing the moral sciences, which teach the virtues, indeed, there is not the slightest doubt that moral education amends and ennobles them. How could anyone think or believe that whoever follows good teaching or doctrine is the worse for it? Such an opinion cannot be expressed or maintained. I do not mean that it would be good for a man or a woman to study the art of divination or those fields of learning which are forbidden—for the holy Church did not remove them from common use without good reason—but it should not be believed that women are the worse for knowing what is good.

Quintus Hortensius, a great rhetorician and consummately skilled orator in Rome, did not share this opinion. He had a daughter, named Hortensia, whom he greatly loved for the subtlety of her wit. He had her learn letters and study the science of rhetoric, which she mastered so thoroughly that she resembled her father Hortensius not only in wit and lively memory but also in her excellent delivery and order of speech—in fact, he surpassed her in nothing. . . . That is, during the time when Rome was governed by three men, this Hortensia began to support the cause of women and to undertake what no man dared to undertake. There was a question whether certain taxes should be levied on women and on their jewelry during a needy period in Rome. This woman's eloquence was so compelling that she was listened to, no less readily than her father would have been, and she won her case.

From Christine de Pizan, *The Book of the City of Ladies*, trans. Earl Jeffrey Richards (New York: Persea Books, 1982), pp. 153–155.

Similarly, to speak of more recent times, without searching for examples in ancient history, Giovanni Andrea, a solemn law professor in Bologna not quite sixty years ago, was not of the opinion that it was bad for women to be educated. He had a fair and good daughter, named Novella, who was educated in the law to such an advanced degree that when he was occupied by some task and not at leisure to present his lectures to his students, he would send Novella, his daughter, in his place to lecture to the students from his chair. And to prevent her beauty from distracting the concentration of her audience, she had a little curtain drawn in front of her. In this manner she could on occasion supplement and lighten her father's occupation. . . .

Thus, not all men (and especially the wisest) share the opinion that it is bad for women to be educated. But it is very true that many foolish men have claimed this because it displeased them that women knew more than they did. [My] father, who was a great scientist and philosopher, did not believe that women were worth less by knowing science; rather, as you know, he took great pleasure from seeing your inclination to learning.

### READING QUESTIONS

1. How does de Pizan defend a woman's ability to learn?

2. According to de Pizan, why do some men not want to see women educated? What other reasons might have motivated them?

3. How and why does Pizan couch her arguments that women should be educated within accepted moral norms of the fifteenth century?

### SOURCES IN CONVERSATION

# A Female Painter Tells Stories About Women

Renaissance and early modern artists drew heavily for their inspiration on Christianity and the classical past, but this does not mean that they were uninterested in the present. In the hands of a skilled artist, the past became a vehicle for commenting on what was important to the artist, his or her patron, and the community to which they both belonged. The work of the Roman painter Artemisia Gentileschi (1593–ca. 1656) is a case in point. The daughter of painter Orazio Gentileschi, Artemisia was perhaps the most successful female artist of her day. Her paintings *Susannah and the Elders* and *Judith and Holofernes,* both depicting scenes from the Old Testament, demonstrate how deeply personal such works could be. *Susannah and the Elders,* Artemisia's first work, was completed in 1610 when she was seventeen. Between that time and the completion of *Judith and Holofernes* in 1612, Artemisia was raped by one of her father's colleagues, Agostino Tassi. As you examine these two works, consider the connections between the content and themes of the paintings and Gentileschi's own experiences.

How did she use these paintings to comment on the power dynamics that shaped women's lives?

1. Compare the power relationships being portrayed in the two paintings. How are they different?

2. How do you think seventeenth-century Europeans would have reacted to the stories being told in the two paintings? If the reactions would have been different, why would they have differed?

## 12-6 | ARTEMISIA GENTILESCHI, *Susannah and the Elders* (1610)

Taken from the book of Daniel, the story of *Susannah and the Elders* centers on a false accusation of adultery. As Susannah, a young wife, bathes in her garden, two elders of her community watch secretly. Filled with lust, the two men threaten to denounce her as an adulteress if she refuses to have sex with them. When she resists their attempts at blackmail, they follow through on their threat. Only the intervention of Daniel, who exposes inconsistencies in their story, saves Susannah from execution. As you examine the painting, pay particular attention to the way Gentileschi composed it. How does the placement of the three figures amplify its message?

Fine Art Images/Superstock.

## READING QUESTIONS

1. How would you describe Gentileschi's Susannah? How does the position of her arms and head help to convey her reaction to the unwanted advances of the elders?

2. How would you characterize the two elders? How does their placement in the painting reflect their power? What might explain Gentileschi's decision to depict them whispering to one another at the very moment they accost Susannah?

## 12-7 | ARTEMISIA GENTILESCHI, *Judith and Holofernes* (1612)

Like *Susannah and the Elders*, *Judith and Holofernes* depicts a scene from the Old Testament, this time from the book of Judith. In order to save Israel from Assyrian domination, Judith seduces the Assyrian general Holofernes. After he falls asleep drunk, Judith and her maidservant cut off his head. The personal importance of the story to Gentileschi is underscored by the fact that she chose to depict herself as Judith and Agostino Tassi, her rapist, as Holofernes.

Fratelli Alinari IDEA S.p.A./Corbis/Getty Images.

## READING QUESTIONS

1. How would you describe Gentileschi's Judith? How would you characterize her facial expression?

2. What might explain Gentileschi's decision to focus attention on Judith's arms and those of her maid?

3. Compare this work to *Susannah and the Elders*. Taken together, what do the two paintings tell us about the connections Gentileschi made between gender, power, and violence?

---

# ■ COMPARATIVE AND DISCUSSION QUESTIONS ■

1. Compare and contrast Petrarch and Machiavelli. Should they both be considered humanists? Why or why not?

2. Compare and contrast Erasmus's depiction of the successful prince with Machiavelli's. How does each one envision the Renaissance state? What does each think is necessary for a government to function well?

3. What light do the works of Christine de Pizan and Artemisia Gentileschi shed on the challenges faced by women of their day? How would you explain the success of each in male-dominated fields?

4. What marks Erasmus's *Education of a Christian Prince* as a work of the northern Renaissance? How does it differ from some of the other works included in this chapter?

# 13

# Reformations and Religious Wars

## 1500–1600

Even before Martin Luther posted his "Ninety-five Theses on the Power of Indulgences," numerous Catholic practices had come under widespread criticism. The specific political situation in the Holy Roman Empire enabled Luther and other reformers to spread their ideas. Strong local governments and high nobles, who exercised more power in their territories than did the central government of the Holy Roman Empire, welcomed Lutheran ideas and offered safe havens to the Protestants. Protestant reform extended to social thought as well—for example, priests were no longer required to remain celibate in the Protestant tradition. Some reformers adopted beliefs that were far more radical than those of Luther or other reformers and were condemned by Protestants and Catholics alike. Meanwhile, the Catholic Church developed its own plans for reform, both to counter Protestant attacks and to revitalize the church. The age of reformation was also an age of religious violence, as religious and political conflicts merged and overlapped, fueling war, riots, and the persecution of dissenters and outsiders.

## 13-1 | Martin Luther Takes a Stand

### MARTIN LUTHER, *Ninety-five Theses on the Power of Indulgences* (1517)

Martin Luther (1483–1546) composed his "Ninety-five Theses" in response to Pope Leo X's decision to raise funds for the construction of a new cathedral in Rome through the sale of indulgences in Germany. An indulgence was a document issued by the Catholic Church lessening a person's penance or time in purgatory. Many believed that the purchase of an indulgence was an effective substitute for genuine repentance, a belief that papal agents did little or nothing to discourage. Luther's attack on this practice went far beyond a simple accusation of papal corruption. Instead, it struck directly at the power of the church, suggesting that priests had no necessary role in salvation.

1. Our Lord and Master Jesus Christ in saying "Repent ye" etc., intended that the whole life of believers should be penitence.
2. This word cannot be understood as sacramental penance, that is, of the confession and satisfaction which are performed under the ministry of priests.
3. It does not, however, refer solely to inward penitence; nay such inward penitence is naught, unless it outwardly produces various mortifications of the flesh.
4. The penalty thus continues as long as the hatred of self (that is, true inward penitence); namely, till our entrance into the kingdom of heaven.
5. The pope has neither the will nor the power to remit any penalties except those which he has imposed by his own authority, or by that of the canons.
6. The pope has no power to remit any guilt, except by declaring and warranting it to have been remitted by God; or at most by remitting cases reserved for himself; in which cases, if his power were despised, guilt would certainly remain.
7. Certainly God remits no man's guilt without at the same time subjecting him, humbled in all things, to the authority of his representative the priest. . . .
20. Therefore the pope, when he speaks of the plenary remission of all penalties, does not mean really of all, but only of those imposed by himself.
21. Thus those preachers of indulgences are in error who say that by the indulgences of the pope a man is freed and saved from all punishment.
22. For in fact he remits to souls in purgatory no penalty which they would have had to pay in this life according to the canons.
23. If any entire remission of all penalties can be granted to any one it is certain that it is granted to none but the most perfect, that is to very few.

---

From Martin Luther, "Ninety-five Theses," in *Translations and Reprints from the Original Sources of European History* (Philadelphia: University of Pennsylvania Press, 1898), 2/6:12–18.

24. Hence, the greater part of the people must needs be deceived by this indiscriminate and high-sounding promise of release from penalties. . . .

26. The pope acts most rightly in granting remission to souls not by the power of the keys (which is of no avail in this case) but by the way of intercession.[1]

27. They preach man [rather than God] who say that the soul flies out of Purgatory as soon as the money thrown into the chest rattles.[2]

28. It is certain that, when the money rattles in the chest, avarice and gain may be increased, but the effect of the intercession of the Church depends on the will of God alone. . . .

30. No man is sure of the reality of his own contrition, much less of the attainment of plenary remission. . . .

35. They preach no Christian doctrine who teach that contrition is not necessary for those who buy souls [out of purgatory] or buy confessional licenses.

36. Every Christian who feels true compunction has of right plenary remission of punishment and guilt even without letters of pardon.

37. Every true Christian, whether living or dead, has a share in all the benefits of Christ and of the Church, given him by God, even without letters of pardon. . . .

38. The remission, however, imparted by the pope is by no means to be despised, since it is, as I have said, a declaration of the divine remission.

39. It is a most difficult thing, even for the most learned theologians, to exalt at the same time in the eyes of the people the ample effect of pardons and the necessity of true contrition.

40. True contrition seeks and loves punishment; while the ampleness of pardons relaxes it, and causes men to hate it, or at least gives occasion for them to do so. . . .

43. Christians should be taught that he who gives to a poor man, or lends to a needy man, does better than if he bought pardons.

44. Because by works of charity, charity increases, and the man becomes better; while by means of pardons, he does not become better, but only freer from punishment. . . .

49. Christians should be taught that the pope's pardons are useful if they do not put their trust in them, but most hurtful if through them they lose the fear of God. . . .

54. Wrong is done to the Word of God when, in the same sermon, an equal or longer time is spent on pardons than on it.

55. The mind of the pope necessarily is that, if pardons, which are a very small matter, are celebrated with single bells, single processions, and single ceremonies, the Gospel, which is a very great matter, should be preached with a hundred bells, a hundred processions, and a hundred ceremonies.

---

[1]**intercession**: Prayer to God on another's behalf.

[2]**They preach . . . rattles**: This was the claim being made by the indulgence seller Tetzel in Luther's Saxony.

56. The treasures of the Church, whence the pope grants indulgences, are neither sufficiently named nor known among the people of Christ.

57. It is clear that they are at least not temporal treasures, for these are not so readily lavished, but only accumulated, by many of the preachers. . . .

67. Those indulgences, which the preachers loudly proclaim to be the greatest graces, are seen to be truly such as regards the promotion of gain.

68. Yet they are in reality most insignificant when compared to the grace of God and the piety of the cross. . . .

75. To think that the papal pardons have such power that they could absolve a man even if — by an impossibility — he had violated the Mother of God, is madness.

76. We affirm on the contrary that papal pardons cannot take away even the least of venial sins, as regards its guilt. . . .

79. To say that the cross set up among the insignia of the papal arms is of equal power with the cross of Christ, is blasphemy.

80. Those bishops, priests, and theologians who allow such discourses to have currency among the people will have to render an account. . . .

82. As for instance: Why does not the pope empty purgatory for the sake of most holy charity and of the supreme necessity of souls — this being the most just of all reasons — if he redeems an infinite number of souls for the sake of that most fatal thing, money, to be spent on building a basilica — this being a very slight reason?

83. Again; why do funeral masses and anniversary masses for the deceased continue, and why does not the pope return, or permit the withdrawal of, the funds bequeathed for this purpose, since it is a wrong to pray for those who are already redeemed?

84. Again; what is this new kindness of God and the pope, in that, for money's sake, they permit an impious man and an enemy of God to redeem a pious soul which loves God, and yet do not redeem that same pious and beloved soul out of free charity on account of its own need?

85. Again; why is it that the penitential canons, long since abrogated and dead in themselves, in very fact and not only by usage, are yet still redeemed with money, through the granting of indulgences, as if they were full of life?

86. Again; why does not the pope, whose riches are at this day more ample than those of the wealthiest of the wealthy, build the single Basilica of St. Peter with his own money rather than with that of poor believers? . . .

89. Since it is the salvation of souls, rather than money, that the pope seeks by his pardons, why does he suspend the letters and pardons granted long ago, since they are equally efficacious? . . .

91. If all these pardons were preached according to the spirit and mind of the pope, all these questions would be resolved with ease; nay, would not exist.

## READING QUESTIONS

1. In Thesis 36, Luther writes, "Every Christian who feels true compunction has of right plenary remission of punishment and guilt even without letters of pardon." Why would many interpret this as an attack on the papacy?

2. According to the theses, in what ways have the leaders of the church failed to teach true Christian doctrine?

3. Based on your reading of Theses 82–91, how would you classify the sorts of reform that Luther would like to see within the church?

## 13-2 | Reformation Propaganda

### HANS HOLBEIN THE YOUNGER, *Luther as the German Hercules* (ca. 1519)

One of Martin Luther's greatest assets was the printing press. Print technology facilitated the rapid dissemination of Lutheran ideas to a wide variety of audiences. The propaganda campaign waged by Luther's supporters included inexpensive print versions of his tracts, pamphlets, and treatises. It also included images aimed at the illiterate and semi-literate. A majority of sixteenth-century Europeans could not read, and woodcuts like this one, created by Hans Holbein the Younger (1498–1543), helped common people take part in the religious debates that dominated much of the century. Here, Luther is depicted as the Greek hero Hercules, who killed the hydra, a beast with nine heads. The artist has replaced the hydra with nine churchmen, including the theologian Thomas Aquinas (see Document 10-6), monks, and priests. The strangled pope, identifiable by his triple crown, dangles from the rope in Luther's mouth.

De Agostini Picture Library/Getty Images.

## READING QUESTIONS

1. How would you describe the way Luther is depicted here? What about the church leaders?

2. How would you sum up the intended message of this image in a single sentence? What group or groups might it have been meant to influence?

3. What light does this image shed on the nature of religious conflict during the Reformation? What room, if any, did such images leave for compromise between Protestants and Catholics?

## SOURCES IN CONVERSATION

# The War on Witches

Starting around 1560, prosecutions of alleged witches rose dramatically. The next century would see between 100,000 and 200,000 people tried for witchcraft, which resulted in 40,000 to 60,000 executions. Seventy-five to eighty percent of the accused witches of the early modern period were women, suggesting the role of deep-seated biases against females in European society and medieval Christianity in particular. Possible explanations for this phenomenon include changes in legal procedures, the religious upheaval of the Reformation, the social and economic dislocation created by a changing agricultural economy, the efforts of early modern states to assert greater control over their subjects, and new definitions of witchcraft. It should be stressed, however, that each witchcraft trial was different and that a different combination of factors was in play in each case. While shaped by larger social and cultural trends, witchcraft trials were, in the end, local events, and the relationships and personal histories of the individuals involved were at the heart of each outbreak of accusations.

### READ AND COMPARE

1. What do these two documents reveal about aspects of human nature that society and church officials feared most?

2. Why do you suppose women were overwhelmingly the majority of accused witches? Are there any clues you can detect in these documents? What aspects of the Judeo-Christian tradition might have contributed to targeting women as suspected witches?

## 13-3 | HEINRICH KRAMER, *Malleus Maleficarum* (The Hammer of Witches) (1487)

Roughly thirty years before Martin Luther wrote his "Ninety-five Theses" and started the Protestant Reformation, a clergy member named Heinrich Kramer tried to start persecuting people for witchcraft in Tyrol, but he failed and was discredited by the local bishop. He then successfully appealed to the pope Innocent VIII, who wrote a papal bull in 1484 that gave the Inquisition, a church organization created to root out heresy, the authority to try people accused of witchcraft. Kramer then wrote his famous and hugely influential treatise that defined the practices of witchcraft, identified the practices as criminal heresy, and offered instructions for determining the guilt or innocence of accused witches.

The method of beginning an examination by torture is as follows: First, the jailers prepare the implements of torture, then they strip the prisoner (if it be a woman, she has already been stripped by other women, upright and of good report). This stripping is lest some means of witchcraft may have been sewed into the clothing — such as often, taught by the Devil, they prepare from the bodies of unbaptized infants, [murdered] that they may forfeit salvation. And when the implements of torture have been prepared, the judge, both in person and through other good men zealous in the faith, tries to persuade the prisoner to confess the truth freely; but, if he will not confess, he bid attendants make the prisoner fast to the strappado or some other implement of torture. The attendants obey forthwith, yet with feigned agitation. Then, at the prayer of some of those present, the prisoner is loosed again and is taken aside and once more persuaded to confess, being led to believe that he will in that case not be put to death.

Here it may be asked whether the judge, in the case of a prisoner much defamed, convicted both by witnesses and by proofs, nothing being lacking but his own confession, can properly lead him to hope that his life will be spared when, even if he confess his crime, he will be punished with death.

It must be answered that opinions vary. Some hold that even a witch of ill repute, against whom the evidence justifies violent suspicion, and who, as a ringleader of the witches, is accounted very dangerous, may be assured her life, and condemned instead to perpetual imprisonment on bread and water, in case she will give sure and convincing testimony against other witches; yet this penalty of perpetual imprisonment must not be announced to her, but only that her life will be spared, and that she will be punished in some other fashion, perhaps by exile. And doubtless such notorious witches, especially those who prepare witch-potions or who by magical methods cure those bewitched, would be peculiarly suited to be thus preserved, in order to aid the bewitched or to accuse other witches, were it not that their accusations

From George L. Burr, ed., *Translations and Reprints from the Original Sources of European History*, vol. 3, part 4 (Philadelphia: University of Pennsylvania Press, 1897), pp. 11–13.

cannot be trusted, since the Devil is a liar, unless confirmed by proofs and witnesses.

Others hold, as to this point, that for a time the promise made to the witch sentenced to imprisonment is to be kept, but that after a time she should be burned.

A third view is, that the judge may safely promise witches to spare their lives, if only he will later excuse himself from pronouncing the sentence and will let another do this in his place. . . .

But if, neither by threats nor by promises such as these, the witch can be induced to speak the truth, then the jailers must carry out the sentence, and torture the prisoner according to the accepted methods, with more or less of severity as the delinquent's crime may demand. And, while he is being tortured, he must be questioned on the articles of accusation, and this frequently and persistently, beginning with the lighter charges — for he will more readily confess the lighter than the heavier. And, while this is being done, the notary must write down everything in his record of the trial — how the prisoner is tortured, on what points he is questioned and how he answers.

And note that, if he confesses under the torture, he must afterward be conducted to another place, that he may confirm it and certify that it was not due alone to the force of the torture.

But, if the prisoner will not confess the truth satisfactorily, other sorts of tortures must be placed before him, with the statement that unless he will confess the truth, he must endure these also. But, if not even thus he can be brought into terror and to the truth, then the next day or the next but one is to be set for a continuation of the tortures — not a repetition, for it must not be repeated unless new evidences produced.

The judge must then address to the prisoners the following sentence: We, the judge, etc., do assign to you, such and such a day for the continuation of the tortures, that from your own mouth the truth may be heard, and that the whole may be recorded by the notary.

And during the interval, before the day assigned, the judge, in person or through approved men, must in the manner above described try to persuade the prisoner to confess, promising her (if there is aught to be gained by this promise) that her life shall be spared. The judge shall see to it, moreover, that throughout this interval guards are constantly with the prisoner, so that she may not be alone; because she will be visited by the Devil and tempted into suicide.

## READING QUESTIONS

1. Setting aside that these people are being interrogated for the crime of suspected witchcraft, how likely would it be that this process of questioning could result in an honest confession for any crime? Why do you think so?

2. What do you think was the most important societal factor that moved witchcraft trials from the status of marginalized and discredited phenomena to mainstream, widespread occurrences?

## 13-4 | JEAN BODIN, *On the Demon-Mania of Witches* (1580)

Jean Bodin (1529/30–1596) was one of the foremost political theorists of his time. A professor of law and adviser to kings, he is best known for his *Six livres de la République* (1576), in which he developed a case for royal absolutism that rested on a belief in the divine right of kings. It might be surprising that a man of such erudition and international status was also a leading proponent of aggressive efforts to detect and punish witchcraft. For Bodin, however, concern about witchcraft was a natural extension of his interest in politics and government. As he saw it, the "status and greatness of the state" depended on the "punishment of the bad," and there was no greater evil than witchcraft.

Now if ever there was a way to appease the anger of God, to obtain His blessing, to dismay some by the punishment of others, to preserve some from the infection of others, to reduce the number of the wicked, to secure the safety of the good, and to punish the most despicable wickednesses that the human mind can imagine, it is to chastise witches with the utmost rigour. However, the word "rigour" is a misnomer, since there is no penalty cruel enough to punish the evils of witches, since all their wickednesses, blasphemies, and all their designs rise up against the majesty of God to vex and offend Him in a thousand ways. . . . Some people raise objections to burning witches, even witches who have a formal pact with Satan. For it is principally against those witches that one must seek vengeance with the greatest diligence and utmost rigour, in order to bring an end to the wrath of God, and His vengeance upon us. And especially since those who have written on it interpret a magic spell as heresy, and nothing more—although true heresy is the crime of treason against God, and punishable by the fire. It is necessary, however, to note the difference between this crime and simple heresy. For we showed initially that the first occupation of witches is to deny God and all religion. The law of God condemns that person who has left the true God for another to be stoned, which all the Hebrew commentators say is the most terrible form of execution. This point is very significant. For the witch whom I have described does not just deny God in order to change and take up another religion, but he renounces all religion, either true or superstitious, which can keep men in the fear of committing offence.

The second crime of witches is, after having renounced God, to curse, blaspheme and scorn Him, and any other god or idol which he feared. Now the law of God declares as follows, "Whoever curses his God shall bear his sin. He who blasphemes the name of the Lord shall be put to death." . . .

For it seems that God wants to show that those who blaspheme what they think is God, do blaspheme God, with respect to their intention, which is the foundation of the hearts and minds of men: like the witches described above who broke the arms and legs on crucifixes, which they thought were gods. They also offered toads the host[1] to feed on. One sees then a double outrage of impiety

---

Excerpt (pp. 208–213) from Jean Bodin, *On the Demon-Mania of Witches,* translated by Randy A. Scott, with an introduction by Jonathan L. Pearl. Reprinted by permission of the Centre for Reformation & Renaissance Studies, Victoria University.

[1] **the host**: The sanctified bread that signifies the body of Christ.

with witches who blaspheme the true God, and anything they think has some divinity, so as to uproot all pious conviction and fear of offence.

The third crime is even more abominable. Namely, they do homage to the Devil, worship him, offer sacrifice, and the most despicable make a trench and put their face in the ground praying and worshiping him with all their heart. . . . This abomination surpasses any penalty that man can conceive, considering the formal text of the law of God, which requires that one who only bows down to pay honour to images, which the Greeks call "idols," be put to death. . . . Now witches are not content to worship, or only to bow down before Satan, but they offer themselves to Satan, pray to him and invoke him.

The fourth crime is even greater: many witches have been convicted, and have confessed to promising their children to Satan. The fifth is even worse; that is, that witches are frequently convicted by their confession of having sacrificed to the Devil their infant children before they are baptised. They raise them in the air, and then insert a large pin into their head, which causes them to die and is a crime more bizarre than the one before. In fact Sprenger[2] relates that he had one burned who had killed forty-one of them in this way.

The sixth crime is even more horrible. For witches are not satisfied to offer their own children to the Devil and burn them as a sacrifice . . . but they even dedicate them right from the mother's womb . . . which is a double parricide with the most abominable idolatry imaginable.

The seventh and the most common is that witches make an oath and promise the Devil to lure as many as they can into his service, which they customarily do, as we showed earlier. Now the law of God states that that person who is called this way, must stone the one who tried to entice him.

The eighth crime is to call upon and swear by the name of the Devil as a mark of honour, as witches do having it always on their lips, and swearing only by him, except when they renounce God. This is directly against the law of God, which forbids swearing by anything other than the name of God. This, Scripture says, gives glory to God. Thus judges said in taking the oath of parties or witnesses, "Glory be to God."

The ninth is that witches are incestuous, which is the crime they have been charged with and convicted of from earliest times. For Satan gives them to understand that there was never a perfect sorcerer or enchanter who was not born from father and daughter, or mother and son. . . . All these impieties are directly against God and His honour, which judges must avenge with the utmost rigour, and bring an end to God's wrath against us. As for the other crimes of witches, they concern injuries done to men, which they will avenge whenever they can. Now there is nothing so displeasing to God as to see judges avenge the smallest offences committed against themselves or others, but dissemble the horrible blasphemies against the majesty of God, such as those I have cited about witches.

---

[2]**Sprenger**: Jacob Sprenger (1436–1495). A Dominican inquisitor and coauthor with Heinrich Kramer of the *Malleus Maleficarum*, or *The Hammer of Witches* (1487), an influential handbook for the investigation of witchcraft.

Let us continue then with the other crimes. The tenth is that witches make a profession of killing people, and worse of murdering little children, then boiling them to render their humours and flesh drinkable, which Sprenger says he learned from their confessions; and the Neopolitan Battista della Porta[3] writes about it in his book on magic. And still another fact to underline, is that they put children to death before they are baptised. These are four circumstances which make the murder very much worse.

The eleventh crime is that witches eat human flesh, especially of little children, and of course drink their blood. . . . But one sees that it is a vile belief the Devil puts into the hearts of men in order to make them kill and devour each other, and destroy the human race. Again it must be noted that all witches customarily make poisons, which is enough to justify the death sentence. . . .

Now murder, according to the law of God and the laws of men, merits death. And those who eat human flesh, or have others eat it, also deserve death: as for example, a baker in Paris who made a business of making pies from the flesh of people hanged. He was burned, and his house razed to the ground. . . .

The twelfth is particular, killing with poisons or spells, which is distinct from simple homicide. . . . For it is a much more serious offence to kill with poison than with overt violence, as we shall presently point out; and even more serious to cause death by sorcery than by poison. . . .

The thirteenth crime of witches is to kill livestock, something which is customary. . . . The fourteenth is common, and recognised by law, namely, killing crops and causing famine and sterility in an entire region. The fifteenth is that witches have carnal copulation with the Devil, (and very often near their husbands, as I remarked earlier), a wickedness they all confess to.

There then are fifteen detestable crimes, the least of which merits a painful death. This does not mean that all witches are guilty of such evils, but it has been well established that witches who have a formal compact with the Devil are normally guilty of all or of most of these evil deeds.

### READING QUESTIONS

1. What crimes does Bodin attribute to witches?

2. Why does Bodin believe that it was essential for the state to aggressively pursue witchcraft allegations?

3. What does Bodin's discussion of witchcraft tell us about his religious views? What about his political views?

---

[3]**Battista della Porta**: Giambattista della Porta (1535–1615). Italian natural philosopher and author of *Magiae Naturalis,* or *Natural Magic* (1558).

## 13-5 | Calvin Defines His Protestant Vision

### JOHN CALVIN, *The Institutes of Christian Religion* (1559)

Martin Luther may have initiated the Protestant Reformation, but once it began it quickly moved beyond his control. Over the course of the sixteenth century, Protestantism splintered into numerous sects, some largely conforming to Luther's views, others deviating from them in important ways. The most important alternative to Lutheranism was developed by the French theologian John Calvin (1509–1564). At the core of Calvin's theology was a belief in the omnipotence of God and the utter powerlessness of human beings. It was on this foundation that he built the principle of predestination, the idea that the salvation or damnation of every person is foreordained by God and there is nothing any individual can do to alter his or her ultimate fate. In this excerpt from *The Institutes of Christian Religion*, Calvin defines predestination and offers the history of the Jews as evidence of its veracity.

When we attribute foreknowledge to God, we mean that all things always were, and perpetually remain, under His eyes, so that to His knowledge there is nothing future or past, but all things are present. And they are present in such a way that He not only conceives them through ideas, as we have before us those things which our minds remember, but He truly looks upon them and discerns them as things placed before Him. And this foreknowledge is extended throughout the universe to every creature. We call predestination God's eternal decree, by which He determined with Himself what He willed to become of each man. For all are not created in equal condition; rather, eternal life is foreordained for some, eternal damnation for others. Therefore, as any man has been created to one or the other of these ends, we speak of him as predestined to life or to death.

God has attested this not only in individual persons but has given us an example of it in the whole offspring of Abraham, to make it clear that in His choice rests the future condition of each nation. "When the Most High divided the nations, and separated the sons of Adam . . . the people of Israel were His portion, . . . the cord of His inheritance" [Deut. 32:8–9]. The separation is apparent to all men: in the person of Abraham, as in a dry tree trunk, one people is peculiarly chosen, while the others are rejected; but the cause does not appear except that Moses, to cut off from posterity any occasion to boast, teaches that they excel solely by God's freely given love. For he declares this the cause of their deliverance: that God loved the patriarchs, "and chose their seed after them" [Deut. 4:37].

More explicitly, in another chapter: "Not because you surpassed all other peoples in number did He take pleasure in you to choose you, . . . but because He loved you" [Deut. 7:7–8]. . . . Believers also proclaim this with one voice: "He chooses our heritage for us, the glory of Jacob, whom He has loved" [Psalms 47:4]. For all who have been adorned with gifts by God credit them to His freely given love because they knew not only that they had not merited them but that even the holy patriarch himself was not endowed with such virtue as to acquire such a high honor for himself and his descendants. And in order more effectively to crush all pride,

From Hans J. Hillerbrand, *The Protestant Reformation* (New York: Harper and Row, 1968), pp. 184–185.

he reproaches them as deserving no such thing, since they were a stubborn and stiff-necked people [Ex. 32:9; cf. Deut. 9:6]. Also, the prophets often confront the Jews with this election, to the latters' displeasure and by way of reproach, since they had shamefully fallen away from it [cf. Amos 3:2].

Be this as it may, let those now come forward who would bind God's election either to the worthiness of men or to the merit of works. Since they see one nation preferred above all others, and hear that God was not for any reason moved to be more favorably inclined to a few, ignoble — indeed, even wicked and stubborn — men, will they quarrel with Him because He chose to give such evidence of His mercy? But they shall neither hinder His work with their clamorous voices nor strike and hurt His righteousness by hurling the stones of their insults toward heaven. Rather, these will fall back on their own heads!

### READING QUESTIONS

1. How did Calvin define predestination? What about foreknowledge?
2. Why did Calvin believe that the history of the Jews provided evidence in support of predestination?
3. Why did Calvin believe it was a mistake to "bind God's election either to the worthiness of men or to the merit of works"?
4. How could the principle of predestination be used for political purposes, or to reinforce social hierarchy or inequality?

## 13-6 | Training the Soldiers of Christ

### IGNATIUS OF LOYOLA, *Rules for Right Thinking* (1548)

While recovering from an injury, the Spanish soldier Ignatius (ig-NAY-shus) of Loyola (1491–1556) had a religious experience that inspired him to found a new monastic order unlike most others. Conceived as frontline troops in the battle against Protestantism, members of this order, which became known as the Society of Jesus, or the Jesuits, rejected monastic isolation and instead served as teachers and missionaries. Loyola's *Rules for Right Thinking* was designed to help individuals prepare to serve as Catholic soldiers in the Counter-Reformation. As you read this excerpt, consider what it reveals about how Loyola saw the conflict between Protestantism and Catholicism. Why did he believe that strict obedience to church teachings was critical to the ultimate triumph of Catholicism?

**First Rule.** The first: All judgment laid aside, we ought to have our mind ready and prompt to obey, in all, the true Spouse of Christ our Lord, which is our holy Mother the Church. . . .

   **Fifth Rule.** The fifth: To praise vows of Religion, of obedience, of poverty, of chastity, and of other perfections. . . .

From Father Elder Mullen, S. J., trans., *The Spiritual Exercises of St. Ignatius of Loyola* (New York: P. J. Kennedy & Sons, 1914), p. 39. Christian Classics Ethereal Library, Web, February 24, 2010.

**Sixth Rule.** To praise relics of the Saints, giving veneration to them and praying to the Saints; and to praise . . . pilgrimages, indulgences, . . . and candles lighted in the churches. . . .

**Eighth Rule.** To praise the ornaments and the buildings of churches; likewise images, and to venerate them according to what they represent.

**Ninth Rule.** Finally, to praise all precepts of the Church, keeping the mind prompt to find reasons in their defense and in no manner against them.

**Tenth Rule.** We ought to be more prompt to find good and praise as well the . . . recommendations as the ways of our Superiors. Because, although some are not or have not been [upright], to speak against them, whether preaching in public or discoursing before the common people, would rather give rise to fault-finding and scandal than profit; and so the people would be incensed against their Superiors, whether temporal or spiritual. So that, as it does harm to speak evil to the common people of Superiors in their absence, so it can make profit to speak of the evil ways to the persons themselves who can remedy them. . . .

**Twelfth Rule.** We ought to be on our guard in making comparison of those of us who are alive to the blessed passed away, because error is committed not a little in this; that is to say, in saying, this one knows more than St. Augustine; he is another, or greater than, St. Francis; he is another St. Paul in goodness, holiness, etc.

**Thirteenth Rule.** To be right in everything, we ought always to hold that the white which I see, is black, if the Church so decides it, believing that between Christ our Lord, . . . and the Church, . . . there is the same Spirit which governs and directs us for the salvation of our souls. Because by the same Spirit and our Lord Who gave the ten Commandments, our holy Mother the Church is directed and governed.

**Fourteenth Rule.** Although there is much truth in the assertion that no one can save himself without being predestined and without having faith and grace; we must be very cautious in the manner of speaking and communicating with others about all these things.

**Fifteenth Rule.** We ought not, by way of custom, to speak much of predestination; but if in some way and at some times one speaks, let him so speak that the common people may not come into any error, as sometimes happens, saying: Whether I have to be saved or condemned is already determined, and no other thing can now be, through my doing well or ill; and with this, growing lazy, they become negligent in the works which lead to the salvation and the spiritual.

**Sixteenth Rule.** In the same way, we must be on our guard that by talking much and with much insistence of faith, without any distinction and explanation, occasion be not given to the people to be lazy and slothful in works, whether before faith is formed in charity or after.

## READING QUESTIONS

1. What rules should the Jesuits follow to be faithful to the church?
2. What things should not be spoken of to the people? Why?

3. How do you think Ignatius's career as a soldier prepared him for founding this order?

4. Why might the methods and practices of the Jesuit order be more effective in fighting Protestantism than those of earlier, more insular monastic orders? Why would the papacy particularly value the Jesuits' actions?

5. What potential problems might the tactics of the Jesuit order cause that might undermine their goal to resist Protestantism?

## ■ COMPARATIVE AND DISCUSSION QUESTIONS ■

1. In what ways did Luther's and Calvin's versions of Protestantism differ? Which version might have seemed more threatening to secular rulers? Why?

2. Review Loyola's comments on predestination, as well as Calvin's explanation of the term. Why did Loyola consider it wise for Jesuits to remain silent on this subject?

3. What connections can you make between religious upheaval and the surge in witchcraft prosecutions that began in the mid-sixteenth century?

4. Compare and contrast the image of the pope in the woodcut (ca. 1519) with what Luther said of him in his "Ninety-five Theses" (1517). How would you explain the differences?

# 14

# European Exploration and Conquest

## 1450–1650

In the mid-1400s, western Europe faced a rapidly expanding Muslim power in the east. The Ottoman Empire captured Constantinople in 1453 and over time came to rule, directly or indirectly, much of eastern Europe. Now cut off from direct access to Asian trade via the eastern Mediterranean, Europeans turned south and west in search of new trade routes to India and China. Portugal led the way in the fifteenth century, launching expeditions to explore the west coast of Africa and eventually rounding the tip of Africa and reaching India. After Columbus's voyages, Spain and Portugal began to explore and conquer the Americas. Portuguese exploration of Africa, combined with the establishment of colonial empires in the Americas, led to a new era of worldwide trade in African slaves. Through trade, travel, and missionary work, Europeans increasingly came into contact with peoples of whom they had previously had little or no knowledge. For many Europeans, this new experience only reinforced their sense of cultural and religious superiority. For others, it prompted a re-evaluation of basic assumptions about their own society and its place in the world.

## 14-1 | Columbus Sets the Context for His Voyage
### CHRISTOPHER COLUMBUS, *Diario* (1492)

The year 1492 was a momentous one in Spanish history. With the fall of the Muslim state of Granada, Ferdinand of Aragon and Isabella of Castille completed the Christian *reconquista* (reconquest) of the Iberian Peninsula. Having driven the "infidel" from its last stronghold,

From *The Diario of Christopher Columbus's First Voyage to America*, trans. Oliver Dunn and James E. Kelly Jr. (Norman: University of Oklahoma Press, 1989), pp. 17, 19, 21.

they turned to the "enemy within," issuing a proclamation expelling all Jews from their lands. It was at this moment, fired with a crusading spirit and eager to gain access to the wealth of Asia, that Ferdinand and Isabella chose to sponsor the exploratory westward voyage of Christopher Columbus. As you read the introduction from Columbus's *Diario* (diary), compiled at the request of his sponsors, notice the connections Columbus makes between the events described above and his own voyage. What does his introduction suggest about the role of religion in sparking Spain's involvement in westward expansion?

Whereas, Most Christian and Very Noble and
Very Excellent and Very Powerful Princes, King
and Queen of the Spains and of the Islands of
the Sea, our Lords: This present year of 1492,
after Your Highnesses had brought to an end
the war with the Moors who ruled in Europe and
had concluded the war in the very great city
of Granada, where this present year on the
second day of the month of January I saw the
Royal Standards of Your Highnesses placed by
force of arms on the towers of the Alhambra,
which is the fortress of the said city; and I
saw the Moorish King come out to the gates of
the city and kiss the Royal Hands of Your
Highnesses and of the Prince my Lord; and
later in that same month, because of the
report that I had given to Your Highnesses about
the lands of India and about a prince who is
called "Grand Khan," which means in our
Spanish language "King of Kings"; how, many times,
he and his predecessors had sent to Rome to
ask for men learned in our Holy Faith in order
that they might instruct him in it and how the
Holy Father had never provided them; and thus
so many peoples were lost, falling into idolatry
and accepting false and harmful religions;
and Your Highnesses, as Catholic Christians
and Princes, lovers and promoters of the Holy
Christian Faith, and enemies of the false
doctrine of Mahomet and of all idolatries and
heresies, you thought of sending me, Christóbal
Colón, to the said regions of India to see
the said princes and the peoples and the lands,
and the characteristics of the lands and of
everything, and to see how their conversion to
our Holy Faith might be undertaken. And you
commanded that I should not go to the East by
land, by which way it is customary to go, but

by the route to the West, by which route we do
not know for certain that anyone previously
has passed. So, after having expelled all the
Jews from all of your Kingdoms and Dominions,
in the same month of January Your Highnesses
commanded me to go, with a suitable fleet, to
the said regions of India. And for that you
granted me great favors and ennobled me so
that from then on I might call myself "Don"
and would be Grand Admiral of the Ocean Sea
and Viceroy and perpetual Governor of all the
islands and lands that I might discover and
gain and [that] from now on might be discovered
and gained in the Ocean Sea; and likewise my
eldest son would succeed me and his son him,
from generation to generation forever. And I
left the city of Granada on the twelfth day of
May in the same year of 1492 on Saturday, and
I came to the town of Palos, which is a seaport,
where I fitted out three vessels very
well suited for such exploits; and I left the
said port, very well provided with supplies
and with many seamen, on the third day of
August of the said year, on a Friday, half an
hour before sunrise; and I took the route to
Your Highnesses' Canary Islands, which are in
the said Ocean Sea, in order from there to
take my course and sail so far that I would
reach the Indies and give Your Highnesses'
message to those princes and thus carry out
that which you had commanded me to do. And
for this purpose I thought of writing on this
whole voyage, very diligently, all that I
would do and see and experience, as will be
seen further along. Also, my Lord Princes,
besides writing down each night whatever I
experience during the day and each day what I
sail during the night, I intend to make a new
sailing chart. In it I will locate all of the
sea and the lands of the Ocean Sea in their
proper places under their compass bearings
and, moreover, compose a book and similarly
record all of the same in a drawing, by latitude
from the equinoctial line and by longitude
from the west; and above all it is very

important that I forget sleep and pay much
attention to navigation in order thus to carry
out these purposes, which will be great labor.

### READING QUESTIONS

1. How did Columbus explain Ferdinand and Isabella's decision to sponsor his voyage?

2. What does the document suggest about the Spanish monarchs' motives for sponsoring Columbus? What does it suggest about Columbus's motives for conducting the expedition?

3. What might explain Columbus's decision to focus on the reconquista and the expulsion of the Jews in the introduction to the *Diario*?

## 14-2 | Cortés Describes the Conquest of the Aztecs

### HERNÁN CORTÉS, *Two Letters to Charles V: On the Conquest of the Aztecs* (1521)

Hernán Cortés (1485–1547) described his conquest of the Aztec Empire of Mexico in a number of letters to his sovereign and king of Spain, the Holy Roman emperor Charles V. While Cortés was surprised, even impressed, by the advanced culture he encountered, his conquests were not without considerable violence. In one incident, one of his men ordered the massacre of thousands of unarmed members of the Aztec nobility who had assembled peaceably. Under examination, Cortés claimed that this act was done to instill fear and prevent future treachery. Some contemporaries speculated that Cortés embellished his accounts to retain the favor of the king.

### [Second Letter]

This great city of Tenochtitlan is built on the salt lake. . . . It has four approaches by means of artificial causeways. . . . The city is as large as Seville or Cordoba. Its streets . . . are very broad and straight, some of these, and all the others, are one half land, and the other half water on which they go about in canoes. . . . There are bridges, very large, strong, and well constructed, so that, over many, ten horsemen can ride abreast. . . . The city has many squares where markets are held. . . . There is one square, twice as large as that of Salamanca, all surrounded by arcades, where there are daily more than sixty thousand souls, buying and selling . . . in the service and manners of its people, their fashion of living was almost the same as in Spain, with just as much harmony and order; and considering that these people were barbarous, so cut off from the knowledge of God

From *Letters of Cortés*, trans. Francis A. MacNutt (New York: G. P. Putnam's Sons, 1908), 1:256–257, 2:244.

and other civilized peoples, it is admirable to see to what they attained in every respect.

## [Fifth Letter]

It happened . . . that a Spaniard saw an Indian . . . eating a piece of flesh taken from the body of an Indian who had been killed. . . . I had the culprit burned, explaining that the cause was his having killed that Indian and eaten him which was prohibited by Your Majesty, and by me in Your Royal name. I further made the chief understand that all the people . . . must abstain from this custom. . . . I came . . . to protect their lives as well as their property, and to teach them that they were to adore but one God . . . that they must turn from their idols, and the rites they had practiced until then, for these were lies and deceptions which the devil . . . had invented. . . . I, likewise, had come to teach them that Your Majesty, by the will of Divine Providence, rules the universe, and that they also must submit themselves to the imperial yoke, and do all that we who are Your Majesty's ministers here might order them.

### READING QUESTIONS

1. Although Cortés described the people of Tenochtitlan as "barbarous" and lamented that they are "cut off from the knowledge of God and other civilized peoples," what positive qualities did he attribute to the city and its people?

2. Why do you think Cortés chose to describe an act of cannibalism? Why might he have believed that such an account would find favor with his royal reader?

3. What different images of Mexico was Cortés trying to impress upon Charles V?

# The Slave Trade in Africa

Slavery and the slave trade existed in West Africa long before the arrival of Europeans in the fifteenth and sixteenth centuries. For centuries, Africans had enslaved other Africans, both to use as slaves in Africa and to sell to Muslim merchants as part of the international trade that connected Africa to the Arab world. Nonetheless, European participation altered the African slave trade in profound ways. Most important, it resulted in a surge in demand for African slaves. As European empires in the New World grew, so, too, did the demand for slave labor. Over time, the combined efforts of Africans and Europeans to meet that demand would distort and destabilize African societies and economies.

## READ AND COMPARE

1. What do these documents demonstrate about the competing interests and agendas of the Portuguese king and merchants interested in acquiring slaves, and King Affonso of Congo who provided them?

## 14-3 | ALVISE DA CA' DA MOSTO, *Description of Capo Bianco and the Islands Nearest to It: Fifteenth-Century Slave Trade in West Africa* (1455–1456)

Alvise da Ca' da Mosto (ca. 1428–1483) was an Italian trader and explorer. After his father was banished from Venice, Ca' da Mosto took up service with Prince Henry of Portugal, a key promoter of Portuguese exploration of the West African coast. In 1455, he traveled to the Canary and Madeira Islands and sailed past Cape Verde to the Gambia River. During another voyage in 1456, Ca' da Mosto discovered islands off Cape Verde and sailed sixty miles up the Gambia River. In the excerpt that follows, Ca' da Mosto describes the African Muslims who served as middlemen in the Atlantic slave trade. As you read it, notice both the details he chose to include and those he chose to leave out. What do these choices tell you about the nature of his interest in the communities he visited? What do they tell you about his readers' interests?

You should also know that behind this Cauo Bianco[1] on the land, is a place called Hoden,[2] which is about six days inland by camel. This place is not walled, but is frequented by Arabs, and is a market where the caravans arrive from Tanbutu [Timbuktu], and from other places in the land of the Blacks, on their way to our nearer Barbary. The food of the peoples of this place is dates, and barley, of which there is sufficient, for they grow in some of these places, but not abundantly. They drink the milk of camels and other animals, for they have no wine. They also have cows and goats, but not many, for the land is dry. Their oxen and cows, compared with ours, are small.

They are Muhammadans, and very hostile to Christians. They never remain settled, but are always wandering over these deserts. These are the men who go to the land of the Blacks, and also to our nearer Barbary. They are very numerous, and have many camels on which they carry brass and silver from Barbary and other things to Tanbutu and to the land of the Blacks. Thence they carry away gold and pepper, which they bring hither. They are brown complexioned, and wear white cloaks edged with a red stripe: their women also dress thus, without shifts. On their heads the men wear turbans in the Moorish fashion, and they always go barefooted. In these sandy districts there are many lions, leopards, and ostriches, the eggs of which I have often eaten and found good.

From Alvise da Ca' da Mosto, "Description of Capo Bianco and the Islands Nearest to It," in *European Reconnaissance: Selected Documents*, ed. J. H. Parry (New York: Walker, 1968), pp. 59–61.

[1]**Cauo Bianco**: West African port.
[2]**Hoden**: Wadan, an important desert market about 350 miles east of Arguim. Later, in 1487, when the Portuguese sought to penetrate the interior, they attempted to establish a trading factory at Wadan that acted as a feeder to Arguim, tapping the northbound caravan traffic and diverting some of it to the west coast.

You should know that the said Lord Infante of Portugal [the crown prince, Henry the Navigator] has leased this island of Argin to Christians [for ten years], so that no one can enter the bay to trade with the Arabs save those who hold the license. These have dwellings on the island and factories where they buy and sell with the said Arabs who come to the coast to trade for merchandise of various kinds, such as woollen cloths, cotton, silver, and "alchezeli," that is, cloaks, carpets, and similar articles and above all, corn, for they are always short of food. They give in exchange slaves whom the Arabs bring from the land of the Blacks, and gold tiber [gold dust]. The Lord Infante therefore caused a castle to be built on the island to protect this trade for ever. For this reason, Portuguese caravels are coming and going all the year to this island.

These Arabs also have many Berber horses, which they trade, and take to the land of the Blacks, exchanging them with the rulers for slaves. Ten or fifteen slaves are given for one of these horses, according to their quality. The Arabs likewise take articles of Moorish silk, made in Granata and in Tunis of Barbary, silver, and other goods, obtaining in exchange any number of these slaves, and some gold. These slaves are brought to the market and town of Hoden; there they are divided: some go to the mountains of Barcha, and thence to Sicily, [others to the said town of Tunis and to all the coasts of Barbary], and others again are taken to this place, Argin, and sold to the Portuguese leaseholders. As a result every year the Portuguese carry away from Argin a thousand slaves. Note that before this traffic was organized, the Portuguese caravels, sometimes four, sometimes more, were wont to come armed to the Golfo d'Argin, and descending on the land by night, would assail the fisher villages, and so ravage the land. Thus they took of these Arabs both men and women, and carried them to Portugal for sale: behaving in a like manner along all the rest of the coast, which stretches from Cauo Bianco to the Rio di Senega and even beyond.

### READING QUESTIONS

1. Why do you think Ca' da Mosto wrote this account?
2. What were the principal patterns of commerce in northern Africa?
3. What groups were involved in the various facets of the slave trade?
4. In what ways did the arrival of the Portuguese change West African slavery and the slave trade?

## 14-4 | KING NZINGA MBEMBA AFFONSO OF CONGO,
### *Letters on the Slave Trade* (1526)

In 1491, the Portuguese granted the right to send merchants and missionaries into the West African kingdom of Congo. King Affonso, the king of Congo, converted to Christianity, and the trading relationship between Portugal and Congo created many lucrative opportunities

From Basil Davidson, *The African Past: Chronicles from Antiquity to Modern Times* (Boston: Little, Brown, 1964), pp. 191–193; reissued by Africa World Press in 1990 as *African Civilization Revisited: From Antiquity to Modern Times.*

for merchants from both countries. By the 1520s, however, Affonso had grown increasingly concerned about the negative impact that the slave trade was having on his kingdom. The following selection contains two letters from Affonso to the king of Portugal, written in July and October 1526.

## [First Letter]

Sir, Your Highness should know how our Kingdom is being lost in so many ways that it is convenient to provide for the necessary remedy, since this is caused by the excessive freedom given by your agents and officials to the men and merchants who are allowed to come to this Kingdom to set up shops with goods and many things which have been prohibited by us, and which they spread throughout our Kingdoms and Domains in such an abundance that many of our vassals, whom we had in obedience, do not comply because they have the things in greater abundance than we ourselves; and it was with these things that we had them content and subjected under our vassalage and jurisdiction, so it is doing a great harm not only to the service of God, but the security and peace of our Kingdoms and State as well.

And we cannot reckon how great the damage is, since the mentioned merchants are taking every day our natives, sons of the land and the sons of our noblemen and vassals and our relatives, because the thieves and men of bad conscience grab them wishing to have the things and wares of this Kingdom which they are ambitious of; they grab them and get them to be sold; and so great, Sir, is the corruption and licentiousness that our country is being completely depopulated, and Your Highness should not agree with this nor accept it as in your service. And to avoid it we need from those [your] Kingdoms no more than some priests and a few people to teach in schools, and no other goods except wine and flour for the holy sacrament. That is why we beg of Your Highness to help and assist us in this matter, commanding your factors that they should not send here either merchants or wares, because it is *our will that in these Kingdoms there should not be any trade of slaves nor outlet for them.* . . .

## [Second Letter]

Moreover, Sir, in our Kingdoms there is another great inconvenience which is of little service to God, and this is that many of our people, keenly desirous as they are of the wares and things of your Kingdoms, which are brought here by your people, and in order to satisfy their voracious appetite, seize many of our people, freed and exempt men, and very often it happens that they kidnap even noblemen and the sons of noblemen, and our relatives, and take them to be sold to the white men who are in our Kingdoms; and for this purpose they have concealed them; and others are brought during the night so that they might not be recognized.

And as soon as they are taken by the white men they are immediately ironed and branded with fire, and when they are carried to be embarked, if they are caught by our guards' men the whites allege that they have bought them but they cannot say from whom, so that it is our duty to do justice and to restore to the freemen their freedom, but it cannot be done if your subjects feel offended, as they claim to be.

And to avoid such a great evil we passed a law so that any white man living in our Kingdoms and wanting to purchase goods in any way should first inform three of our noblemen and officials of our court whom we rely upon in this matter, and these are Dom Pedro Manipanza and Dom Manuel Manissaba, our chief usher, and Gonçalo Pires our chief freighter, who should investigate if the mentioned goods are captives or free men, and if cleared by them there will be no further doubt nor embargo for them to be taken and embarked. But if the white men do not comply with it they will lose the aforementioned goods. And if we do them this favor and concession it is for the part Your Highness has in it, since we know that it is in your service too that these goods are taken from our Kingdom, otherwise we should not consent to this.

### READING QUESTIONS

1. What negative effects did King Affonso argue that the slave trade was having on his kingdom?

2. In the king's view, who profited from the slave trade? Who bore the social and economic costs of that trade?

3. What did King Affonso propose to do about the slave trade in the first letter? In the second letter? Why do you think he changed his plan?

## 14-5 | Circumnavigating the Globe

### *Navigation and Voyage Which Ferdinand Magellan Made from Seville to Maluco in the Year 1519* (1519–1522)

Ferdinand Magellan was a Portuguese explorer who sought to access the riches offered by the Spice Islands, as European markets were clamoring for spices that could flavor and preserve foods but that would not grow in the relatively cold, dry climate of Europe. After he was rejected by King Manuel of Portugal, he petitioned the young and ambitious King Charles I of Spain, who granted Magellan the support he needed. Magellan was successful in sailing around the globe, though he was killed in the Philippines in 1521, and his initial five ships and 270 crew members dwindled to one ship and 18 members when they limped back to Spain three years later in 1522.

[Magellan] sailed from Seville on the 10th day of August of the said year [1519], and remained at the bar until the 21st day of September . . . they entered the said Rio [de Janeiro] on the day of St. Lucy, which was the 13th December. . . .

. . .

From Oliver J. Thatcher, ed., *The Library of Original Sources*, vol. 5: *Ninth to Sixteenth Centuries* (Milwaukee, Wisc.: University Research Extension Co., 1907), pp. 41–55.

Thence they navigated along the said coast, and arrived on the last day of March of the year 1520 at the Port of St. Julian. . . .

In this port three of the ships rose up against the Captain-major, their captains saying that they intended to take him to Castile in arrest, as he was taking them all to destruction. Here, through the exertions of the said Captain-major, and the assistance and favor of the foreigners whom he carried with him, the Captain-major went to the said three ships which were already mentioned, and there the captain of one of them was killed, who was treasurer of the whole fleet, and named Luis de Mendoça; he was killed in his own ship by stabs with a dagger by the chief constable of the fleet, who was sent to do this by Fernando de Magelhaes [i.e., Magellan] in a boat with certain men. The said three ships having thus been recovered, five days later Fernando de Magelhaes ordered Gaspar de Queixada to be decapitated and quartered; he was captain of one of the ships, and was one of those who had mutinied.

. . .

They sailed on the 24th day of the month of August of the said year from this port of St. Julian . . . and they continued collecting the goods which had remained there during August and up to the 18th September, and there they took in water and much fish which they caught in this river; and in the other, where they wintered, there were people like savages, and the men are from nine to ten spans in height, very well made; they have not got houses, they only go about from one place to another with their flocks, and eat meat nearly raw: they are all of them archers and kill many animals with arrows, and with the skins they make clothes, that is to say, they make the skins very supple, and fashion them after the shape of the body, as well as they can, then they cover themselves with them, and fasten them by a belt round the waist. When they do not wish to be clothed from the waist upwards, they let that half fall which is above the waist, and the garment remains hanging down from the belt which they have girt round them. They wear shoes which cover them four inches above the ankle, full of straw inside to keep their feet warm. They do not possess any iron, nor any other ingenuity of weapons, only they make the points of their arrows of flints, and so also the knives with which they cut, and the adze and awls with which they cut and stitch their shoes and clothes. They are very agile people, and do no harm, and thus they follow their flocks: wherever night finds them there they sleep; they carry their wives along with them with all the chattels which they possess. The women are very small and carry heavy burdens on their backs; they wear shoes and clothes just like the men. Of these men they obtained three or four and brought them in the ships, and they all died except one, who went to Castile in a ship which went thither.

. . .

Fernan de Magalhaes would not make any further stay, and at once set sail, and ordered the course to be steered west, and a quarter south-west; and so they made land [i.e., in the Philippines], which is in barely eleven degrees.

. . .

This king conducted them thence a matter of thirty leagues to another island named Cabo, which is in ten degrees, and in this island Fernando de Magalhaes did what he pleased with the consent of the country, and in one day eight hundred people became Christian, on which account Fernan de Magalhaes desired that the other kings, neighbors to this one, should become subject to this who had become Christian: and these did not choose to yield such obedience. Fernan de Magalhaes seeing that, got ready one night with his boats, and burned the villages of those who would not yield the said obedience; and a matter of ten or twelve days after this was done he sent to a village about half a league from that which he had burned, which is named Matam, and which is also an island, and ordered them to send him at once three goats, three pigs, three loads of rice, and three loads of millet for provisions for the ships. . . . Because they did not choose to grant what he demanded of them, Fernan de Magalhaes ordered three boats to be equipped with a matter of fifty or sixty men, and went against the said place, which was on the 28th day of April, in the morning; there they found many people, who might well be as many as three thousand or four thousand men, who fought with such a good will that the said Fernan de Magalhaes was killed there, with six of his men, in the year 1521.

. . .

When Fernan de Magelhaes was dead the Christians got back to the ships, where they thought fit to make two captains and governors whom they should obey; and having done this, they took counsel and decided that the two captains should go ashore where the people had turned Christians to ask for pilots to take them to Borneo, and this was on the first day of May of the said year; when the two captains went, being agreed upon what had been said, the same people of the country who had become Christians, armed themselves against them, and whilst they reached the shore let them land in security as they had done before. Then they attacked them, and killed the two captains and twenty-six gentlemen, and the other people who remained got back to the boats, and returned to the ships, and finding themselves again without captains they agreed, inasmuch as the principal persons were killed, that one John Lopez, who was the chief treasurer, should be captain-major of the fleet, and the chief constable of the fleet should be captain of one of the ships; he was named Gonzalo Vaz Despinosa.

Having done this they set sail, and ran about twenty-five leagues with three ships, which they still possessed; they then mustered, and found that they were altogether one hundred and eight men in all these three ships, and many of them were wounded and sick, on which account they did not venture to navigate the three ships, and thought it would be well to burn one of them — the one that should be most suitable for that purpose — and to take into the two ships those that remained: this they did out at sea, out of sight of any land.

. . .

As soon as they arrived at the island of Tydor, which is in half a degree, the King thereof did them great honor, which could not be exceeded: there they treated with the King for their cargo, and the King engaged to give them a cargo and whatever there was in the country for their money . . . the inhabitants of the country gave them information that further on, in another island near, there was a Portuguese man. This island might be two leagues distant, and it was named

Targatell; this man was the chief person of Maluco; there we now have got a fortress. They then wrote letters to the said Portuguese, to come and speak with them, to which he answered that he did not dare, because the King of the country forbade it; that if they obtained permission from the King he would come at once; this permission they soon got, and the Portuguese came to speak with him. They gave him an account of the prices which they had settled, at which he was amazed, and said that on that account the King had ordered him not to come, as they did not know the truth about the prices of the country; and whilst they were thus taking in cargo there arrived the King of Baraham, which is near there, and said that he wished to be a vassal of the King of Castile, and also that he had got four hundred bahars of cloves, and that he had sold it to the King of Portugal, and that they had bought it, but that he had not yet delivered it, and if they wished for it, he would give it all to them; to which the captains answered that if he brought it to them, and came with it, they would buy it, but otherwise not. The King, seeing that they did not wish to take the cloves, asked them for a flag and a letter of safe conduct, which they gave him, signed by the captains of the ships.

While they were thus waiting for the cargo, it seemed to them, from the delay in the delivery, that the King was preparing some treachery against them, and the greater part of the ships' crews made an uproar and told the captains to go, as the delays which the King made were nothing else than treachery: as it seemed to them all that it might be so, they were abandoning everything, and were intending to depart; and being about to unfurl the sails, the King, who had made the agreement with them, came to the flagship and asked the captain why he wanted to go, because that which he had agreed upon with him he intended to fulfill it as had been settled. The captain replied that the ships' crews said they should go and not remain any longer, as it was only treachery that was being prepared against them. To this the King answered that it was not so, and on that account he at once sent for his Koran, upon which he wished to make oath that nothing such should be done to them. They at once brought him this Koran, and upon it he made oath, and told them to rest at ease with that. At this the crews were set at rest, and promised them that he would give them their cargo by the 1st December 1521, which he fulfilled within the said time without being wanting in anything.

## READING QUESTIONS

1. How are the people of the Philippines and the "Moors" treated by Magellan's crew, and how are they described by the "Genoese pilot" that wrote this account?

2. What role do Christian and Muslim beliefs play in this account? What religious assumptions did Magellan make in the Philippines that ultimately got him killed?

3. How do you think this voyage might have changed the perceptions of Magellan's crew about the people they encountered? Why do you think so?

## 14-6 | A Critique of European "Superiority"
### MICHEL DE MONTAIGNE, *Of Cannibals* (1580)

Michel de Montaigne (duh mahn-TAYN) (1533–1592), a French lawyer and government official, wrote about his personal experiences and travels in his *Essays* of 1580. Writing during a period of religious warfare in Europe and the expansion of the European presence around the world, Montaigne offered a critique of European assumptions of social and cultural superiority. In his essay "Of Cannibals," Montaigne pointed out the virtues of Native American society as he saw them. As you read this excerpt from the essay, consider how Montaigne's own assumptions and cultural commitments shaped his view of Native American society. How did Montaigne's diagnosis of the ills of his own society affect his perception of the peoples of the Americas?

When King Pyrrhus[1] invaded Italy, having viewed and considered the order of the army the Romans sent out to meet him; "I know not," said he, "what kind of barbarians" (for so the Greeks called all other nations) "these may be; but the disposition of this army that I see has nothing of barbarism in it." . . . By which it appears how cautious men ought to be of taking things upon trust from vulgar opinion, and that we are to judge by the eye of reason, and not from common report.

I long had a man in my house that lived ten or twelve years in the New World, discovered in these latter days, and in that part of it where Villegaignon landed, which he called Antarctic France.[2] This discovery of so vast a country seems to be of very great consideration. I cannot be sure, that hereafter there may not be another, so many wiser men than we having been deceived in this. I am afraid our eyes are bigger than our bellies, and that we have more curiosity than capacity; for we grasp at all, but catch nothing but wind. . . .

This man that I had was a plain ignorant fellow, and therefore the more likely to tell truth: for your better-bred sort of men are much more curious in their observation; . . . they never represent things to you simply as they are, but rather as they appeared to them, or as they would have them appear to you. . . . I would have every one write what he knows, and as much as he knows, but no more; and that not in this only but in all other subjects. . . .

Now, to return to my subject, I find that there is nothing barbarous and savage in this nation, by anything that I can gather, excepting, that every one gives

From *Essays of Montaigne*, trans. Charles Cotton, ed. William Carew Hazlitt, vol. 1 (London: Reeves and Turner, 1902), pp. 237–252.

[1]**Pyrrhus**: Greek king of Sicily (319–272 B.C.E.) who attempted to prevent Roman armies from advancing into southern Italy.

[2]**and in that part . . . Antarctic France**: Nicolas Durand de Villegaignon (1510–1571) was an officer in the French navy who in 1555 captured the region surrounding what is now Rio de Janeiro, Brazil, from the Portuguese. In addition to creating new trading opportunities, his goal was to build a refuge for the French Calvinists to escape religious persecution in France. Portugal retook the colony in 1567.

the title of barbarism to everything that is not in use in his own country. As, indeed, we have no other level of truth and reason than the example and idea of the opinions and customs of the place wherein we live: there is always the perfect religion, there the perfect government, there the most exact and accomplished usage of all things. . . .

These nations then seem to me to be so far barbarous, as having received but very little form and fashion from art and human invention, and consequently to be not much remote from their original simplicity. The laws of nature, however, govern them still, not as yet much [corrupted] with any mixture of ours: but 'tis in such purity, that I am sometimes troubled we were not sooner acquainted with these people, and that they were not discovered in those better times, when there were men much more able to judge of them than we are. . . . To my apprehension, what we now see in those nations, does not only surpass all the pictures with which the poets have adorned the golden age, and all their inventions in feigning a happy state of man, but, moreover, the fancy and even the wish and desire of philosophy itself; so native and so pure a simplicity, as we by experience see to be in them, could never enter into their imagination, nor could they ever believe that human society could have been maintained with so little artifice and human patchwork. I should tell Plato[3] that it is a nation wherein there is no manner of traffic, no knowledge of letters, no science of numbers, no name of magistrate or political superiority; no use of service, riches or poverty, no contracts, no successions, no dividends, no properties, no employments, but those of leisure, no respect of kindred, but common, no clothing, no agriculture, no metal, no use of corn or wine; the very words that signify lying, treachery, dissimulation, avarice, envy, detraction, pardon, never heard of. How much would he find his imaginary Republic short of his perfection? . . .

As to the rest, they live in a country very pleasant and temperate, so that, as my witnesses inform me, 'tis rare to hear of a sick person, and they moreover assure me, that they never saw any of the natives, either paralytic, bleary-eyed, toothless, or crooked with age. The situation of their country is along the sea-shore. . . . They have great store of fish and flesh that have no resemblance to those of ours: which they eat without any other cookery, than plain boiling, roasting, and broiling. The first that rode a horse thither, though in several other voyages he had contracted an acquaintance and familiarity with them, put them into so terrible a fright, with his centaur[4] appearance, that they killed him with their arrows before they could come to discover who he was. Their buildings are very long, and of capacity to hold two or three hundred people. . . . They have wood so hard, that they cut with it, and make their swords of it, and their grills of it to broil their meat. Their beds are of cotton, hung swinging from the roof, like our seamen's hammocks, every man his own, for the wives lie apart from their husbands. They rise with the sun, and so soon as they are up, eat for all day, for they have no more meals but that; they do not then drink, . . . but drink

---

[3]**Plato**: Greek philosopher (427–347 B.C.E.) and author of *The Republic*, who wrote about an ideal city in which people were ruled by philosophers.

[4]**centaur**: Half-human, half-horse creature from Greek mythology.

very often all day after, and sometimes to a rousing pitch. . . . The whole day is spent in dancing. Their young men go a-hunting after wild beasts with bows and arrows; one part of their women are employed in preparing their drink the while, which is their chief employment. One of their old men, in the morning before they fall to eating, preaches to the whole family, walking from the one end of the house to the other, and several times repeating the same sentence, till he has finished the round, for their houses are at least a hundred yards long. Valor towards their enemies and love towards their wives, are the two heads of his discourse. . . . They believe in the immortality of the soul, and that those who have merited well of the gods are lodged in that part of heaven where the sun rises, and the accursed in the west. . . .

They have continual war with the nations that live further within the main-land, beyond their mountains, to which they go naked, and without other arms than their bows and wooden swords, fashioned at one end like the head of our javelins. The obstinacy of their battles is wonderful, and they never end without great effusion of blood: for as to running away, they know not what it is. Every one for a trophy brings home the head of an enemy he has killed, which he fixes over the door of his house. After having a long time treated their prisoners very well, and given them all the regales they can think of, he to whom the prisoner belongs, invites a great assembly of his friends. They being come, he ties a rope to one of the arms of the prisoner, of which, at a distance, out of his reach, he holds the one end himself, and gives to the friend he loves best the other arm to hold after the same manner; which being done, they two, in the presence of all the assembly, dispatch him with their swords. After that, they roast him, eat him amongst them, and send some chops to their absent friends. They do not do this, as some think, for nourishment, . . . but as a representation of an extreme revenge; as will appear by this: that having observed the Portuguese, who were in league with their enemies, to inflict another sort of death upon any of them they took prisoners, which was . . . to shoot at [them] till [they were] stuck full of arrows, and then to hang them, they thought those people of the other world . . . did not exercise this sort of revenge without a meaning, and that it must needs be more painful than theirs, they began to leave their old way, and to follow this. I am not sorry that we should here take notice of the barbarous horror of so cruel an action, but that, seeing so clearly into their faults, we should be so blind to our own. I conceive there is more barbarity in eating a man alive, than when he is dead; in tearing a body limb from limb by racks and torments, that is yet in perfect sense; in roasting it by degrees; in causing it to be bitten and worried by dogs and swine (as we have not only read, but lately seen, not amongst invet-erate and mortal enemies, but among neighbors and fellow-citizens, and, which is worse, under color of piety and religion), than to roast and eat him after he is dead. . . .

We may then call these people barbarous, in respect to the rules of rea-son: but not in respect to ourselves, who in all sorts of barbarity exceed them. Their wars are throughout noble and generous, and carry as much excuse and fair pretence, as that human malady is capable of; having with them no other foundation than the sole jealousy of valor. Their disputes are not for the conquest of new lands, for these they already possess are so fruitful by nature, as to supply them without labor or concern, with all things necessary, in such abundance that they have no need to enlarge their borders. And they are, moreover, happy in this, that they only covet so much as their natural necessities require: all beyond that is superfluous to them. . . . If their neighbors pass over the mountains to assault them, and obtain a victory, all the victors gain by it is glory only, and the advantage of having proved themselves the better in valor and virtue: for they never meddle with the goods of the conquered, but presently return into their own country, where they have no want of anything necessary, nor of this greatest of all goods, to know happily how to enjoy their condition and to be content. And those in turn do the same; they demand of their prisoners no other ransom, than acknowledgment that they are overcome. . . . There is not a man amongst them who had not rather be killed and eaten, than so much as to open his mouth to entreat he may not. They use them with all liberality and freedom, to the end their lives may be so much the dearer to them; but frequently entertain them with menaces of their approaching death, of the torments they are to suffer, of the preparations making in order to it, of the mangling of their limbs, and of the feast that is to be made, where their carcass is to be the only dish. All which they do, to no other end, but only to extort some gentle or submissive word from them, or to frighten them so as to make them run away, to obtain this advantage that they were terrified, and that their constancy was shaken; and indeed, if rightly taken, it is in this point only that a true victory consists. . . .

But to return to my story: these prisoners are so far from discovering the least weakness, for all the terrors that can be represented to them, that, on the contrary, during the two or three months they are kept, they always appear with a cheerful countenance; importune their masters to make haste to bring them to the test, defy, rail at them, and reproach them with cowardice, and the number of battles they have lost against those of their country. I have a song made by one of these prisoners, wherein he bids them "come all, and dine upon him, and welcome, for they shall withal eat their own fathers and grandfathers, whose flesh has served to feed and nourish him. These muscles," says he, "this flesh and these veins, are your own: poor silly souls as you are, you little think that the substance of your ancestors' limbs is here yet; notice what you eat, and you will find in it the taste of your own flesh": in which song there is to be observed an invention that nothing relishes of the barbarian. Those that paint these people dying after this manner, represent the prisoner spitting in the faces of his executioners and making wry mouths at them. And 'tis most certain, that to the very last gasp, they never cease to brave and defy them both in word and gesture. In plain truth, these men are very savage in comparison of us; of necessity, they must either be absolutely so or else we are savages; for there is a vast difference betwixt their manners and ours.

## READING QUESTIONS

1. Why does Montaigne write that the words of a "plain ignorant fellow" are more reliable than the words of someone who has been educated? Why does he think it important that reason should be the guide to understanding?

2. How does Montaigne use the word *barbarian* in this essay? To him, what makes someone a barbarian, and why?

3. On what points does Montaigne compare and contrast Native American society with Portuguese society? In what ways does he find the Portuguese to be more barbarous than the cannibals? Why?

# ■ COMPARATIVE AND DISCUSSION QUESTIONS ■

1. What light do Cortés and Columbus shed on the motives behind Spanish exploration and colonization of the Americas?

2. Compare and contrast the two documents on the African slave trade (Documents 14-3 and 14-4). What do these documents reveal about the nature of Portuguese participation?

3. Based on your reading of the documents in these chapters, which distinctions among peoples seemed most important for Europeans of the fifteenth and sixteenth centuries?

4. How do Montaigne's impressions of non-Europeans contrast with those in other European accounts in this chapter? Why do you think they are different?

# 15

# Absolutism and Constitutionalism
## ca. 1589–1725

Sixteenth- and seventeenth-century Europe witnessed a prolonged struggle between monarchs seeking to consolidate and extend their power, and social groups and institutions opposing those efforts. Many factors—political, social, and economic—influenced the course of this struggle, and the outcome varied from country to country. France's kings managed to suppress some of the opposition to royal power and thus are termed "absolutist" monarchs, although even the greatest of them, Louis XIV, lacked the power and authority to exert his unchallenged will over all of his subjects, in particular the great nobles. Eastern European rulers in Prussia, Austria, and Russia also augmented their power and authority, although there were significant differences from state to state, and none matched Louis XIV's achievement. Still, all experienced greater success in expanding royal authority than did their counterparts in the Netherlands and England. Two English kings, Charles I and James II, lost their thrones as a consequence of political revolutions, and the former was also tried and executed for crimes against his subjects.

## 15-1 | A French King Establishes Limited Religious Toleration
### HENRY IV, *Edict of Nantes* (1598)

Prince Henry of Navarre (1553–1610) was a Huguenot, or Protestant, in an overwhelmingly Roman Catholic country. He ascended to the French throne as Henry IV in 1589 in the midst of the French Wars of Religion. A pragmatist, Henry realized that the country's Catholic

From King Henry of Navarre, "Edict of Nantes," in *Readings in European History*, ed. James Harvey Robinson, vol. 2 (Boston: Ginn, 1906), pp. 183–185.

majority would never accept a Protestant as their legitimate ruler, so he converted to Catholicism. However, to protect the Huguenots against religiously motivated attacks, as well as to establish peace among the people he was determined to rule, he issued the Edict of Nantes. In so doing, Henry legally sanctioned a degree of religious tolerance in a Europe previously characterized by the formula "one king, one people, one faith."

Among the infinite benefits which it has pleased God to heap upon us, the most signal and precious is his granting us the strength and ability to withstand the fearful disorders and troubles which prevailed on our advent in this kingdom. The realm was so torn by innumerable factions and sects that the most legitimate of all the parties[1] was fewest in numbers. God has given us strength to stand out against this storm; we have finally surmounted the waves and made our port of safety,—peace for our state. For which his be the glory all in all, and ours a free recognition of his grace in making use of our instrumentality in the good work. . . . We implore and await from the Divine Goodness the same protection and favor which he has ever granted to this kingdom from the beginning. . . .

We have, by this perpetual and irrevocable edict, established and proclaimed and do establish and proclaim:

I. First, that the recollection of everything done by one party or the other between March, 1585, and our accession to the crown, and during all the preceding period of troubles, remain obliterated and forgotten, as if no such things had ever happened. . . .

III. We ordain that the Catholic Apostolic and Roman religion shall be restored and reestablished in all places and localities of this our kingdom and countries subject to our sway, where the exercise of the same has been interrupted, in order that it may be peaceably and freely exercised, without any trouble or hindrance; forbidding very expressly all persons, of whatsoever estate, quality, or condition, from troubling, molesting, or disturbing ecclesiastics in the celebration of divine service, in the enjoyment or collection of tithes, fruits, or revenues of their benefices, and all other rights and dues belonging to them; and that all those who during the troubles have taken possession of churches, houses, goods, or revenues, belonging to the said ecclesiastics, shall surrender to them entire possession and peaceable enjoyment of such rights, liberties, and sureties as they had before they were deprived of them. . . .

VI. And in order to leave no occasion for troubles or differences between our subjects, we have permitted, and herewith permit, those of the said religion called Reformed [Protestant] to live and abide in all the cities and places of this our kingdom and countries of our sway, without being annoyed,

---

[1]**the most legitimate of all the parties**: Faction supporting Valois king Henry III (r. 1574–1589) during the French Wars of Religion (1561–1598). Henry's subsequent reference to "one party or the other" refers to the three factions, two of them Catholic, one of them Protestant, that struggled for control of the French throne.

molested, or compelled to do anything in the matter of religion contrary to their consciences, . . . upon conditions that they comport themselves in other respects according to that which is contained in this our present edict.

VII. It is permitted to all lords, gentlemen, and other persons making profession of the said religion called Reformed, holding the right of high justice [or a certain feudal tenure], to exercise the said religion in their houses. . . .

IX. We also permit those of the said religion to make and continue the exercise of the same in all villages and places of our dominion where it was established by them and publicly enjoyed several and divers times in the year 1597, up to the end of the month of August, notwithstanding all decrees and judgments to the contrary. . . .

XIII. We very expressly forbid to all those of the said religion its exercise, either in respect to ministry, regulation, discipline, or the public instruction of children, or otherwise, in this our kingdom and lands of our dominion, otherwise than in the places permitted and granted by the present edict.

XIV. It is forbidden as well to perform any function of the said religion on our court or retinue, or in our lands and territories beyond the mountains, or in our city of Paris, or within five leagues of the said city. . . .

XVIII. We also forbid all our subjects, of whatever quality and condition, from carrying off by force or persuasion, against the will of their parents, the children of the said religion, in order to cause them to be baptized or confirmed in the Catholic Apostolic and Roman Church; and the same is forbidden to those of the said religion called Reformed, upon penalty of being punished with special severity. . . .

XXI. Books concerning the said religion called Reformed may not be printed and publicly sold, except in cities and places where the public exercise of the said religion is permitted.

XXII. We ordain that there shall be no difference or distinction made in respect to the said religion, in receiving pupils to be instructed in universities, colleges, and schools; or in receiving the sick and poor into hospitals, retreats and public charities.

XXIII. Those of the said religion called Reformed shall be obliged to respect the laws of the Catholic Apostolic and Roman Church, recognized in this our kingdom, for the consummation of marriages contracted, or to be contracted, as regards to the degrees of consanguinity and kinship.

### READING QUESTIONS

1. Why was Henry so intent on "obliterating" the memory of "everything done by one party or the other" in the years immediately prior to his coronation as king of France?

2. Is the Edict of Nantes consistent with Henry's aim of increasing the monarchy's and the state's power? Why or why not?

3. Why might Henry's son, Louis XIII, have regarded the Huguenots as "a state within a state"?

4. Based on the details of the edict regarding ceremonies, property, literature, and education, what sorts of practices defined a religion before and during Henry's reign? What, if any, practices did he consider irreligious, or purely civil?

## 15-2 | An Argument for the Divine Right of Kings

### JEAN DOMAT, *Of the Government and General Policy of a State* (1689)

Jean Domat was a French legal scholar who became one of the foremost experts on Roman law in seventeenth-century Europe. He compiled a massive and systematic guidebook for the French legal system that had enormous long-term influence, and in the process he defined and supported the basis of absolute monarchy, not surprisingly while in the service of the most successful absolute monarch of the period, the French Louis XIV. In these excerpts, he first lays out the rational roots of government in general, and then proceeds to explain why absolute monarchy was a legitimate form of political leadership.

There is nobody who does not appreciate the need for good order in a state, and who does not sincerely wish to see the state that he lives in well regulated. For everyone comprehends and feels within himself by experience and by reason, that the order of society concerns and affects him in many different ways. . . .

Everybody knows that every person is a member of society: and this Truth which the Scripture teaches us, and which the Light of Reason makes clear and evident, is the foundation of all the duties which respect the conduct of every member towards all the other members in particular, and towards the body in general. For a person's duties are nothing else but the functions which are proper to the relationships he has due to his rank in society.

It is from this principle that we draw all the rules of the duties of those who govern, and of those who are subject to the government. For it is by the rank that each person holds in society, that God, who determines the societal place of everyone, also determines their functions and duties. This includes the functions and duties between individual people and also between a person and society as a whole.

Because all men are equal by nature, simply because they are all human, nature does not allow for any person to dominate anyone else. . . . But within this natural equality, there are things that make people unequal, and create relationships and dependencies between them that determine the various duties of each toward the others, and make government necessary. . . .

The first distinction that makes some people able to dominate others is the relationship between parents and children. And this distinction lends itself to a sort of government in families, where children must obey their parents, who lead the family.

From Jean Domat, *The Civil Law in Its Natural Order Together with the Public Law*, trans. William Strahan (London: E. Bell et al., 1722), pp. 289–319.

The second distinction between people derives from the various jobs necessary to be done within a society, and which unite them all into a group that they all are part of. For just as God has made each person dependent upon others for certain things, He has varied their status and their occupations to meet all these needs, assigning people their roles and functions in society. And it is through these interdependent jobs and roles that the connections within human society are formed, as well as the ties among its people. This also makes it necessary to have a leader to unite and rule the society created by these various occupations, and to maintain the order of the relationships that give the public the benefit of the different duties of people that have various social ranks.

It also follows that, since not every person does their duties, and some actually commit injustices, in order to prevent societal chaos, injustices and anything that threatens the social order must be repressed: which was possible only by granting some people authority over others, and which made government necessary.

## Causes of the Necessity of a Government

This necessity of government over people equal by their nature, distinguished from each other only by the differences that God established among them according to their stations and professions, makes it clear that government arises from His will; and because only He is the natural sovereign of men, it is from Him that all those who govern derive their power and all their authority, and it is God Himself Whom they represent in their functions.

## The Duties of the Governed

Since government is necessary for the health of society, and God has established it, it is therefore also necessary that subjects of a government be submissive and obedient. For if they were not obedient they would resist God, and government, which should preserve societal peace and unity, would foster conflicts that would cause it to collapse.

The first duty of obedience to government is to obey those who have the most powerful roles, monarchs or others who lead society, and to obey them as the limbs of the human body obey the head of their body.

This obedience to the leader should be considered as obedience to the power of God, Who has installed [the leader] as His viceregent here on Earth.

. . .

Obedience to government includes observing the laws, not doing anything contrary to them, executing commands, avoiding things that are forbidden, bearing public burdens, whether they are performing occupations or paying taxes; and in general everyone is obliged not only not to disturb public order in any way, but to contribute everything that is necessary to maintain order.

Since this obedience is necessary to maintain the order and peace that should unite the sovereign and the members of society, it is a duty for all subjects in all cases to obey the orders of the prince, without passing judgment on the orders they should obey. For otherwise, the right to inquire what is just or not would make everyone a master, and it would encourage rebellions.

Thus each individual must obey even laws and orders that seem unjust and [even] to unjust orders, provided he can obey and follow them without being unjust in their own actions. And the only exception that where people could choose to disobey is limited to cases in which one could not obey without disobeying the divine law.

. . .

## The Power, Rights, and Duties of Sovereigns

The sovereign power of government should be proportionate to its ministerial function, and in the rank he holds in a society that comprises a state, the sovereign should represent God. For since God is the only natural governor of men, their judge, their lawgiver, their king, no man can have lawful authority over others unless if comes from the hand of God. . . .

Since the power of sovereigns thus comes to them from God, and since He gives it to them only through His providence and His rule over the states whose government He delegates to them, it follows that they should use this power in alignment with the aims that divine providence and rule have established for them; and that the exercises of their authority should reflect the operation of the will of God. . . .

Among the rights of the sovereign, the first is the right to administer justice, the foundation of public order, whether he exercises it himself when necessary or whether he delegates others to exercise it. . . .

This same right to enforce the laws, and to maintain order in general by administering justice and exercising sovereign power, gives the prince the right to use his authority to enforce the laws of the Church, whose *protector, conservator, and defender* [*sic*] he should be; so that through his authority, religion rules all his subjects. . . .

Among the rights that the laws give the sovereign should be the ability to display all the signs of grandeur and majesty necessary to display his authority and power, and to make his subjects respect that power. . . .

The first and most essential of all the duties of God-appointed sovereigns is acceptance of this fact: that *it is from God that they hold all their power* [*sic*], that it is His authority they represent, that it is through Him they should reign, and that it is to Him they should look for the knowledge and wisdom needed to govern well. . . .

These general obligations . . . concern all the specific duties of sovereigns. For . . . everything that concerns administering justice, policing of the state, public order, the repose of subjects, peace of mind in families, vigilance over everything that can contribute to the common good, *the choice of able and just ministers*, the appointment of good men whom he knows to the dignities and offices, observing regulations for filling other offices with people that he cannot personally choose, using severity or mercy in those cases where the rigor of justice may be tempered, wisely distributing benefits, rewards, exemptions, privileges, and other favors; good administration of the public finances, wisdom in conducting relations with foreign states, and lastly everything that can make government favorable to good people, terrible to wicked people, and worthy in all respects of the divine mandate to govern men, and of the use of a power which, coming only from God, shares in His own Authority. . . .

We may add as a last duty of the sovereign, which follows from the first and includes all the others, that although his power seems to place him above the law, with no one able to make him accountable to the law, nevertheless he should follow the laws as they may apply to him. And he needs to do this not only to set a good example for his subjects and make them love their duty, but because his sovereign power does not free him from his own duty, and his station requires him to privilege the general good of the state above his personal interests, and it is a glory for him to look upon the general good as his own.

### READING QUESTIONS

1. Why does Domat argue that government is necessary?

2. What is the basis for the power of monarchs, or where do they get their authority?

3. According to Domat, are there any limits to the absolute power of kings? If so, what are they? How likely is it that French kings would be hampered by those limits in practice?

4. How does this document differ from the parameters of monarchical power set in the English Bill of Rights (Document 15-3)?

5. What do you see as the benefits and drawbacks of the absolute authority that Domat describes?

## 15-3  |  The English Place Limits on Monarchical Power
### *The Bill of Rights* (1689)

Almost a century of struggle between the forces of constitutionalism and absolutism in England culminated in the Bill of Rights. The Bill of Rights was an unequivocal statement that Parliament, not the monarch, was the source of English law and that all Englishmen, including the monarch, were subject to the law. Acceptance of the Bill of Rights was a non-negotiable condition of the ascendency of William and Mary to the English throne. Thus, the very first act of the new monarchs was to acknowledge the limits of their power. As you read this excerpt, think about what it reveals about late-seventeenth-century notions of freedom and tyranny. What kinds of abuses of power did Parliament fear? What rights and liberties did it seek to protect?

Whereas the late King James the Second, by the assistance of divers evil counsellors, judges and ministers employed by him, did endeavour to subvert and extirpate the Protestant religion and the laws and liberties of this kingdom;

By assuming and exercising a power of dispensing with and suspending of laws and the execution of laws without consent of Parliament;

By committing and prosecuting divers worthy prelates for humbly petitioning to be excused from concurring to the said assumed power;

By issuing and causing to be executed a commission under the great seal for erecting a court called the Court of Commissioners for Ecclesiastical Causes;

By levying money for and to the use of the Crown by pretence of prerogative for other time and in other manner than the same was granted by Parliament;

By raising and keeping a standing army within this kingdom in time of peace without consent of Parliament, and quartering soldiers contrary to law;

By causing several good subjects being Protestants to be disarmed at the same time when papists were both armed and employed contrary to law;

By violating the freedom of election of members to serve in Parliament;

By prosecutions in the Court of King's Bench for matters and causes cognizable only in Parliament, and by divers other arbitrary and illegal courses;

And whereas of late years partial corrupt and unqualified persons have been returned and served on juries in trials, and particularly divers jurors in trials for high treason which were not freeholders;

And excessive bail hath been required of persons committed in criminal cases to elude the benefit of the laws made for the liberty of the subjects;

And excessive fines have been imposed;

And illegal and cruel punishments inflicted;

And several grants and promises made of fines and forfeitures before any conviction or judgment against the persons upon whom the same were to be levied;

All which are utterly and directly contrary to the known laws and statutes and freedom of this realm;

And whereas the said late King James the Second having abdicated the government and the throne being thereby vacant, his Highness the prince of Orange (whom it hath pleased Almighty God to make the glorious instrument of delivering this kingdom from popery and arbitrary power) did (by the advice of the Lords Spiritual and Temporal and divers principal persons of the Commons) cause letters to be written to the Lords Spiritual and Temporal being Protestants, and other letters to the several counties, cities, universities, boroughs and cinque ports, for the choosing of such persons to represent them as were of right to be sent to Parliament, to meet and sit at Westminster upon the two and twentieth day of January in this year one thousand six hundred eighty and eight [old-style date], in order to such an establishment as that their religion, laws and liberties might not again be in danger of being subverted, upon which letters elections having been accordingly made;

And thereupon the said Lords Spiritual and Temporal and Commons, pursuant to their respective letters and elections, being now assembled in a full and free representative of this nation, taking into their most serious consideration the best means for attaining the ends aforesaid, do in the first place (as their ancestors in like case have usually done) for the vindicating and asserting their ancient rights and liberties declare

That the pretended power of suspending the laws or the execution of laws by regal authority without consent of Parliament is illegal;

That the pretended power of dispensing with laws or the execution of laws by regal authority, as it hath been assumed and exercised of late, is illegal;

That the commission for erecting the late Court of Commissioners for Ecclesiastical Causes, and all other commissions and courts of like nature, are illegal and pernicious;

That levying money for or to the use of the Crown by pretence of prerogative, without grant of Parliament, for longer time, or in other manner than the same is or shall be granted, is illegal;

That it is the right of the subjects to petition the king, and all commitments and prosecutions for such petitioning are illegal;

That the raising or keeping a standing army within the kingdom in time of peace, unless it be with consent of Parliament, is against law;

That the subjects which are Protestants may have arms for their defence suitable to their conditions and as allowed by law;

That election of members of Parliament ought to be free;

That the freedom of speech and debates or proceedings in Parliament ought not to be impeached or questioned in any court or place out of Parliament;

That excessive bail ought not to be required, nor excessive fines imposed, nor cruel and unusual punishments inflicted;

That jurors ought to be duly impanelled and returned, and jurors which pass upon men in trials for high treason ought to be freeholders;

That all grants and promises of fines and forfeitures of particular persons before conviction are illegal and void;

And that for redress of all grievances, and for the amending, strengthening and preserving of the laws, Parliaments ought to be held frequently.

### READING QUESTIONS

1. According to the authors, in what ways did James II abuse his power?

2. What steps did the authors take to protect the power of Parliament? To ensure the impartial application of the law?

3. What restrictions did the Bill of Rights place on the rights of Catholics? How might the authors have justified their inclusion of discriminatory provisions in a law meant to protect the rights of the English people?

## 15-4 | A Tsar Imposes Western Styles on the Russians

### PETER THE GREAT, *Edicts and Decrees* (1699–1723)

Peter the Great's reign (1682–1725) marked Russia's emergence as a major European power. Russia defeated Sweden in the grueling Great Northern War (1700–1721) and acquired a "window on Europe" at the head of the Gulf of Finland, where Peter built a new capital, St. Petersburg. In order to defeat the Swedes, who had routed his ill-trained army at Narva in 1700, Peter had reformed and modernized his military along western European lines. His enthusiasm for Western technology and tactics extended also to other realms, including

From Marthe Blinoff, *Life and Thought in Old Russia* (University Park: Pennsylvania State University Press, 1961), pp. 49–50; Eugene Schuyler, *Peter the Great*, vol. 2 (New York: Charles Scribner's Sons, 1884), pp. 176–177; L. Jay Oliva, *Peter the Great* (Englewood Cliffs, N.J.: Prentice-Hall, 1970), p. 50; George Vernadsky et al., *A Source Book for Russian History from Early Times to 1917*, vol. 2 (New Haven, Conn.: Yale University Press, 1972), pp. 329, 347, 357.

education, dress, and economic programs, as can be seen from the following excerpts. As you read them, ask yourself why the West was of such interest to Peter. What did he hope to accomplish through his program of "westernization"?

## Decree on the New Calendar, 1699

It is known to His Majesty that not only many European Christian lands, but also Slavic nations which are in total accord with our Eastern Orthodox Church . . . agree to count their years from the eighth day after the birth of Christ, that is from the first day of January, and not from the creation of the world,[1] because of the many difficulties and discrepancies of this reckoning. It is now the year 1699 from the birth of Christ, and from the first of January will begin both the new year 1700 and a new century; and so His Majesty has ordered, as a good and useful mea-sure, that from now on time will be reckoned in government offices and dates be noted on documents and property deeds, starting from the first of January 1700. And to celebrate this good undertaking and the new century . . . in the sovereign city of Moscow . . . let the reputable citizens arrange decorations of pine, fir, and juniper trees and boughs along the busiest main streets and by the houses of emi-nent church and lay persons of rank. . . . Poorer persons should place at least one shrub or bough on their gates or on their house. . . . Also . . . as a sign of rejoic-ing, wishes for the new year and century will be exchanged, and the following will be organized: when fire-works are lit and guns fired on the great Red Square, let the boyars [nobles], the Lords of the Palace, of the Chamber, and the Council, and the eminent personages of Court, Army, and Merchant ranks, each in his own grounds, fire three times from small guns, if they have any, or from muskets and other small arms, and shoot some rockets into the air.

## Decree on the Invitation of Foreigners, 1702

Since our accession to the throne all our efforts and intentions have tended to govern this realm in such a way that all of our subjects should, through our care for the general good, become more and more prosperous. For this end we have always tried to maintain internal order, to defend the state against invasion, and in every possible way to improve and to extend trade. With this purpose we have been compelled to make some necessary and salutary changes in the administration, in order that our subjects might more easily gain a knowledge of matters of which they were before ignorant, and become more skillful in their commercial relations.

We have therefore given orders, made dispositions, and founded institu-tions indispensable for increasing our trade with foreigners, and shall do the same in the future. Nevertheless we fear that matters are not in such a good condition as we desire, and that our subjects cannot in perfect quietness enjoy

---

[1]**agree to count their years . . . world**: Before January 1, 1700, the Russian calendar started from the date of the creation of the world, which was reckoned at 5508 B.C.E. The year began on September 1.

the fruits of our labors, and we have therefore considered still other means to protect our frontier from the invasion of the enemy, and to preserve the rights and privileges of our State, and the general peace of all Christians. . . .

To attain these worthy aims, we have endeavored to improve our military forces, which are the protection of our State, so that our troops may consist of well-drilled men, maintained in perfect order and discipline. In order to obtain greater improvement in this respect, and to encourage foreigners, who are able to assist us in this way, as well as artisans profitable to the State, to come in numbers to our country, we have issued this manifesto, and have ordered printed copies of it to be sent throughout Europe. . . . And as in our residence of Moscow, the free exercise of religion of all other sects, although not agreeing with our church, is already allowed, so shall this be hereby confirmed anew in such manner that we, by the power granted to us by the Almighty, shall exercise no compulsion over the consciences of men, and shall gladly allow every Christian to care for his own salvation at his own risk.

## An Instruction to Russian Students Abroad Studying Navigation, 1714

1. Learn how to draw plans and charts and how to use the compass and other naval indicators.

2. Learn how to navigate a vessel in battle as well as in a simple maneuver, and learn how to use all appropriate tools and instruments; namely, sails, ropes, and oars, and the like matters, on row boats and other vessels.

3. Discover . . . how to put ships to sea during a naval battle. . . . Obtain from foreign naval officers written statements, bearing their signatures and seals, of how adequately you are prepared for naval duties.

4. If, upon his return, anyone wishes to receive from the Tsar greater favors, he should learn, in addition to the above enumerated instructions, how to construct those vessels [aboard] which he would like to demonstrate his skills.

5. Upon his return to Moscow, every foreign-trained Russian should bring with him at his own expense, for which he will later be reimbursed, at least two experienced masters of naval science. They [the returnees] will be assigned soldiers, one soldier per returnee, to teach them what they have learned abroad. . . .

## Decree on Western Dress, 1701

Western ["German"] dress shall be worn by all the boyars, okol'nichie,[2] members of our councils and of our court . . . gentry of Moscow, secretaries . . . provincial gentry, boiarskie,[3] gosti,[4] government officials, strel'tsy,[5] members of the guilds purveying for our household, citizens of Moscow of all ranks, and residents of provincial cities . . . excepting the clergy (priests, deacons, and church attendants) and peasant tillers of the soil. The upper dress shall

---

[2]**boyars, okol'nichie**: Nobles of the highest and second-highest rank, respectively.
[3]**boiarskie**: Sons of boyars.
[4]**gosti**: Merchants who often served the tsar in some capacity.
[5]**strel'tsy**: Members of the imperial guard stationed in Moscow.

be of French or Saxon cut, and the lower dress — [including] waistcoat, trou-sers, boots, shoes, and hats — shall be of the German type. They shall also ride German saddles. [Likewise] the womenfolk of all ranks, including the priests', deacons', and church attendants' wives, the wives of the dragoons, the soldiers, and the strel'tsy and their children, shall wear Western ["German"] dresses, hats, jackets, and underwear — undervests and petticoats — and shoes. From now on no one [of the abovementioned] is to wear Russian dress or Circassian coats,[6] sheepskin coats, or Russian peasant coats, trousers, boots, and shoes. It is also forbidden to ride Russian saddles, and the craftsmen shall not manufacture them or sell them at the marketplaces.

## Decree on Shaving, 1705

A decree to be published in Moscow and in all the provincial cities: Henceforth, in accordance with this, His Majesty's decree, all court attendants . . . provincial service men, government officials of all ranks, military men, all the gosti, members of the wholesale merchants' guild, and members of the guilds purveying for our house-hold must shave their beards and moustaches. But, if it happens that some of them do not wish to shave their beards and moustaches, let a yearly tax be collected from such persons. . . . Special badges shall be issued to them from the Administrator of Land Affairs [of Public Order] . . . which they must wear. . . . As for the peasants, let a toll of two half-copecks[7] per beard be collected at the town gates each time they enter or leave a town; and do not let the peasants pass the town gates, into or out of town, without paying this toll.

## Decree on Promotion to Officer's Rank, 1714

Since there are many who promote to officer rank their relatives and friends — young men who do not know the fundamentals of soldiering, not having served in the lower ranks — and since even those who serve [in the ranks] do so for a few weeks or months only, as a formality; therefore . . . let a decree be promulgated that henceforth there shall be no promotion [to officer rank] of men of noble extraction or of any others who have not first served as privates in the Guards. This decree does not apply to soldiers of lowly origin who, after long service in the ranks, have received their commissions through honest service or to those who are promoted on the basis of merit, now or in the future; it applies exclusively to those who have remained in the ranks for a short time, only as a formality, as described above.

## Statute for the College of Manufactures, 1723

His Imperial Majesty is diligently striving to establish and develop in the Russian Empire such manufacturing plants and factories as are found in other states, for the general welfare and prosperity of his subjects. He [therefore] most

---

[6]**Circassian coats**: Traditional outer garments worn by the people of Circassia, a Russian territory between the Caspian and Black Seas. The style was evidently adopted by the nobility.

[7]**half-copecks**: One-twentieth of a ruble, the basic unit of Russian money.

graciously charges the College of Manufactures[8] to exert itself in devising the means to introduce, with the least expense, and to spread in the Russian Empire these and other ingenious arts, and especially those for which materials can be found within the empire; [the College of Manufactures] must also consider the privileges that should be granted to those who might wish to found manufacturing plants and factories.

His Imperial Majesty gives permission to everyone, without distinction of rank or condition, to open factories wherever he may find suitable. . . .

Factory owners must be closely supervised, in order that they have at their plants good and experienced [foreign] master craftsmen, who are able to train Russians in such a way that these, in turn, may themselves become masters, so that their produce may bring glory to the Russian manufactures. . . .

By the former decrees of His Majesty commercial people were forbidden to buy villages [i.e., to own serfs], the reason being that they were not engaged in any other activity beneficial for the state save commerce; but since it is now clear to all that many of them have started to found manufacturing establishments and build plants, both in companies and individually, which tend to increase the welfare of the state . . . therefore permission is granted both to the gentry and to men of commerce to acquire villages for these factories without hindrance. . . .

In order to stimulate voluntary immigration of various craftsmen from other countries into the Russian Empire, and to encourage them to establish factories and manufacturing plants freely and at their own expense, the College of Manufactures must send appropriate announcements to the Russian envoys accredited at foreign courts. The envoys should then, in an appropriate way, bring these announcements to the attention of men of various professions, urge them to come to settle in Russia, and help them to move.

### READING QUESTIONS

1. Why do you think Peter decreed that the nobles, merchants, and townspeople wear German, rather than French, clothes, seeing as the French kings and their palaces were objects of emulation throughout Europe?

2. What does Peter's decree encouraging foreign soldiers and artisans to emigrate to Russia and his Statute for the College of Manufactures suggest about the state of Russia's military forces and economy as of the early 1700s?

3. Why didn't Russia have a navy prior to 1700?

4. What, according to Peter, was wrong with the system of promotion in the Russian army, and how did he intend to redress it? What does his decree on promotion suggest about the power and benefits granted to the Russian nobility?

---

[8]**College of Manufactures**: One of several administrative boards created by Peter in 1717, modeled on Swedish practice.

SOURCES IN CONVERSATION

# The Commonwealth and the State of Nature

Over the course of the seventeenth century, England experienced two civil wars, the execution of a king, and the forced abdication of another. These dramatic events raised fundamental political questions: What limitations exist on monarchical authority? What rights do subjects enjoy, and under what conditions can those rights be abridged? What means of redress, if any, do subjects have if their leaders abuse their power? The political philosophers Thomas Hobbes and John Locke developed the two most important theoretical responses to these questions. While their answers differed, they framed their analyses in similar ways. Both addressed two overarching questions: How and why do governments form? And what do the origins of the state imply for contemporary political conflicts?

## READ AND COMPARE

1. How do these two documents explain the reason that government exists, and how do those explanations differ? Why do you think they are different, based upon the identity of the authors?

2. Which people in society would benefit most from Hobbes's system on the one hand, and Locke's on the other?

## 15-5 | THOMAS HOBBES, *Leviathan* (1651)

Thomas Hobbes (1588–1679), the son of a Church of England clergyman, was educated at Oxford University and spent the years between 1608 and 1637 chiefly as a tutor to aristocratic families. Rising religious and political tensions in England drove Hobbes to flee to Paris in 1640, and there he remained until the publication of *Leviathan*, which aroused so much anger among English royalists that he was forced to seek protection from Cromwell's republican government. Leviathan originally referred to a biblical sea monster, but Hobbes used it as a synonym for the commonwealth; the frontispiece to his book depicts a gargantuan human figure made up of smaller people (members of the commonwealth) with the head of a monarch. *Leviathan* itself is based on the premise that without a sovereign authority invested with absolute power, human society is in a state of perpetual violence. Faced with such a prospect, he argued, individuals voluntarily relinquish their personal rights and liberties in return for protection.

Nature hath made men so equal, in the faculties of body and mind, as that though there be found one man sometimes manifestly stronger in body, or of quicker mind than another; yet when all is reckoned together, the difference between man and man is not so considerable, as that one man can thereupon claim to himself any benefit, to which another may not pretend, as well as he.

From Thomas Hobbes, *Leviathan, or the Matter, Form, and Power of a Commonwealth, Ecclesiastical and Civil* (London: George Routledge and Sons, 1886), pp. 64–66, 82, 84–85.

For as to the strength of body, the weakest has strength enough to kill the strongest, either by secret machination or by confederacy with others that are in the same danger with himself. . . .

From this equality of ability, ariseth equality of hope in the attaining of our ends. And therefore if any two men desire the same thing, which nevertheless they cannot both enjoy, they become enemies, and in the way to their end, . . . endeavor to destroy, or subdue one another. . . .

So that in the nature of man, we find three principal causes of quarrel. First, competition; secondly, diffidence; thirdly, glory.

The first maketh men invade for gain; the second, for safety; and the third, reputation. The first use violence to make themselves masters of other men's persons, wives, children, and cattle; the second, to defend them; the third, for trifles, as a word, a smile, a different opinion, and any other sign of undervalue, either direct in their persons, or by reflection in their kindred, their friends, their nation, their profession, or their name.

Hereby it is manifest, that during the time men live without a common power to keep them all in awe, they are in that condition which is called war; and such a war, as is of every man, against every man. . . .

[On "the state of nature":]

Whatsoever therefore is consequent to a time of war, where every man is enemy to every man; the same is consequent to the time wherein men live without other security, than what their own strength and their own invention shall furnish them withall. In such condition, there is no place for industry, because the fruit thereof is uncertain, and consequently no culture of the earth; no navigation, nor use of the commodities that may be imported by sea; no commodious building; no instruments of moving and removing such things as require much force; no knowledge of the face of the earth; no account of time; no arts; no letters; no society; and, which is worst of all, continual fear, and danger of violent death; and the life of man, solitary, poor, nasty, brutish, and short. . . .

The passions that incline men to peace, are fear of death; desire of such things as are necessary to commodious living; and a hope by their industry to obtain them. And reason suggesteth convenient articles of peace, upon which men may be drawn to agreement. . . .

And because the condition of man, as hath been declared in the precedent chapter, is a condition of war of everyone against everyone; in which case everyone is governed by his own reason, and there is nothing he can make use of, that may not be a help unto him, in preserving his life against his enemies; It followeth that, in such a condition, every man has a right to every thing, even to one another's body. And therefore, as long as this natural right of every man to everything endureth, there can be no security to any man, how strong or wise soever he be, of living out the time, which Nature ordinarily alloweth men to live. . . .

If there be no power erected, or not great enough for our security, every man will and may lawfully rely on his own strength and art, for caution against all other men. . . .

The only way to erect such a common power, as may be able to defend them from the invasion of foreigners, and the injuries of one another, and thereby to secure them in such sort as that by their own industry and by the fruits of the earth they may nourish themselves and live contentedly, is to confer all their power and strength upon one man, or upon one assembly of men, that may reduce all their wills, by plurality of voices, unto one will: which is as much as to say, to appoint one man, or assembly of men, to bear their person; and every one to own and acknowledge himself to be author of whatsoever he that so beareth their person shall act, or cause to be acted, in those things which concern the common peace and safety; and therein to submit their wills, every one to his will, and their judgments to his judgment. This is more than consent, or concord; it is a real unity of them all in one and the same person, made by covenant of every man with every man, in such manner as if every man should say to every man: "I authorize and give up my right of governing myself to this man, or to this assembly of men, on this condition, that thou give up thy right to him, and authorize all his actions in like manner." This done, the multitude so united in one person is called a "commonwealth," in Latin, *civitas*. This is the generation of that great "leviathan," or rather, to speak more reverently, of that "mortal god," to which we owe under the "immortal God," our peace and defense. For by this authority, given him by every particular man in the commonwealth, he hath the use of so much power and strength conferred on him that by terror thereof, he is enabled to perform the wills of them all, to peace at home, and mutual aid against their enemies abroad. And in him consisteth the essence of the commonwealth; which, to define it, is "one person, of whose acts a great multitude, by mutual covenants one with another, have made themselves every one the author, to the end he may use the strength and means of them all as he shall think expedient, for their peace and common defense."

And he that carryeth this person is called "sovereign," and said to have "sovereign power"; and every one besides, his "subject." . . .

They that have already instituted a commonwealth, being thereby bound by covenant to own the actions and judgments of one, cannot lawfully make a new covenant, amongst themselves, to be obedient to any other, in anything whatsoever, without his permission. And therefore, they that are subjects to a monarch cannot without his leave cast off monarchy, and return to the confusion of a disunited multitude; nor transfer their person from him that beareth it to another man, other assembly of men . . . [he] that already is their sovereign shall do and judge fit to be done: so that any one man dissenting, all the rest should break their covenant made to that man, which is injustice: and they have also every man given the sovereignty to him that beareth their person; and therefore if they depose him, they take from him that which is his own, and so again it is injustice. . . . And whereas some men have pretended for their disobedience to their sovereign, a new covenant, made not with men but with God; this also is unjust: for there is no covenant with God but by mediation of somebody that representeth God's person; which none doth but God's lieutenant, who hath the sovereignty under God. But this pretense of covenant with God is so evident a lie, even in the pretenders' own consciences, that it is not only an act of an unjust, but also of a vile and unmanly disposition. . . .

Consequently none of [the sovereign's] subjects, by any pretence of forfeiture, can be freed from his subjection.

### READING QUESTIONS

1. How does Hobbes characterize human existence without the peace and order afforded by a ruler vested with absolute authority?

2. What is Hobbes's view of religious or divine justifications for absolute power?

3. Having placed themselves under the sovereign power of a ruler, what freedom of action do individuals have to govern their own affairs?

4. What options, according to Hobbes, do a sovereign's subjects have in the event that he abuses his power?

## 15-6 | JOHN LOCKE, *Second Treatise of Civil Government: Vindication for the Glorious Revolution* (1690)

John Locke (1632–1704) was, along with Thomas Hobbes, one of the two greatest English political theorists of the seventeenth century. Unlike Hobbes, however, who provided a justification for monarchical absolutism, Locke's *Second Treatise of Civil Government*, published anonymously in 1690, argued that government is an agreement between governors and the governed. The people submit to governmental authority in return for protection of their life, liberty, and property, and the governors' fundamental task is to provide those essential protections. According to Locke, a government that failed to do so or became tyrannical lost its claim to legitimacy, and could therefore be cast off by the governed.

87. Man being born, as has been proved, with a title to perfect freedom and an uncontrolled enjoyment of all the rights and privileges of the law of Nature, equally with any other man, or number of men in the world, hath by nature a power not only to preserve his property — that is, his life, liberty and estate against the injuries and attempts of other men; but to judge of and punish the breaches of that law in others, as he is persuaded the offense deserves, even with death itself, in crimes where the heinousness of the fact, in his opinion, requires it. But because no political society can be, nor subsist, without having in itself the power to preserve the property, and in order thereunto punish the offenses of all those of that society, there, and there only is political society where every one of the members hath quitted this natural power, resigned it up into the hands of the community in all cases that exclude him not from appealing for protection to the law established by it. And thus all private judgment of every particular member being excluded, the community comes to be umpire, and by understanding indifferent rules and men authorized by the community for their

From John Locke, *Two Treatises on Civil Government* (London: George Routledge and Sons, 1887), pp. 234–238.

execution, decides all the differences that may happen between any members of that society concerning any matter of right, and punishes those offenses which any member hath committed against the society with such penalties as the law has established; whereby it is easy to discern, who are, and are not, in political society together. Those who are united into one body, and have a common established law and judicature to appeal to, with authority to decide controversies between them and punish offenders, are in civil society one with another; but those who have no such common appeal, I mean on earth, are still in the state of Nature, each being where there is no other, judge for himself and executioner; which is, as I have before showed it, the perfect state of Nature.

88. And thus the commonwealth comes by a power to set down what punishment shall belong to the several transgressions they think worthy of it, committed amongst the members of that society (which is the power of making laws) as well as it has the power to punish any injury done unto any of its members by any one that is not of it (which is the power of war and peace); and all this for the preservation of the property of all the members of that society, as far as is possible. But though every man entered into society has quitted his power to punish offenses against the law of Nature in prosecution of his own private judgment, yet with the judgment of offenses which he has given up to the legislative, in all cases where he can appeal to the magistrate, he has given up a right to the commonwealth to employ his force, for the execution of the judgments of the commonwealth whenever he shall be called to it, which, indeed, are his own judgments, they being made by himself or his representative. And herein we have the original of the legislative and executive power of civil society, which is to judge by standing laws how far offenses are to be punished when committed within the commonwealth; and also by occasional judgments founded on the present circumstances of the fact, how far injuries from without are to be vindicated; and in both these to employ all the force of all the members when there shall be need.

89. Wherever, therefore, any number of men so unite into one society as to quit every one his executive power of the law of Nature, and to resign it to the public, there and there only is a political or civil society. And this is done wherever any number of men, in the state of nature, enter into society to make one people one body politic under one supreme government; or else when any one joins himself to, and incorporates with any government already made. For hereby he authorizes the society, or which is all one, the legislative thereof, to make laws for him as the public good of the society shall require; to the execution whereof his own assistance (as to his own decrees) is due. And this puts men out of a state of Nature into that of a commonwealth, by setting up a judge on earth with authority to determine all the controversies and redress the injuries that may happen to any member of the commonwealth; which judge is the legislative or magistrates appointed by it. And wherever there are any number of men, however associated, that have no such decisive power to appeal to, there they are still in the state of Nature.

90. And hence it is evident that absolute monarchy, which by some men is counted for the only government in the world, is indeed inconsistent with civil

society, and so can be no form of civil government at all. For the end of civil society being to avoid and remedy those inconveniencies of the state of nature which necessarily follow from every man's being judge in his own case by setting up a known authority to which every one of that society may appeal upon any injury received, or controversy that may arise, and which every one of the society ought to obey. Wherever any persons are who have not such an authority to appeal to, and decide any difference between them there, those persons are still in the state of Nature. And so is every absolute prince in respect of those who are under his dominion.

91. For he being supposed to have all, both legislative and executive, power in himself alone, there is no judge to be found, no appeal lies open to any one, who may fairly and indifferently, and with authority decide, and from whence relief and redress may be expected of any injury or inconveniency that may be suffered from him, or by his order. So that such a man, however entitled, Czar, or Grand Signior, or how you please, is as much in the state of Nature, with all under his dominion, as he is with the rest of mankind. For wherever any two men are, who have no standing rule and common judge to appeal to on earth, for the determination of controversies of right betwixt them, there they are still in the state of Nature, and under all the inconveniencies of it, with only this woeful difference to the subject, or rather slave of an absolute prince. That whereas, in the ordinary state of nature, he has a liberty to judge of his right, and according to the best of his power to maintain it; but whenever his property is invaded by the will and order of his monarch, he has not only no appeal, as those in society ought to have, but as if he were degraded from the common state of rational creatures, is denied a liberty to judge of, or to defend his right, and so is exposed to all the misery and inconveniencies that a man can fear from one, who being in the unrestrained state of Nature, is yet corrupted with flattery and armed with power.

92. For he that thinks absolute power purifies men's bloods, and corrects the baseness of human nature, need read but the history of this, or any other age, to be convinced of the contrary.

## READING QUESTIONS

1. What, according to Locke, distinguishes "political, or civil society" from "a state of nature"?

2. What, in Locke's opinion, led to the creation of "political, or civil society"?

3. Why does he argue that "absolute monarchy, which by some men is counted for the only government in the world, is indeed inconsistent with civil society, and so can be no form of civil government at all"?

4. Why do you think Locke published this work anonymously, rather than publicly claiming credit for what is now generally regarded as one of the classics of Western political theory?

## ▪ COMPARATIVE AND DISCUSSION QUESTIONS ▪

1.  What would Hobbes say of Domat's justification for absolute royal authority? What would Domat say of Hobbes's?

2.  How does Hobbes's "social contract" theory differ from Locke's? How do Hobbes and Locke use "the state of nature" to further their arguments?

3.  In what ways are Locke's views reflected in the English Bill of Rights?

4.  What do Henry IV's and Peter the Great's edicts tell you about their attitudes toward monarchy and their roles in the lives of their subjects?

# Toward a New Worldview
## 1540–1789

For the most part, medieval scholars turned to authoritative texts for information and ideas about the natural world. Placing their faith in the Bible and in the insights of ancient scholars, they forged a vision of the universe and its workings that infused classical models with Christian implications. Those models were first challenged and then overturned over the course of the sixteenth and seventeenth centuries, as direct observation and experiment combined with increasingly sophisticated mathematics to produce a revolution in the study of the natural world. This process culminated at the end of the seventeenth century in the discoveries of Isaac Newton, whose work would provide the fundamental framework for Western physics well into the twentieth century. By the eighteenth century, the spirit of this "scientific revolution" had spread to human affairs. Philosophers and scientists of the European Enlightenment, particularly in France, began to question traditional forms of social and political organization. Some thinkers rejected the legitimacy of absolutism and divine right. Others challenged the authority of the Roman Catholic Church. In the climate of the age, even absolutist monarchs saw advantages to embracing aspects of Enlightenment thought, though with varying degrees of enthusiasm and success.

## 16-1 | A New Model of the Solar System

### NICOLAUS COPERNICUS, *On the Revolutions of the Heavenly Spheres* (1542)

There was nothing revolutionary about Polish cleric and astronomer Nicolaus Copernicus's (1473–1543) motives for developing a heliocentric (sun-centered) model of the universe. Frustrated by the cumbersome calculations and inaccuracies of the Ptolemaic model, Copernicus sought an alternative that overcame these limitations and, in his view, offered a better reflection of the perfection of God's creation. Moreover, he retained many elements of earlier systems. For example, Copernicus still imagined the stars embedded in crystalline spheres. For all the conservatism of his approach, however, Copernicus was well aware of the stir his work might produce. Fearful of the response of church authorities, he waited to publish his findings until 1542, more than a decade after his work was complete and shortly before his death. As you read this excerpt, consider its mix of traditional and revolutionary ideas. In what ways does Copernicus seem like a medieval scholar? In what ways does he seem closer to what we think of as a scientist?

### That the Universe Is Spherical

First we must remark that the universe is globe-shaped, either because that is the most perfect shape of all, needing no joint, an integral whole; or because that it is the most capacious of shapes, which is most fitting because it is to contain and preserve all things; or because the most finished parts of the universe, I mean the Sun, Moon, and stars, are observed to have that shape, or because everything tends to take on this shape, which is evident in drops of water and other liquid bodies, when they take on their natural shape. There should therefore be no doubt that this shape is assigned to the heavenly bodies.

### That the Earth Is Also Spherical

The Earth is also globe-shaped, because every part of it tends towards its center. Although it is not immediately apparent that it is a perfect sphere, because the mountains project so far and the valleys are so deep, they produce very little variation in the complete roundness of the Earth. That is evident from the fact that as one moves northward from any point that pole [the North Pole] of the diurnal [daily] rotation rises little by little, while the other pole on the contrary sinks to the same extent, and several stars round the North Pole seem not to set, while some in the South no longer rise. . . .

From Nicolaus Copernicus, *De Revolutionibus Orbium Celestium*, trans. A. M. Duncan (Newton Abbot, Devonshire: David and Charles, 1976), pp. 36, 37, 40–41, 43–44, 45–46.

## Whether the Earth Has a Circular Motion, and Concerning the Location of the Earth

As it has now been shown that the Earth also has the shape of a globe, I believe we must consider whether its motion too follows its shape, and what place it holds in the universe, without which it is impossible to find a reliable explanation of celestial phenomena. Among the authorities it is generally agreed that the Earth is at rest in the middle of the universe, and they regard it as inconceivable and even ridiculous to hold the opposite opinion. However, if we consider it more closely the question will be seen to be still unsettled, and so decidedly not to be despised. For every apparent change in respect of position is due to motion of the object observed, or of the observer, or indeed to an unequal change of both. (Between objects which move equally in the same direction no motion is perceived, I mean between that which is observed and the observer.) Now the Earth is the point from which the rotation of the heavens is observed, and brought into our view. If therefore some motion is imputed to the Earth, the same motion will appear in all that is external to the Earth, but in the opposite direction, as if it were passing by. The first example of this is the diurnal rotation. This seems to whirl round the whole universe, except the Earth and the things on it. But if you grant that the heaven has no part in this motion, but that the Earth revolves from west to east, as far as the apparent rising and setting of the Sun, Moon, and stars is concerned, if you consider the point seriously, you will find that this is the way of it. And as the heaven is that which contains and cloaks all things, where everything has its place, it is not at once apparent why motion is attributed to that which is contained rather than to the container, to that which is located rather than that which locates it. . . . If this assumption is made there follows another and no lesser problem about the position of the Earth, although almost everyone admits and believes the Earth to be the center of the universe. For if one argues that the Earth does not occupy the center or middle of the universe, not claiming that its distance is great enough to be comparable with the sphere of the fixed stars, but that it is appreciable and significant compared with the orbits of the Sun and other stars,[1] and believing that on this account their motion seems to be variable, as if they were regular with respect to [i.e., revolved around] some center other than the center of the Earth, he would perhaps be able to put forward a not unreasonable account of the apparently variable motion. For the fact that the wandering stars are observed to be sometimes nearer to the Earth and sometimes further away from it necessarily shows that the center of the Earth is not the center of their orbits. It is also undecided whether the Earth veers toward them and away from them or they towards and away from the Earth. It would also not be surprising if in addition to this daily revolution another motion should be supposed for the Earth. Indeed that the

---

[1]**not claiming . . . other stars:** Copernicus is arguing here that the diameter of the earth's orbit is insignificant compared to the distance of the earth from the "fixed stars," which he, like his contemporaries, believed to be embedded in an invisible crystalline sphere, but is comparable to that of the "wandering stars," i.e., the visible planets.

Earth revolves, wanders with several motions, and is one of the stars [i.e., planets] is said to have been the opinion of Philolaus the Pythagorean,[2] no mean mathematician. . . .

## Refutation of the Arguments Quoted, and Their Insufficiency[3]

From this and similar arguments, then, they say that the Earth is at rest in the middle of the universe, and that such is undoubtedly the state of affairs. Yet if anyone should hold the opinion that the Earth revolves, he will surely assert that its motion is natural, not violent. What is natural produces contrary effects to what is violent. For objects to which force or impulse is applied must necessarily be destroyed and cannot long subsist; but objects which exist naturally are in their proper state, and continue in their perfect form. There is therefore no need for Ptolemy to fear the scattering of the Earth and of all terrestrial objects in a revolution brought about through the workings of nature, which is far different from artifice, or what can be achieved by human abilities. Further, why is not the same question raised even more strongly about the universe, the motion of which must be much swifter in proportion as the heaven is greater than the Earth? Or has heaven become so immense, because it is drawn outwards from the middle by a motion of ineffable strength [i.e., centrifugal force], that it would collapse if it were not at rest? Certainly if this reasoning were to be accepted, the magnitude of the heaven will rise to infinity. For in proportion it is thrown higher by the impulse of the motion, so the motion will be swifter, on account of the continual increase in the circumference which it must traverse in the space of twenty-four hours; and on the other hand as the motion increased, so would the immensity of the heaven. So the velocity would increase the magnitude, and the magnitude the velocity, to infinity. But according to that axiom in physics, that what is infinite cannot be traversed, nor moved by any means, the heaven will necessarily be at rest. But they say that outside the heaven there is no body, no place, no empty space, in fact nothing whatsoever, and therefore there is nothing to which the heaven can go out. In that case it is remarkable indeed if something can be restrained by nothing. But if the heaven is infinite, and finite only in its hollow interior, perhaps it will be more clearly proved that there is nothing outside the heaven, since every single thing will be within, whatever amount of space it occupies, but the heaven will remain immovable. For the strongest argument by which they try to establish that the universe is finite, is its motion. Therefore let us leave the question whether the universe is finite or infinite for the natural philosophers[4] to argue. What we

---

[2]**Philolaus the Pythagorean**: Greek mathematician and philosopher (ca. 470–385 B.C.E.).
[3]**the arguments quoted . . . insufficiency**: Arguments by ancient authorities, maintaining that "the Earth was at rest in the middle of the universe as if it was the center."
[4]**natural philosophers**: Scientists.

do know for certain is that the Earth is limited by its poles and bounded by a globular surface. . . .

Surely Aristotle's division of simple motion into three types, away from the middle, towards the middle, and round the middle, will be regarded merely as an intellectual division; just as we distinguish between a line, a point, and a surface, although one cannot exist without the other, and none of them without a body. A further point is that immobility is considered a more noble and divine state than that of change and instability, which is for that reason more appropriate to the Earth than to the universe. I also add that it would seem rather absurd to ascribe motion to that which contains and locates, and not rather to that which is contained and located, that is the Earth. Lastly, since it is evident that the wandering stars are sometimes nearer, sometimes further from the Earth, this will also be an example of motion of a single body which is both round the middle, by which they mean the center, away from the middle, and towards it. Motion round the midpoint must therefore be accepted more generally, and as satisfactory, provided that each motion is motion about its own midpoint. You will see then that from all these arguments the mobility of the Earth is more probable than its immobility, especially in the daily revolution, as that is particularly fitting for the Earth.

### READING QUESTIONS

1. What justification does Copernicus offer for his opening premise that the universe is spherical? What is his justification for the premise that the earth, too, is spherical?

2. Why does Copernicus accuse Ptolemy of logical inconsistency?

3. On what grounds does Copernicus argue that the heavens (or universe) are of finite extent? Does his logic on this score convince you? Why or why not?

4. Why does Copernicus argue that the earth, like the other planets, is in motion? Why did scientists before him accept the idea that the earth was stationary?

## 16-2 | A Defense of Science

### FRANCIS BACON, *On Superstition and the Virtue of Science* (1620)

Trained as a lawyer, Sir Francis Bacon (1561–1626) served in the court of the English king James I (r. 1603–1625) and conducted numerous experiments designed to explain the natural world. Bacon's most important contribution was to the scientific method itself. He was a

From Francis Bacon, "Aphorisms Concerning the Interpretation of Nature and the Kingdom of Man," in *The Works of Francis Bacon: Popular Edition, Based upon the Complete Edition of Spedding, Ellis, and Heath*, vol. 1 (New York: Hurd and Houghton, 1877), pp. 70–71, 124–126.

proponent of inductive reasoning, the arrival at general principles though the collection and analysis of empirical evidence. He contrasted his method with deductive reasoning, the use of general principles to interpret particular events and phenomena. In this excerpt from his writing, Bacon lays out his general method and seeks to defend it against critics who saw in his work a threat to religion.

There is no soundness in our notions, whether logical or physical. Substance, quality, action, passion, essence itself are not sound notions; much less are heavy, light, dense, rare, moist, dry, generation, corruption, attraction, repulsion, element, matter, form, and the like; but all are fantastical and ill-defined. . . .

The discoveries which have hitherto been made in the sciences are such as lie close to vulgar notions, scarcely beneath the surface. In order to penetrate into the inner and further recesses of nature, it is necessary that both notions and axioms [be] derived from things by a more sure and guarded way, and that a method of intellectual operation be introduced altogether better and more certain. . . .

There are and can be only two ways of searching into and discovering truth. The one flies from the senses and particulars to the most general axioms, and from these principles, the truth of which it takes for settled and immovable, proceeds to judgment and the discovery of middle axioms. And this way is now in fashion. The other derives axioms from the senses and particulars, rising by a gradual and unbroken ascent, so that it arrives at the most general axioms last of all. This is the true way, but as yet untried. . . .

It is not to be forgotten that in every age natural philosophy has had a troublesome adversary and hard to deal with — namely, superstition and the blind and immoderate zeal of religion. For we see among the Greeks that those who first proposed to man's uninitiated ears the natural causes for thunder and for storms were thereupon found guilty of impiety. Nor was much more forbearance shown by some of the ancient fathers of the Christian Church to those who, on most convincing grounds (such as no one in his senses would now think of contradicting), maintained that the earth was round and, of consequence, asserted the existence of the antipodes.[1]

Moreover, as things now are, to discourse of nature is made harder and more perilous by the summaries and systems of the schoolmen; who, having reduced theology into regular order as well as they were able, and fashioned it into the shape of an art, ended in incorporating the contentious and thorny philosophy of Aristotle, more than was fit, with the body of religion. . . .

Lastly . . . some are weakly afraid lest a deeper search into nature should transgress the permitted limits of sobermindedness; wrongfully wresting and

---

[1]**maintained that the earth was round . . . antipodes**: Bacon refers to an ancient debate relating to the shape of the earth; if the earth was round, some Greek theorists argued, then there would be lands (or ocean) on the side of the world directly opposite the one they inhabited. The debate was largely resolved by the fifteenth-century voyages of European explorers, culminating in the 1492 discovery of the New World, when the theorists were proven correct.

transferring what is said in Holy Writ [the Christian Bible] against those who pry into sacred mysteries to the hidden things of nature, which are barred by no prohibition. Others, with more subtlety, surmise and reflect that if secondary causes are unknown everything can be more readily referred to the divine hand and rod,—a point in which they think religion greatly concerned; which is, in fact, nothing else but to seek to gratify God with a lie. Others fear from past example that movements and changes in philosophy will end in assaults on religion; and others again appear apprehensive that in the investigation of nature something may be found to subvert, or at least shake, the authority of religion, especially with the unlearned. But these two last fears seem to me to savor utterly of carnal wisdom; as if men in the recesses and secret thoughts of their hearts doubted and distrusted the strength of religion, and the empire of faith over the senses, and therefore feared that the investigation of truth in nature might be dangerous to them. But if the matter be truly considered, natural philosophy is, after the word of God, at once the surest medicine against superstition and the most approved nourishment for faith; and therefore she is rightly given to religion as her most faithful handmaid, since the one displays the will of God, the other his power.

## READING QUESTIONS

1. In Bacon's view, what was, and had always been, the most important adversary of the natural philosopher?

2. Why, according to Bacon, did some observers see natural philosophy as a threat to religion? How did Bacon counter this criticism?

3. What do Bacon's assertions about natural philosophy suggest about the larger relationship between science and faith in the seventeenth century?

## 16-3 | A Defense of a Sun-Centered Universe

### GALILEO GALILEI, *Letter to the Grand Duchess Christina of Tuscany* (1615)

The heliocentric (sun-centered) universe that Nicolaus Copernicus described was defended several decades after his death by Italian astronomer Galileo Galilei. Galileo also made groundbreaking discoveries in mathematics, engineering, and physics and is considered an important contributor to the scientific method. He is probably most famous, however, for the conflict that he had with the Catholic Church over his defense of Copernican heliocentrism. Ultimately, church authorities forced him to publicly recant his defense of heliocentric theory, but the church eventually removed the ban on books concerning the theory centuries later. Galileo refutes the critiques of his ideas in the following letter to the Grand Duchess of Florence, who had recently become interested in the controversy between Copernican theory and the traditional geocentric theory mandated by the Catholic Church.

From Galileo Galilei, trans. Stillman Drake, "Letter to the Grand Duchess Christina," in *Discoveries and Opinions of Galileo* (Garden City, Doubleday, 1957), 175–179, 181–183, 209–211.

As Your Most Serene Highness knows very well, a few years ago I discovered in the heavens many particulars which had been invisible until our time. Because of their novelty, and because of some consequences deriving from them which contradict certain physical propositions commonly accepted in philosophical schools, they roused against me no small number of such professors, as if I had placed these things in heaven with my hands in order to confound nature and the sciences. These people seemed to forget that a multitude of truths contribute to inquiry and to the growth and strength of disciplines rather than to their diminution or destruction, and at the same time they showed greater affection for their own opinions than for the true ones; thus they proceeded to deny and to try to nullify these novelties, about which the senses themselves could have rendered them certain, if they had wanted to look at those novelties carefully. To this end they produced various matters, and they published some writings full of useless discussions and sprinkled with quotations taken from the Holy Scripture, taken from passages which they do not properly understand and which they inappropriately adduce. This was a very serious error, and they might not have fallen into it had they paid attention to Saint Augustine's very useful advice concerning how to proceed with care in reaching definite decisions about things which are obscure and difficult to understand by means of reason alone. For, speaking also about a particular physical conclusion pertaining to heavenly bodies, he writes this: "Now then, always practicing a pious and serious moderation, we ought not to believe anything lightly about an obscure subject, lest we reject (out of love for our error) something which later may be truly shown not to be in any way contrary to the holy books of either the Old or New Testament."

. . .

These people are aware that in my astronomical and philosophical studies, on the question of the constitution of the world's parts, I hold that the sun is located at the center of the revolutions of the heavenly orbs and does not change place, and that the earth rotates on itself and moves around it. Moreover, they hear how I confirm this view not only by refuting Ptolemy's and Aristotle's arguments, but also by producing many for the other side, especially some pertaining to physical effects whose causes perhaps cannot be determined in any other way, and other astronomical ones dependent on many features of the new celestial discoveries; these discoveries clearly confute the Ptolemaic system, and they agree admirably with this other position and confirm it. Now, these people are perhaps confounded by the known truth of the other propositions different from the ordinary which I hold, and so they may lack confidence to defend themselves as long as they remain in the philosophical field. Therefore, since they persist in their original self-appointed task of beating down me and my findings by every imaginable means, they have decided to try to shield the fallacies of their arguments with the cloak of simulated religiousness and with the authority of the Holy Scriptures, unintelligently using the latter for the confutation of arguments they neither understand nor have heard.

. . .

They alleviate their task as much as they can by making it look, at least among common people, as if this opinion were new and especially mine, pretending not to know that Nicolaus Copernicus was its author or rather its reformer and confirmer. Now, Copernicus was not only a Catholic, but also a clergyman and a canon, and he was so highly regarded that he was called to Rome from the remotest parts of Germany when under Leo X the Lateran Council was discussing the reform of the ecclesiastical calendar; at that time this reform remained unfinished only because there was still no exact knowledge of the precise length of the year and of the lunar month. Thus he was charged by the Bishop of Fossombrone, who was then supervising this undertaking, to try by repeated studies and efforts to acquire more understanding and certainty about those celestial motions; and so he undertook this study, and, by truly Herculanean labor and by his admirable mind, he made so much progress in this science and acquired such an exact knowledge of the periods of celestial motions that he earned the title of supreme astronomer; then, in accordance with his doctrine not only was the calendar regularized, but tables of all planetary motions were constructed. . . .

So the reason they advance to condemn the opinion of the earth's mobility and sun's stability is this: since in many places in the Holy Scripture one reads that the sun moves and the earth stands still, and since Scripture can never lie or err, it follows as a necessary consequence that the opinion of those who want to assert the sun to be motionless and the earth moving is erroneous and damnable. . . .

Therefore I think that in disputes about natural phenomena one must begin not with the authority of scriptural passages, but with sense experiences and necessary demonstrations. For the Holy Scripture and nature derive equally from the Godhead, the former as the dictation of the Holy Spirit and the latter as the most obedient executrix of God's orders; moreover, to accommodate the understanding of the common people it is appropriate for Scripture to say many things that are different (in appearance and in regard to the literal meaning of the words) from the absolute truth; on the other hand, nature is inexorable and immutable, never violates the terms of the laws imposed upon her, and does not care whether or not her recondite reasons and ways of operating are disclosed to human understanding; but not every scriptural assertion is bound to obligations as severe as every natural phenomenon; finally, God reveals Himself to us no less excellently in the effects of nature than in the sacred words of Scripture, as Tertullian perhaps meant when he said, "We postulate that God ought first to be known by nature, and afterwards further known by doctrine—by nature through His works, by doctrine through official teaching" . . .

However, I do not think one has to believe that the same God who has given us senses, language, and intellect would want us to set aside the use of these and give us by other means the information we can acquire with them, so that we would deny our senses and reason even in the case of those physical conclusions which are placed before our eyes and intellect by our sense experiences or by necessary demonstrations. This is especially implausible for those sciences discussed in Scripture to a very minor extent and with disconnected statements; such is precisely the case of astronomy, so little of which is contained therein that one does not find there even the names of the planets, except for the sun, the moon, and only once or twice Venus, under the name of Morning Star. Thus, if the sacred authors had had in mind to teach people about the arrangement and motions of the heavenly bodies, and consequently to have us acquire this information from Holy Scripture, then, in my opinion, they would not have discussed so little of the topic — that is to say, almost nothing in comparison with the innumerable admirable conclusions which are contained and demonstrated in this science.

Indeed, it is the opinion of the holiest and most learned Fathers that the writers of Holy Scripture not only did not pretend to teach us about the structure and the motions of the heavens and of the stars, and their shape, size, and distance, but that they deliberately refrained from doing so, even though they knew all these things very well. For example, on reads the following words in Saint Augustine: "It is also customary to ask what one should believe about the shape and arrangement of heaven according to our Scriptures. In fact, many people argue a great deal about these things, which with greater prudence our authors omitted, which are of no use for eternal life to those who study them, and (what is worse) which take up a lot of time that ought to be spent on things pertaining to salvation. For what does it matter to me whether heaven, like a sphere, completely surrounds the earth, which is balanced at the center of the universe, or whether like a discus it covers the earth on one side from above? However, since the issue here is the authority of Scripture, let me repeat a point I have made more than once; that is, there is a danger that someone who does not understand the divine words may find in our books or infer from them something about these topics which seems to contradict received opinions, and then he might not believe at all the other useful things contained in its precepts, stories, and assertions; therefore, briefly, it should be said that our authors did know the truth about the shape of heaven, but that the Spirit of God, which was speaking through them, did not want to teach men these things which are of no use to salvation." . . .

This let these people apply themselves to refuting the arguments of Copernicus and of the others, and let them leave its condemnation as erroneous and heretical to the proper authorities. . .

## READING QUESTIONS

1. According to Galileo, why did Catholic theologians reject the notion of a heliocentric universe?

2. How did Galileo define the relationship between science and religion?

3. How does Galileo use the Bible, St. Augustine, and the history of the Catholic Church itself to rebut the argument that his defense of a heliocentric universe is heretical?

4. How does Galileo say that truth can be established in science, on the one hand, and religion on the other?

SOURCES IN CONVERSATION

# Monarchical Power and Responsibility

Enlightenment reformers offered critiques of almost all aspects of European society, from education to religion to economics. For the most part, however, *philosophes* were not revolutionaries. In the determined application of rational thought, they saw a tool for the improvement of human life, not a weapon for destroying all that had come before. Thus, most philosophes supported monarchical government, the European norm in the eighteenth century. Certainly, they saw countless ways in which such governments could be made more efficient, less arbitrary, and more productive of the common good. They did not, however, want to do away with kings.

## READ AND COMPARE

1. Which reading would be more threatening to monarchs in Europe? Why do you think so?

2. How do the two excerpts reflect the social status of their authors, who do you suppose was the intended audience for each (aristocracy or commoners), and which reading would appeal better to each class?

## 16-4 | CHARLES DE SECONDAT, BARON DE MONTESQUIEU, *The Spirit of Laws: On the Separation of Governmental Powers* (1748)

The writings of Frenchman Charles de Secondat (1689–1755), better known as Baron de Montesquieu (mahn-tuhs-KYOO), were composed as the spirit of the Enlightenment swept over Europe in the early eighteenth century. Montesquieu's political writings, excerpted here, were concerned with the makeup of the state and the effect of a government on the lives of those it ruled. In this excerpt from *The Spirit of Laws*, Montesquieu argues for the importance of the separation of powers, or the assignment of executive, legislative, and judicial powers to different individuals or political bodies. As you read, consider the implications for political reform. Why, despite Montesquieu's avowed support of European monarchies, might monarchs have seen his work as a threat?

In every government there are three sorts of power: the legislative; the executive in respect to things dependent on the law of nations; and the executive in regard to matters that depend on the civil law.

From Baron de Montesquieu, *The Spirit of Laws*, trans. T. Nugent (New York: Hafner, 1949), pp. 151–152.

By virtue of the first, the prince or magistrate enacts temporary or perpetual laws, and amends or abrogates those that have been already enacted. By the second, he makes peace or war, sends or receives embassies, establishes the public security, and provides against invasions. By the third, he punishes criminals, or determines the disputes that arise between individuals. The latter we shall call the judiciary power, and the other simply the executive power of the state.

The political liberty of the subject is a tranquility of mind arising from the opinion each person has of his safety. In order to have this liberty, it is requisite the government be so constituted as one man need not be afraid of another.

When the legislative and executive powers are united in the same person, or in the same body of magistrates, there can be no liberty; because apprehensions may arise, lest the same monarch or senate should enact tyrannical laws, to execute them in a tyrannical manner.

Again, there is no liberty, if the judiciary power be not separated from the legislative and executive. Were it joined with the legislative, the life and liberty of the subject would be exposed to arbitrary control; for the judge would be then the legislator. Were it joined to the executive power, the judge might behave with violence and oppression.

There would be an end of everything, were the same man or the same body, whether of the nobles or of the people, to exercise those three powers, that of enacting laws, that of executing the public resolutions, and of trying the causes of individuals.

Most kingdoms in Europe enjoy a moderate government because the prince who is invested with the two first powers leaves the third to his subjects. In Turkey, where these three powers are united in the Sultan's person, the subjects groan under the most dreadful oppression.

In the republics of Italy, where these three powers are united, there is less liberty than in our monarchies. Hence their government is obliged to have recourse to as violent methods for its support as even that of the Turks; witness the state inquisitors, and the lion's mouth into which every informer may at all hours throw his written accusations.

What a situation must the poor subject be in, under those republics! The same body of magistrates are possessed, as executors of the laws, of the whole power they have given themselves in quality of legislators. They may plunder the state by their general determinations; and as they have likewise the judiciary power in their hands, every private citizen may be ruined by their particular decisions.

The whole power is here united in one body; and though there is no external pomp that indicates a despotic sway, yet the people feel the effects of it every moment.

Hence it is that many of the princes of Europe, whose aim has been levelled at arbitrary power, have constantly set out with uniting in their own persons, all the branches of magistracy, and all the great offices of state.

## READING QUESTIONS

1. How did Montesquieu define liberty? Why did he believe that a separation of powers was crucial to the protection of liberty?

2. In Montesquieu's view, under what circumstances could liberty be obtained under a monarchy? Under what circumstances could a republic produce tyranny?

3. How does Montesquieu's essay reflect his cultural biases?

4. How might opponents of absolute monarchy have used Montesquieu's ideas to support their position?

## 16-5 | JEAN-JACQUES ROUSSEAU, *The Social Contract: On Popular Sovereignty and the General Will* (1762)

Jean-Jacques Rousseau (1712–1778) was born in Swiss Geneva and came from the common, not the aristocratic, class. He left Geneva at the age of sixteen; after spending years living on charity and the income from odd jobs, he traveled to Paris seeking to make a name for himself. Rousseau's poverty and origins, combined with his prickly personality, made him something of an outsider in Enlightenment social circles. His 1762 work on political theory, *The Social Contract*, was part of an extended argument in the seventeenth and eighteenth centuries over the sources of governmental power and the conditions, if any, under which one form of government could be replaced with another.

Since no man has any natural authority over his fellow men, and since force is not the source of right, conventions are the basis of all lawful authority among men.

Now, as men cannot create any new forces, but only combine and direct those that exist, they have no other means of preserving themselves than to combine those forces . . . and to make them work in concert.

This sum of forces can be produced only by many people working together; but since every man needs his own strength and freedom to preserve himself, how can he contribute them without injuring himself, and without neglecting to take care of himself? This difficulty, applied to my subject, may be explained this way:

"To find an organization which may use the collective power of the community to defend and protect the person and property of every associate, and while working together, each person may nevertheless obey only himself, and remain as free as he was without the organization." Such is the problem that the social contract addresses. . . .

---

From Jean-Jacques Rousseau, *The Social Contract*, in *Translations and Reprints from the Original Sources of European History* (Philadelphia: University of Pennsylvania Press, 1898), vol. 5, no. 1:14–16. Language modernized by J. Michael Long.

If we set aside things that are not essential in the social contract, we can explain it as follows: "Each of us puts themselves and their power toward the good of the community, and in return everyone is part of that community."

But the political system or sovereign, which only exists because of the contract, can never compromise itself in anything that undermines the contract, such as giving up control of a part of the system, or submitting to the authority of another sovereign. To violate the contract that created it would be to annihilate itself, and what is nothing produces nothing.

Based upon what we just explained, the will of the people is always right and always best for society; but the policies that the people create are not always the best for society. Men always desire their own good, but do not always understand how to achieve it; the people are never corrupted, but they can be deceived, and it is only then that they intend evil things.

The power of the people, then, needs something to concentrate it and put it in action according to the directions of the will of the people, to be able to communicate between the state and the sovereign, to achieve in society what the connection of soul and body achieves in a man. This is, in the State, the purpose of government, which is often confused with the sovereign, who is actually served and advised by the government.

What, then, is the government? It is an intermediate body established between the people and the sovereign so they can communicate, and intended to execute the laws and maintain civil and political liberties.

It is not enough for the assembled people to create the constitution of the state by approving a set of laws; nor is it enough that they establish a permanent government, or that they create a lasting process for electing magistrates. Besides special assemblies that might become necessary due to emergencies, there should also be fixed assemblies that meet periodically that cannot be abolished; so that, on the appointed day, the people are called together by the law, without needing to be formally summoned.

Once the people are lawfully assembled as a sovereign body, the entire jurisdiction of the government ceases, the executive power is suspended, and the most common citizen is as sacred and inviolable as the most powerful magistrate, because the representatives of that assembly do not need anyone else to represent their interests.

These assemblies, which are meant to maintain the social contract, should always begin their business with two proposals, which no one should be able to suppress, and which should pass separately by vote. The first: "Whether the sovereign wants to maintain the present form of government." The second: "Whether the people want to leave the administration to those who now control it."

I assume that I have proved my belief, that there is no fundamental law in the state which cannot be revoked, not even this social compact; for if all the citizens assembled agree to break that compact, no one can doubt that it could be quite legitimately broken.

## READING QUESTIONS

1. What might Rousseau mean when he says "force is not the source of right"?

2. According to Rousseau, what is the origin and reason for the legitimacy of a government?

3. How does Rousseau's concept of the "general will" relate to the concept of majority rule in a representative government?

4. How do you think monarchs and traditional elites would critique the idea of replacing a government that did not represent the will of the people?

## 16-6 | A Philosophe Argues for Religious Toleration

### VOLTAIRE, *A Treatise on Toleration* (1763)

François-Marie Arouet (1694–1778), who used the pen name Voltaire, was arguably the greatest of the Enlightenment philosophes. He was an astonishingly prolific author whose output amounted to hundreds of books and pamphlets. In some respects he was unrepresentative of the general currents of Enlightenment thought, being skeptical of both human rationality and human progress. Like virtually all the philosophes, however, he was an unceasing critic of religious dogma and intolerance. The following excerpts from Voltaire's *Treatise on Toleration* (1763) present the essential components of his argument in favor of religious toleration. As you read, consider what core assumptions form the foundation of his position. How did Voltaire's beliefs about the fundamental equality of human beings and the limits of human knowledge shape his views on religion?

### Chapter XXI. Universal Toleration

It does not require any great art or studied eloquence, to prove, that Christians should tolerate each other. I shall go further, and say, that we should regard all men as our brethren. What! a Turk my brother? a Chinese my brother? a Jew? a Siamese? my brother? Yes, without doubt; for are we not all children of the same father, and creatures of the same God?

But these people despise us and treat us as idolaters! It may be so; but I shall only tell them, they are to blame. It seems to me, I should stagger the haughty obstinacy of an Iman,[1] or a Talapoin,[2] if I spoke to them in the following manner:

This little globe, which is but a point, rolls in universal space, in the same manner as other globes, and we are lost in the immensity. Man, a being about five feet in height, is assuredly a thing of no great importance in the creation.

From Voltaire, *A Treatise on Toleration; The Ignorant Philosopher; and A Commentary on the Marquis of Becaria's [sic] Treatise on Crimes and Punishments*, trans. David Williams (London: Fielding and Walker, 1779), pp. 118–123.

[1]**Iman**: Imam; a Muslim religious leader.
[2]**Talapoin**: Buddhist priest or monk.

One of those beings, called men, and who are hardly perceptible, says to some of his neighbors in Arabia or in the country of the Cafres:[3] "Attend to what I say, for the God of all these worlds has enlightened me. There are about nine hundred millions of little ants, such as we are, on this earth, but my ant-hill alone is [in] the care of God, all the rest have been hateful to him from [i.e., for] all eternity; we only shall be happy; all others will be eternally wretched."

They would stop me, and ask, who is this madman, who utters such folly? I should be obliged to answer each of them, It is you. I might then take occasion to meliorate their dispositions into something like humanity; but that I should find difficult.

I will now address myself to Christians; and venture to say to a Dominican,[4] who is an inquisitor, "My brother, you know, that every province of Italy has its jargon; that they do not speak at Venice and Bergamo as they do at Florence. The Academy de la Crusca[5] has fixed the general disposition and construction of the language; its dictionary is a rule from which no deviations are allowed; and the grammar of Buonmattei's[6] is an infallible guide, which must be followed. But do you think that the consul, president of the Academy, or in his absence, Buonmattei, could have the conscience, to order the tongues of all the Venetians and Bergamese to be cut out, who should persist in their provincial dialects?"

The inquisitor would answer me: "The cases are very different. The question here is the salvation of your soul; it is for your good, that the court of inquisition ordains, that you should be seized, on the deposition of a single person, though he be infamous, and in the hands of justice; that you have no advocate[7] to plead for you; that the very name of your accuser should be unknown to you; that the inquisitor should promise you mercy, and afterwards condemn you; that he apply five different kinds of torture to you, and that afterwards you should be whipt [i.e., whipped] or sent to the galleys, or burnt [at the stake] as a spectacle in a religious ceremony.[8] Father Ivonet, [and] Doctor[s] Cuchalon, Zarchinus, Campegius, Royas, Telinus, Gomarus, Diabarus, and Gemelinus[9] lay down these things as laws, and this pious practice must not be disputed. I would take the liberty to answer, "My brother, perhaps you are right; I am convinced of the good you wish to do me; but, without all this, is it not possible to be saved?"

It is true that these absurd horrors do not always deform the face of the earth; but they have been very frequent; and we might collect materials to compose a volume on these practices, much larger than the gospels which condemn them. It is not only cruel to persecute in this short life those who do not think as

---

[3]**Cafres**: Kaffirs; South Africa.

[4]**Dominican**: The Dominicans were a Roman Catholic religious order who, as Voltaire suggests, conducted the Inquisition.

[5]**Academy de la Crusca**: Accademia della Crusca; an Italian learned society founded in 1582. Its members were chiefly linguists and philologists. In 1612 it sponsored publication of a dictionary of the Italian language.

[6]**Buonmattei**: Benedetto Buommattei (1581–1647), also rendered as Boummattei and Buonmattei; Florentine lexicographer, author of *Della Lingua Toscana*.

[7]**advocate**: Lawyer.

[8]Here Voltaire inserted a footnote instructing his readers to "See that excellent book, intitled [sic], The Manual of the Inquisition."

[9]**Father Ivonet, . . . Gemelinus**: Roman Catholic theologians.

we do, but it is audacious to pronounce their eternal damnation. It seems to me, that it little becomes the atoms of a moment [i.e., such insignificant, ephemeral creatures], such as we are, thus to anticipate the decrees of the Creator. I am very far from opposing that opinion, "that out of [i.e., outside] the church there is no salvation." I respect it, as well as everything taught by the church: but, in truth, are we acquainted with all the ways of God, and the whole extent of his mercy? Is it not permitted that we should hope in him, as well as fear him? Is it not sufficient that we are faithful to the church? Is it necessary that every individual should usurp the power of the Deity, and decide, before him, the eternal lot of all mankind?

When we wear mourning for a king of Sweden, Denmark, England, or Prussia, do we say that we mourn for a reprobate who will burn eternally in hell? There are in Europe forty millions of inhabitants, who are not [members] of the Church of Rome; shall we say to each of them, "Sir, as you are to be infallibly damned, I would neither eat, deal, or converse with you."

Is it to be supposed, that an ambassador of France, presented to the Grand Seignior,[10] would say to himself, His highness will be burnt to all eternity, because he has submitted to circumcision? If he really thought that the Grand Seignior was a mortal enemy to God, and the object of his vengeance, could he have spoken to him? Should he have been sent to him? With whom could we have dealings in trade? What duty of civil life could we ever fulfill, if we were in fact possessed with the idea, that we were conversing with persons eternally reprobated?

O ye followers of a merciful God! if you have cruel hearts. If, in adoring him, whose whole law consists in these words, "Love God and your neighbor," you have encumbered that pure and holy law with sophisms, and incomprehensible disputes! If you have lighted the fires of discord, sometimes for a new word, sometimes for a letter of the alphabet! If you have annexed eternal torments to the omission of some words, or some ceremonies, which other people cannot be [i.e., are not] acquainted with—I must say, while shedding tears for mankind: "Transport yourselves with me to that day, in which all men will be judged, and when God will render to every one according to his works."

"I see all the dead, of past and present ages, appearing in his presence. Are you very sure that our Creator and Father will say to the wise and virtuous Confucius, to the legislator Solon, to Pythagoras, Zaleucus, Socrates, Plato, the divine Antonini, the good Trajan, to Titus the delight of mankind, to Epictetus,[11] and to many others who have been the models of human nature: Go, monsters!

---

[10]**Grand Seignior**: Grand signeur; the Ottoman sultan.

[11]**Confucius, Solon, . . . Titus, Epictetus**: Confucius (551–479 B.C.E.), Chinese philosopher; Solon (638–558 B.C.E.), Athenian statesman and lawgiver; Pythagoras (ca. 570–495 B.C.E.), Greek philosopher, theologian, and mathematician; Zaleucus (seventh century B.C.E.), Greek lawgiver; Socrates (ca. 469–399 B.C.E.), Greek philosopher; Plato (428–348 B.C.E.), Greek philosopher and mathematician; Antoninus Pius (r. 138–161), Roman emperor, and Marcus Aurelius Antoninus (r. 161–180), Roman emperor and Stoic philosopher; Trajan (r. 98–117), Roman emperor; Titus Pomponius Atticus (ca. 112–ca. 35 B.C.E.), Roman editor and man of letters; Epictetus (55–135), Greek Stoic philosopher.

Let your punishments be as eternal as my being!—and you, my well-beloved, Jean Châtel, Ravaillac, Damiens, Cartouche,[12] &c. who have died according to the forms which are enjoined, sit at my right hand and partake of my dominion, and of my felicity!"

You shrink with horror at these words; and after they have escaped me, I have nothing more to say to you.

## Chapter XXII. Prayer to God

I no longer then look up to men; it is to thee, the God of all beings, of all worlds, and of all ages, I address myself—If weak creatures, lost in immensity and imperceptible to the rest of the universe, may dare to ask any thing of thee, who hast given [us] all things, and whose decrees are immutable and eternal! Deign to regard with pity the errors inseparable from our nature; let not these errors prove our calamities! Thou hast not given us hearts to hate, and hands to destroy each other; dispose us to mutual assistance, in supporting the burden of a painful and transitory life! Let the little differences in the garments which cover our frail bodies; in all our imperfect languages, in our ridiculous customs, our imperfect laws, our idle opinions, in our ranks and conditions, so unequal in our eyes, and so equal in thine: let all those little shades which distinguish the atoms called *men*, be no more signals of hatred and persecution! Let those who light tapers [i.e., candles] at noon-day, to glorify thee—bear with those who content themselves with the light of thy sun! Let not those who throw over their garments a white surplice, while they say it is the duty of men to love thee, hate those who say the same thing in a black woolen cloak! Let it be equal, to adore thee in a jargon formed from an ancient, or from a modern language! May those whose vestments are dipped in scarlet, or in purple who domineer over a small parcel of the small heap of the dirt and mud of this world; and those who possess a few round fragments of a certain metal, enjoy without pride, what they call grandeur and riches; and may others regard them without envy: for thou knowest, there is nothing in these things to inspire envy or pride!

May all men remember that they are brethren! May they regard in horror tyranny, the tyranny exercised over the mind, as they do rapine, which carries away by force the fruits of peaceable labor and industry! If the scourges of war be inevitable, let us not hate and destroy each other in the bosom of peace; let us employ the instant of our existence to praise, in a thousand different languages, from Siam to California, thy goodness which hath granted us that instant!

---

[12]**Jean Châtel, Ravaillac, Damiens, Cartouche**: Jean Châtel (1575–1594), tortured and executed for attempting to assassinate Henry IV of France; François Ravaillac (1578–1610), tortured and drawn and quartered for assassinating Henry IV of France; Robert-François Damiens (1715–1757), tortured and drawn and quartered for attempting to assassinate Louis XV of France; Louis Dominique Bourguignon, known as Cartouche (1693–1721), French highwayman tortured to death.

## READING QUESTIONS

1. In Voltaire's view, what important differences, if any, exist between individual human beings? Between different human societies? How did Voltaire's answers to these questions shape his view of religion?

2. What does Voltaire's argument in favor of religious toleration tell you about his beliefs about the limits of human understanding?

3. Do you find Voltaire's argument in favor of universal religious toleration persuasive? Why or why not?

# ■ COMPARATIVE AND DISCUSSION QUESTIONS ■

1. Nicolaus Copernicus and Francis Bacon were separated by a lifetime. (Copernicus died almost twenty years before Bacon was born.) What similarities do you note between their modes of thinking? In what ways did they differ?

2. What was different about how Copernicus and Galileo expressed their supposedly "heretical" views about the universe? Why were their approaches different?

3. What differences do you note between Montesquieu's and Rousseau's theories about the nature of government and how it ought to interact with its citizens? Where do they seem to be in agreement?

4. How did the new vision of the universe created by participants in the Scientific Revolution shape Voltaire's view of human beings and their societies?

5. What would Montesquieu and Rousseau think of Domat's divine-right monarchical theory (Document 15-2), and why?

**Acknowledgments** (*continued from page iv*)

*Chapter 1*

1-1 Republished by permission of Princeton University Press from James B. Pritchard, ed., *Ancient Near Eastern Texts Relating to the Old Testament*, 3rd ed. (Princeton, N.J.: Princeton University Press, 1955); permission conveyed through Copyright Clearance Center, Inc.

1-2 From *The Epic of Gilgamesh*, by Kovacs, Maureen Gallery (Translator). Copyright © 1985, 1989 by the Board of Trustees of the Leland Stanford Jr. University. All rights reserved. Used by permission of the publisher, Stanford University Press, sup.org.

1-3 Republished by permission of Princeton University Press from James B. Pritchard, ed., *Ancient Near Eastern Texts Relating to the Old Testament*, 2d ed. (Princeton, N.J.: Princeton University Press, 1955); permission conveyed through Copyright Clearance Center, Inc.

1-4 Republished with permission of University of California Press from *Ancient Egyptian Literature: A Book of Readings*, Volume 2, edited by Miriam Lichtheim, copyright © 1973 by the Regents of the University of California; permission conveyed through Copyright Clearance Center, Inc.

1-7 Republished with permission from Blackwell Publishing from Mark W. Chavalas, ed., *Historical Sources in Translation: The Ancient Near East* (Malden, Mass.: Blackwell Publishing, 2006); permission conveyed through Copyright Clearance Center, Inc.

*Chapter 2*

2-3 Republished with permission of Blackwell Publishing from Mark W. Chavalas, ed., *The Ancient Near East: Historical Sources in Translation* (Malden, Mass.: Blackwell Publishing, 2006); permission conveyed through Copyright Clearance Center, Inc.

2-4 Republished by permission of Princeton University Press from James B. Pritchard, ed., *Ancient Near Eastern Texts Relating to the Old Testament*, 3rd ed. (Princeton, N.J.: Princeton University Press, 1955); permission conveyed through Copyright Clearance Center, Inc.

*Chapter 3*

3-1 "Book 12: The Cattle of the Sun" from *The Odyssey* by Homer, translated by Robert Fagles, translation copyright © 1996 by Robert Fagles. Used by permsision of Viking Books, an imprint of Penguin Publishing Group, a division of Penguin Random House LLC. All rights reserved.

3-3 Republished with permission of The University of Chicago Press from *The Complete Greek Tragedies*, edited by David Grene and Richmond Lattimore (Chicago: University of Chicago Press, 1954); permission conveyed through Copyright Clearance Center, Inc.

*Chapter 4*

4-6 From M. M. Austin, ed., *The Hellenistic World from Alexander to the Roman Conquest*, copyright © Michael Austin 1981. Reproduced by permission of Cambridge University Press through PLSclear.

*Chapter 5*

5-4 From Naphtali Lewis and Meyer Reinhold, eds., *Roman Civilization: Selected Readings*, vol. 2. Copyright © 1951 Columbia University Press. Reprinted with permission of Columbia University Press.

*Chapter 6*

6-1 From *Tacitus, Agricola and Germania*, translated by Anthony R. Birley. Copyright © 1999 by Oxford University Press. Reproduced with permission of Oxford University Press through PLSclear.

## Chapter 8

8-4 Republished with permission of McGraw-Hill Higher Education from *The Middle Ages, Volume I: Sources of Medieval History*, 3rd Edition, edited by Brian Tierney (1978); permission conveyed through Copyright Clearance Center, Inc.

8-5 Republished with permission of McGraw-Hill Higher Education from *The Middle Ages, Volume I: Sources of Medieval History*, 3rd Edition, edited by Brian Tierney (1978); permission conveyed through Copyright Clearance Center, Inc.

## Chapter 9

9-3 Pope Gregory: *The Correspondence of Pope Gregory VII*, edited and translated by Ephraim Emerton. Copyright © 1932 by Columbia University Press. Reprinted with permission of Columbia University Press.

9-5 From Edward Peters, editor, *The First Crusade: The Chronicle of Fulcher and Other Source Materials*, 2nd Edition. Copyright © 1998 University of Pennsylvania Press. Reprinted by permission of University of Pennsylvania Press.

9-6 Republished with permission of University of California Press from *European Jewry and the First Crusade*, by Robert Chazan, copyright © 1987 by the Regents of the University of California; permission conveyed through Copyright Clearance Center, Inc.

9-7 Ali Ibn Al-Athir, The Complete History (1231) Reproduced from *Arab Historians of the Crusades*, by Francesco Gabrieli, published by Routledge, copyright © 1984 by the Regents of the University of California. Reprinted by permission of the University of California Press and by arrangement with Taylor & Francis Books UK.

## Chapter 11

11-6 Republished with permission of Manchester University Press from Craig Taylor, trans. and ed., *Joan of Arc: La Pucelle* (Manchester, U.K.: Manchester University Press, 2006), pp. 82–83, 125–127; permission conveyed through Copyright Clearance Center, Inc.

## Chapter 12

12-4 From Desiderius Erasmus, *The Education of a Christian Prince*, translated by Lester K. Born. Copyright © 1936 by Columbia University Press. Reprinted with permission of Columbia University Press.

12-5 Christine de Pizan, excerpts from *The Book of the City of Ladies*, translated by Earl J. Richards, pp. 153–155. Copyright © 1982, 1998 by Persea Books, Inc. Reprinted with the permission of Persea Books, Inc. (New York), www.perseabooks.com. All rights reserved.

## Chapter 13

13-4 Excerpt (pp. 208–213) from Jean Bodin, *On the Demon-Mania of Witches*, translated by Randy A. Scott, with an introduction by Jonathan L. Pearl. Reprinted by permission of the Centre for Reformation & Renaissance Studies, Victoria University.

## Chapter 14

14-1 Material originally published in *The Diario of Christopher Columbus's First Voyage to America, 1942–1943*, trans. by Oliver Dunn and James E. Kelly, Jr. Copyright © 1989 by Oliver Dunn and James E. Kelly, Jr. Reprinted by permission of the publisher, University of Oklahoma Press.

14-4 From Basil Davidson, *The African Past: Chronicles from Antiquity to Modern Times* (Boston: Little, Brown and Company, 1964), pp. 191–193; reissued by Africa World Press in 1990 as

African Civilization Revisited: From Antiquity to Modern Times. Reproduced with permission of Curtis Brown Ltd., on behalf of the Beneficiaries of the Estate of Basil Davidson.

*Chapter 16*

16-3 Galileo Galilei, "Letter to the Grand Duchess Christina," in The Galileo Affair: A Documentary History, translated by Maurice A. Finocchiaro. Copyright © 1989 by The Regents of the University of California. Reprinted by permission of the University of California Press.